IN CENTRAL ASIA

D1446659

Central Asia Book Series

Muslims

IN CENTRAL ASIA

Expressions of Identity

and Change

Edited by Jo-Ann Gross

Duke University Press / Durham and London   1992

Second printing, 1994
© 1992 Duke University Press
All rights reserved
Printed in the United States of America
on acid-free paper ∞
Library of Congress Cataloging-in-Publication Data
appear on the last printed page of this book.

To my parents,

Philip W. and Ruth Gross,

with love and gratitude

Contents

Illustrations

Central Asia Book Series

Islam may play two different roles in the dramatic changes affecting contemporary Central Asian society. Through the first, it
surely provides an underpinning today for a culture that until the
late 1920s regarded itself as wholly Muslim. More problematic is
Islam's part in the region's public reidentification set in motion
by Mikhail Gorbachev's program of openness (*glastnost*) insti-
tuted around the mid-1980s.

Analysts or scholars who interpret very recent developments
in Central Asia often seriously disagree about the cultural and political importance of Islam in the area's affairs. But most recognize
the paradox created by the heritage of Islamic civilization per-
sisting in the officially atheistic USSR. Religion played only a
small part in the region's public life between the late 1920s and
at least the mid-1980s. For that reason, by no means all analysts
or scholars favor an "Islamic" approach to current Central Asian
affairs. A few consider that the Communist suppression of religion
in the Soviet Union has only pushed the practice of Islam under-
ground. Some believe that latent forces of Islam merely wait to
burst out at the first chance to dominate the thinking and life of
the area once again.

This divergence in interpretation of the significance of Islam,
together with the intense interest among students and other informed persons concerning Islam and ethnicity in group identity,
reveal the need for systematic inquiries into those linkages at this
time. For the same reasons, the present study benefits noticeably
from bringing to readers more than one author's point of view.
However, this volume generally does not address in a partisan

fashion the disagreement over the degree of significance of today's Islamic religion for Central Asia. Rather, the authors carefully build a case for examining the factor of religion as a component of group identity in the study of contemporary Central Asia. All productive approaches to the study of the culture and society of the region deserve appropriate attention. The editors chose this manuscript for publication in the Central Asia Book Series because it offers insights into those problems. Even more persuasive in this selection were the academic credentials, access to the local-language sources, and experience of these authors as well as their mastery of the subjects they treat.

The Moscow regime's willingness to permit genuine expressions of ethnic pluralism in the territory currently under its management appears to have cooled considerably by 1990 and 1991, in comparison with its attitude toward expression of nationality during the years between 1986 and 1989. That reversal concerns religious practices as well. Whether or not Soviet governmental policy may now aim to counteract the important moves that contributed to removing some of the previous strictures from the practice of religion in Central Asia, the subject deserves more informed discussion. Both outside and inside the USSR, scholars and other informed persons can hardly ignore the potential effects of a revival in religious influence upon the life and art of the majority of Central Asian people, especially among that largest proportion comprising the broad base of society.

The Central Asia Book Series endeavors to issue learned studies, documents, eye-witness accounts, and reference materials that will make a lasting addition to knowledge about the region.

Edward Allworth, General Editor of the Series, Columbia University.

Andras J. E. Bodrogligeti, Advisory Editor, University of California, Los Angeles.

Richard N. Frye, Advisory Editor, Harvard University.

Edward Allworth   March 1991
General Editor, Central Asia Book Series

Preface

The chapters included in this volume originated as papers presented at a workshop on "Approaches to the Study of Islam in Central and Inner Asia," which was sponsored by the Middle East Institute at Columbia University, and held in March 1988. Implicit in the planning and organization of this project was my belief that a comparative interregional, cross-disciplinary discussion of Islam and identity in the Muslim societies of pre-modern and medieval Central Asia would result in a meaningful dialogue through which issues of religious, ethnic, and national identities could be discussed. Current developments in Eastern Europe, the Soviet Union, Central Asia, Africa, and the Middle East have demonstrated the resilience of such identities in the face of social, economic, and political changes. However, as the contributors in this volume demonstrate, issues concerning identity formation and the construction and reconstruction of ethnic, religious, and national identities are by no means a phenomenon confined to the modern era of nation-states. The purpose of this volume is twofold: first, to present a variety of approaches to the process of identity formation which take into consideration the cultural, political, and historical factors involved in that process; and second, to demonstrate the fluidity and multiplicity of concepts of identity in the Muslim societies of Central Asia.

The problems involved in the transliteration of eight languages (Persian, Arabic, Chaghatay, Turkmenian, Uzbek, Tajik, Russian, and Chinese) are considerable. The system employed for Persian, Arabic, and Russian is that of the Library of Congress, except ẓ has been used instead of z̤ for the letter zed in Persian and Arabic.

Khoja rather than *khwaja* has also been used. Words accepted in English such as *ulama, madrasa, Qur'an,* etc., will be spelled as commonly used in English-language journals. Foreign words have been italicized the first time they are used; diacritical marks have been used for Persian and Arabic words throughout the text.

An attempt has been made to spell personal and proper names consistently throughout the book. However, regional and localized spellings have been used whenever appropriate. In the case of Turkic languages, which as yet have no standardized transliteration system, I have tried to respect the systems adopted by individual authors.

In addition to those who have contributed to this volume, other scholars who participated in the original workshop were Edward Allworth, Yuri Bregel, Robert Canfield, Jonathan Lipman, Robert McChesney, Eden Naby, William Roff, Morris Rossabi, Nazif Shahrani, and Maria Subtelny. Their contributions to the workshop, although not explicitly represented in this volume, added a great deal to the final form of the project, and they are much appreciated.

I am grateful to Professor Richard Bulliet, who as director of the Middle East Institute at Columbia University fully supported the project from the planning stages to its completion. I also am grateful to Edward Allworth, who encouraged me to prepare the original manuscript for publication and whose advice, as general editor of the Central Asia Book Series, was indispensable. I would like to express my appreciation to Trenton State College, which provided me with the grant support and time needed to complete the introductory chapter and the editing of the manuscript, and to John Karras, chairman of the history department, whose constant encouragement throughout the project was so helpful. I would also like to thank Haideh Sahim, whose assistance with the Persian transliteration was so valuable, and Mehrdad Izady for his help in drawing the maps. I am particularly indebted to Thomas Allsen, Walter Feldman, Dru Gladney, John Karras, and Robert McChesney for their insightful suggestions and comments on the introductory chapter.

Jo-Ann Gross

Introduction:

Approaches to the Problem

of Identity Formation

Jo-Ann Gross

Central Asia is perhaps most distinctive for its cultural and geo-political position as a frontier region. Historically, Central Asia has served as a point of convergence for nomadic and sedentary civilizations in the pre-Islamic and Islamic periods. This conver-gence resulted in a unique integration of social and cultural tra-ditions. In the post-Mongol period, for example, the convergence of Perso-Islamic and Turko-Mongolian traditions affected the character of the economies, political ideologies, popular religious beliefs, arts and literature, languages, and social organization in Central Asia, parts of Russia, Northwest China, the Eastern Is-lamic world, and even parts of the Arab world. The effects of a dual Turkic/Iranian sociopolitical and cultural framework of tra-ditions is one which persists in many Central Asian societies to-day, as reflected in several of the chapters included in this volume.

Scholars studying the Muslim societies of Central Asia face the dilemma of how to deal with the dynamics of identity formation in so diverse a region.[1] The researcher dealing with Central Asia confronts a cultural and historical field in which knowledge of several languages is imperative, and the sifting of cultural symbols and meanings is a part of the dialectical process of untangling the threads of identity. If, for example, we consider the post-Mongol societies of medieval Khurasan, Transoxiana, or Chinese Turk-istan, the question of ethnicity and group identity is a crucial one. At the heart of studies that deal with such societies are questions

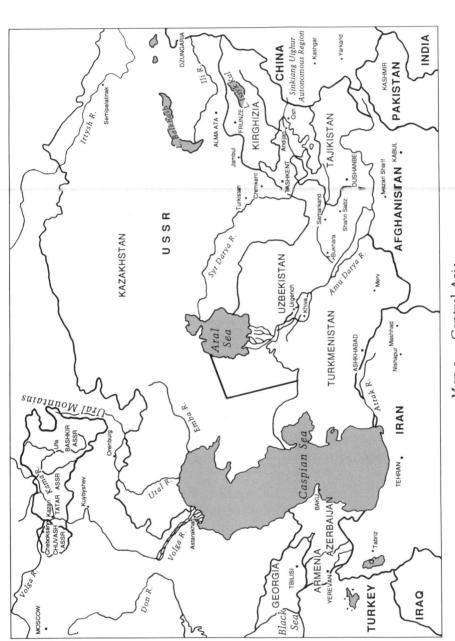

Map 1. Central Asia

concerning ethnogenesis and ethnic identity. How does a group firmly grounded in nomadic steppe traditions, such as the Mongols or Timurids, transform itself into a settled state polity?[2] How does one ethnic group such as the Uzbeks or the Shaybanids define itself in relationship to others?[3] What historiographical patterns may be discerned in the way identity is perceived and represented? What is the relationship between nomadic steppe rulers, such as Khubilai Khan, Möngke, Timur, or Chinggis Khan, and their conquered populations?[4] All of these questions necessitate research which considers the cultural heritage as well as the conceptions of how this heritage is socially and culturally created, defined and expressed, used to attain certain results, and understood by others.

From the nineteenth century to the present, during which time Muslim societies began to be subsumed into larger polities which redefined the identities of groups and posed challenges to the expression of identities, the question of religious, national, and ethnic identity becomes critical to the understanding of historical change. In the wake of colonial rule in much of the Middle East and Central Asia, the nineteenth century posed new problems, threats, and challenges to the Muslim societies of these regions. In Afghanistan, in Iran, in the khanates of Central Asia under tsarist rule, and in China, Muslims were faced with a variety of new and often alien political ideologies, cultural traditions, and technologies. These new influences, challenges, and threats were affected through colonial rule and through the increased presence of Western culture (most effectively through the printed word and educational institutions).[5] In the twentieth century, the Bolshevik revolution and the Chinese Communist revolution resulted in a much more dramatic change for the Muslim populations within those borders. Ethnic definitions were expounded on a political, ideological basis, and geopolitical borders were artificially created on the basis of macroethnic identities. The Soviet Union, in an effort to deal with its non-Russian populations in a newly created Soviet Communist state, created a Union of Socialist Republics, defined primarily in terms of nationalities (based on language and local traditions). The Peoples Republic of China, using the Soviet system as a model, created "minority nationalities," and formed autonomous areas for such minorities.[6] The effects of state-produced ethnic and/or nationality policies and the role played by central governments in assigning and defining identities must be addressed in order to understand fully the processes of identity formation in nineteenth- and twentieth-century Muslim Central Asia.

The timely topics of ethnicity and nationality have become the domain of Soviet politics as well as the everyday reportage in newspapers and magazine articles discussing Gorbachev's reform programs, ongoing ethnic strife in the Soviet republics, or constitutional reform in republics such as Uzbekistan and Tajikistan. China's progression from its liberalization policies, to the emergence of a popular democratization movement in the spring of 1989 and its destruction, to the current atmosphere of political repression is equally relevant to understanding the historical factors involved in the resurgence of Islamic sentiment among the Muslim populations in China. Such rapid changes impose a certain urgency for a reappraisal of the entire question of ethnic, religious, and national identity in the context of Central Asia, and in relationship to similar processes occurring in other parts of the world today.

In such complex societies, how then is the problem of identity to be approached? Is it possible to broach such issues in a comparative context, even comparing problems of identity in medieval Central Asia with contemporary issues in Soviet Central Asia or China, for example? The premise of this book rests on the belief that comparative research on the Muslim regions of Central Asia is indeed justified. The Muslim societies of medieval and premodern eastern Khurasan, Transoxiana, eastern Turkistan, and northwest China, and the present societies of Soviet Central Asia, northwest China, and Afghanistan, among others, share common cultural, social, and political heritages that can and indeed need to be more closely examined on a comparative basis. A corollary to this premise is that comparative approaches to the subject of identity formation in the Muslim societies of Central Asia will raise new questions concerning the dynamics involved in the formation of ethnic, religious, and national identities which are valuable in the study of other cultures and societies.

All of the chapters in this volume, however diverse their methodologies, disciplinary and regional foci, or temporal confines, are concerned with relationships between the cultural reproduction of identities, whether they be expressed through literature, Islamic discourse, historical texts, ethnic labels, genealogies, or Islamic rituals; and the social dimensions of identity, whether routinized through state policy or political manipulation, political parties, social and/or religious institutions, or spiritual activities. In the remainder of this introduction the following topics will be discussed: the current methodologies and the direction of the chapters in this volume, the main issues under consideration and the problems they pose, and some insights as to the directions for research on identity formation in Central Asian studies.

From Boundary Maintenance to Habitus

The primary analytic label (adopted by social scientists and to some extent historians) for the discussion of identity formation is the term *ethnicity,* or *ethnic group.*[7] Although it may be argued that the use of the category "ethnicity" is problematic, particularly in Central Asia, where ethnic, national, and religious identities remain fluid and changing, often intersecting and combining, the evolution of the term's usage illustrates not only the variety of theoretical alternatives, but offers strategies for dealing with historical problems in research on Central Asia.[8] Therefore, it may be useful to survey the theories of ethnicity as they have developed from the 1960s to the present, and to assess the relevance of these approaches for the study of identity in the Muslim societies of Central Asia.

The study of ethnicity and the theoretical positions concerning its definition have been developed primarily within the field of anthropology. Edmund Leach's study *Political Systems of Highland Burma* is a seminal work in which the author reveals the problem of using cultural-based unitary categories to understand ethnicity (Leach, 1954). In his ground-breaking ethnography, Leach illustrates the importance of structural relationships as well as the subjective process of identity formation. However, it was Fredrik Barth's study, *Ethnic Groups and Boundaries* (Barth, 1969) which set the stage for the further development of theories of ethnicity and the ongoing polemical discussions that continue today. His boundary-maintenance approach focuses on the structural differentiation of groups rather than on the cultural basis of group distinction. In Barth's theory, ethnicity is a factor of organizational unity; although he does not entirely dismiss cultural factors, he sees them as the result of structural relationships rather than as any primary characteristic that defines ethnicity.[9]

Following the publication of Barth's study, two divergent approaches to the problem of ethnicity emerged: the situationalist and the primordialist approaches.[10] The first approach, the situationalist (following Barth, and variously named instrumentalist [Bentley, 1987], circumstantialist [Nagata, 1981], or situationalist) focuses on the factors involved in the selection and manipulation of identities and on factors such as self and group interests, political policies, and local interests.

The situationalist approach is useful in trying to understand the critical interaction of groups, particularly in the interaction between sedentary and nomadic populations in the frontier regions, as well as the relationship between state formation and the rise of ethnic identity (Lattimore, 1951, 1962; Fletcher, 1986; Khazanov, 1984; Barfield, 1989; Jagchid and Symons, 1989). Togan, in her chapter on the Khojas of eastern Turkistan, finds that the ecological and geographical conditions of the region together with changes in population render steppe values impractical and provide a favorable environment for religious values to surface as the critical factor in legitimizing political rule.

In Manz's study of the ethnogenesis of Turkic Chaghatay identity, internal structural dynamics are important in the formation of the Ulus Chaghatay as a self-conscious group. In the formation of this group, various "political contests" foster further unity. However, the situational model proves deficient for understanding the actual dynamics of ethnic identity formation. For Togan such a limitation is not crucial, since her concern is with the factors underlying the change from rule based on steppe traditions to rule based on Islam, not in the actual process of identity formation. She is interested in the benefits offered by Khoja rule and how such rule was able to override the tribal leadership and play a central economic role while satisfying the needs of the nomadic as well as the sedentary populations. For Manz, however, understanding the ethnogenesis of Turkic Chaghatay identity necessitates not only understanding the internal structure of the Ulus Chaghatay, but the steps which lead to its formation as a self-conscious group. The situationalist model, therefore, while useful to outline circumstantial data (whose value is in no way degraded) is a limited one for understanding the actual shaping of identities in the Muslim societies of Central Asia.

The second approach, the primordialist approach, largely based on the work of Shils (1957) and Geertz (1963), maintains that culturally distinctive characteristics such as birth, myths of origin, ritual, religion, or genealogical descent distinguish groups from one another. The primordialist approach also accommodates the view that in times of rapid change or conflict, ethnicity may satisfy psychological as well as emotional needs for individuals and groups. Such a model provides the first step in outlining the map of cultural values and indicators, such as language, ethnic labels, and genealogical charters, but stops short of putting them into any historical context or sorting out their meaning and use. Traditional Islamic rituals such as circumcision, funerals, or the observance of Ramadan are important cultural expressions of Muslim identity, but the social and/or political meaning of such expressions, if assessed in isolation, cannot account for historical change. The fact that Hui Muslims have increased their attendance at mosques, for example, is a cultural indicator of their Muslim identity. However, in order to understand the shaping of that identity, we must look to the political, social, and economic changes that have taken place, and how the Hui as well as other Chinese perceive those changes.

Reacting to Barth's emphasis on the structural aspects of group differentiation, and the polarization between primordialist and situational models, Keyes attempted to posit a new approach to the definition of ethnicity, an approach which remains influential in current research (Keyes, 1976). For Keyes, culture is the "primary defining characteristic" of an ethnic group (Keyes, 1976:203; 1981). However, both primordial characteristics and the situational or structural factors are considered in order to provide a full analysis. In a later publication in which Keyes deals with the problem of ethnic change, he expands his model to include the factor of social interaction and the social manipulation of ethnicity (Keyes, 1981; A. Cohen, 1974). At this point, Keyes begins to address the problem of identity formation and its social representation and meaning. In social interaction, Keyes concludes, "ethnicity is salient only insofar as it serves to orient people in the pursuit of their interests vis à vis other people who are seen as holding contrastive ethnic identities" (Keyes, 1981:10). Thus, the process of ethnic change, according to Keyes, is a dialectical one in which "pre-existing patterns of social action often prove to be no longer viable, and new patterns evolve, using newly adapted cultural characteristics" (Keyes, 1981:15).

The Keyesian approach is a valuable model for the study of identity in Central Asian societies since it recognizes the subjective perceptions of ethnic identity and the historical dimension of how such identities are formed, changed, adapted, utilized, or manipulated. The meaning of cultural symbols, the context of ethnogenesis, and the social and political uses of ethnic identities can thus be examined.

It would be fair to say that, whether overtly stated or not, all of the authors in this volume have considered both the cultural representation and the situational context of identity. Feldman, for example, considers the way in which the eighteenth-century Turkmen poet Mäkhtumquli utilizes the primordial characteristics of the Turkmen people to produce a symbol of national consciousness. Atkin, although using a more functionalist approach, is critical of the popular assumption that binds together religious and national identity among the Muslim societies of Soviet Central Asia. Not only does Atkin illustrate the ambiguity and diversity of Tajik identity; she also points to the significance of the sociopolitical arena in which Tajik identity is formed—that is, the complexity of loyalties and manipulative strategies at work which make these identities meaningful in various ways to Tajiks and non-Tajiks. In an environment which rigidly defines nationality, in which the very foundation of the political system is nationality-based, defining one's nationality has crucial advantages and disadvantages both to the rulers and to the individuals who represent those collective identities. The controversial issue of Tajik identity versus Uzbek identity brings to mind not only the complexity of ethnic relations in the present-day Soviet Union, but also in the numerous contemporary societies in which the convergence of ethnic self-definition and outside political forces have become such critical factors in state and local politics.[11]

Two critical appraisals of the primordial-situationalist model have recently been published, both of which raise significant issues relevant to this volume. The first critique, by Carter Bentley, in his review of the models discussed above, concludes that such models "leave unexamined the microprocesses by which collectives of interest and sentiment come into existence" (Bentley, 1987:26). While Keyes explains the relationship between objective and subjective categories, and explains the functions of ethnic identities, Bentley asserts that he does not explain "how people come to recognize their commonalities in the first place" (Bentley, 1987:27). In other words, no theory adequately deals with how "people recognize the commonalities (or interest or sentiment) underlying claims to common identity" (Bentley, 1987:27). How are such claims constructed? The answer, according to Bentley, is to be found in Bourdieu's "theory of practice" (Bourdieu, 1977; Bentley, 1987:28–29). The "theory of practice" model takes into consideration the situational aspects, self and group interests, the cultural expressions that make meaning of distinctiveness, and most importantly, the way in which unconscious knowledge and experience is made conscious and acted upon.

The "theory of practice" is based on the concept of habitus, which represents a "set of generative schemes that produces practices and representations that are regular without reference to overt rules and that are goal directed without requiring conscious selection of goals or mastery of methods of achieving them" (cited by Bentley, 1987:28; Bourdieu, 1977:72). The commonality of experience and the habitus that this engenders is what provides the sense of familiarity and familiality, or the awareness of shared community (Bentley, 1987:33). Thus, the shared habitus or shared common experiences and the significance attached to similarities and differences are important in the formation of identity as well as in understanding the way individuals may use manipulative strategies to exploit such unconscious values. The problem is no longer one of objective or subjective consciousness of identity, but rather the role of habitus in providing a repertoire of habitual responses (Bentley, 1987:40).

In societies in which religious identities sometimes conflict with national identities (often state-sponsored); in which the processes of ethnogenesis often occurs in a multicultural, multiethnic social world understood in a variety of ways by different individuals and groups; in which religious communities and values often function as political forces as well as provide shared sets of values, the "theory of practice" model is particularly appropriate. The primordial-situationalist model may provide a useful route to analyze the structural parameters of identities, the various interests and benefits influencing the formation of and reshaping of identities, and the cultural expression of them. However, as Gladney and Manz demonstrate in their chapters, the process whereby shared ideas, values, or rituals become what Gladney refers to as "an important role text" in defining ethnic identity is an integral part of identity formation which should be considered. In Central Asian societies in which identities have been and continue to be reshaped, whether they be through a politicized process as in the case of the Ulus Chaghatay or the Uzbeks in northern Afghanistan, or through a process of colonialization, as in the case of the Turkmen, or as a result of changing state policies, as in the case of the Hui Muslims in China, it is not enough to look merely for the primordial cultural symbols or the situational manipulation of identity. Rather, preexisting shared values and commonalities, as personalized individual and group experiences, need to be brought back into the picture.

Following this theory, discourse may then be understood as a shared, culturally produced set of values based on common experience and a sense of familiarity.[12] Literature, as a vehicle for expressing shared experience and for reinforcing a sense of the familiar, thus assumes some importance for the historian. The value of literature as an important source for Central Asian social history is well illustrated in Feldman's chapter on the Turkmen poet Mäkhtumquli and in Murphy's on the Uzbek writer Abdullah Qadiriy. In Feldman's analysis of the author's aesthetic choices, use of literary devices, and the historical meaning of his works, he makes a case for the strength of cultural forms as symbols of historical and national consciousness, as well as for the role of a habitus of shared values in the formation of a collective identity of the Turkmen people. Turkmenian poetry is an expression of ethnic, religious, and national identity as well as a personal record of one writer's individual experience and shaping of that identity. Murphy's discussion of the literary career of Qadiriy likewise examines the variant themes and stylistic tools used by that author to convey his own changing values in the period of political transformation from tsarist colonial rule to the Bolshevik revolution.

The importance of habitus is evident also in Algar's study of Shaykh Zaynullah Rasulev, leader of the Khalidi shaykhs in the Volga-Urals region. Zaynullah established his own madrasa in Troitsk, to which Tatars, Bashkirs, and Kazakhs were drawn;

helped to establish a printing press and libraries in Kazan; and maintained important international connections among a network of peers. His ability to arouse Muslim sentiment, particularly among the Kazakhs, made him a controversial figure to those proponents of Russian policies who justifiably saw him as an agent in the Islamicization process which took place in the nineteenth century. Under Zaynullah's influence, Troitsk became a center of learning for the Muslims of the Russian empire as well as a base for the diffusion of the Khalidi Naqshbandi order. One could argue that such a community, in which shared values and traditions were developed and nurtured, was crucial in the formation of Muslim identity among the Tatars, Bashkirs, and Kazakhs.

Manz's chapter on the ethnogenesis of Turkic Chaghatay identity clearly reveals the value of the primordial-situationalist and "theory-of-practice" approaches in outlining the processes involved in the formation of the Ulus Chaghatay as a distinctive group, as an ethnic group, and finally as a ruling group which defined its identity to outsiders. The layers of meaning, the relationship between cultural and political bonds and internal political structure, the formation of a habitus and the meaning of habitual activities, the interests and benefits gained in acquiring status and privilege as a distinctive elitist group, and the political processes at work in the further definition of this group are all discussed. Manz's chapter indicates convincingly the value of applying such models to the historical study of ethnogenesis.

Lazzerini's study of "jadīd-ism" also focuses on the formation of a shared community of values. It is impossible to discuss nineteenth-century Central Asian literary or social history without mentioning the Jadīd movement. Despite the common reference to its importance, there has not as yet been a thorough study which traces the combined literary, political, and social implications of its development. In this volume Lazzerini treats the Jadīd movement, or "jadīd-ism," as he refers to it, as a new sociopolitical discourse. He considers the movement within the wider historical context of Islamic reform and the broad nineteenth-century response to global sociopolitical and economic changes. As a response to Western ideas, "jadīd-ism" is a Central Asian charter which redefines Muslim and Turkic identity by reconciling established Islamic traditions with recent Western achievements. This study raises once again the question of duality, in this instance not a duality of sedentary and nomadic traditions, or Turkic and Iranian heritages, but rather Islamic thought and Western technology and ideals. Can a new understanding of Islam, of ethnic identity, of Western thought and technology be achieved through such a method of discourse? Such questions have been asked for other Islamic reform movements in the Middle East (Voll, 1982; Hourani, 1983; Metcalf, 1982; Keddie, 1972). In the case of Central Asia such a reform movement called for social changes as well as a redefinition of Turkic identity and the place of Islam.

The second critique of the primordial-situationalist approach is that of Williams. Written during the current period of sweeping change, ethnic conflict, and emerging nationalist agendas, this study finds that current theories of ethnicity (specifically A. Cohen, 1974, 1981; R. Cohen, 1978; and Keyes, 1976, 1981; Williams, 1989:405, 423, 426) have neglected to adequately consider nationalist ideologies. Williams faults Keyes for failing to provide "a sense of how state, civil society, and nationalist precepts constrain processes of ethnic identification or how they influence modes of ethnic organization within and across the hierarchy of segments he identifies" (Williams, 1989:426).[13]

In light of the role of what Williams refers to as "state-fostered modes of competition and cooperation" (Williams, 1989:426) in China, Afghanistan, and the Soviet Union, as well as the role of political ideology in the creation of ethnic groups and labels, Williams's remarks should not be taken lightly. As he states, "an adequate theory of ethnicity must account for the historical and contemporary ideological linkages among ethnicity and other categorical aspects of identity formation processes in nation-states" (Williams, 1989:428–29). Rather than gloating over the successful discarding of such seemingly inadequate terms as *tribe, race,* or *barbarian,* Williams reinforces the need to understand the usage of ethnic labels as they have evolved, not only in terms of their scholarly application, but also within the societies themselves.

Roy's chapter, which examines the multiple definitions of ethnicity in present-day northern Afghanistan, reflects the poignancy of such issues. Roy reconfirms the multiple levels of identification, the fluidity of ethnic labels, and the importance and influence of social and political factors in the process of identity formation. But he also examines the interplay of local and nation-wide levels of identity in the context of several local and state-related activities: the relationship between the effect of jihād on group alliances and state-sponsored policies; the relationship between the development of a Pan-Turkic Islamic movement, Azad Beg's party, and Kabul, state-sponsored Turkic nationalism; and the relationship between the Kabul regime and the Uzbek Muja-hidin in northern Afghanistan. The manipulation of nationality policies, and the resulting fragmentation of ethnic loyalties among the peoples of northern Afghanistan, is, as Roy notes, reminiscent of Stalinist as well as present-day Soviet nationality policies. The power relations effected through state policy and the desire for war materiel are only two examples of the importance of power rela-tions as an aspect of ethnic identity formation, as Williams sug-gests.

Ethnicity, Religion and Nationality— Do the Categories Always Fit?

It was suggested earlier that the term *ethnicity* is problematic for the Muslim societies of modern Central Asia because it incor-porates an array of religious, national, and ethnic identities that is often distinctively understood. As historians and anthropol-ogists have shown, religious and national identity cannot simply be considered as a subset of ethnic identity in the modern Muslim societies of Central Asia (Gladney, 1987a; Naby, 1980; Rorlich, 1986; Roy, 1986; Shahrani, 1986; Shalinsky, 1982). Ethnic cate-gories may in fact imply and/or incorporate religious identity. It is an undeniable fact that Tajik identity presumes Muslim iden-tity. However, as Atkin shows, this is not so simple a matter. What does being a Muslim mean to a Tajik?

In medieval Central Asia, membership in a particular ethnic group may have signified religious affiliation. However, religious sentiments were not always so easily distinguishable from ethnic labels. In the fifteenth century, for example, the Turkic military elite identified itself with steppe traditions as well as with Persian traditions and Sunni Islam, but religious identity was not always clearly indicated by membership in the Timurid ruling class (Manz, 1988; Subtelny, 1988; Woods, 1987). Ḥusayn Bāyqarā (ruler of Khurasan, 873–911/1469–1506) for example appears to have had strong 'Alid sentiments and was a key figure in the building and endowment of the rediscovered 'Alid shrine which became Mazar-i Sharif (McChesney, 1991:30–36).

Among the Muslims of Central Asia, who acquired a national identity only under Soviet rule, scholars undoubtedly will continue to ask how Islam has shaped the national identities of Central Asians, and how a variety of identities relate to notions of Uzbek or Turkmen or Tajik nationality (Bennigsen and Wimbush, 1979; Lazzerini, 1982; Allworth, 1971; Rakowska-Harmstone, 1970). However, just how Islam has been and is being reshaped in the face of social, political, and economic change, and how religious identities cross-cut national identities remain to be fully understood. The roles of the Muslim intelligentsia, the Muslim religious leadership, and Sufism in the formation of identities can only be appraised by examining ethnic, religious, and national identities not as closed categories, but categories that represent culturally produced, fluid notions which have a historical, political, social, and often, economic dimension. It may be argued that Islam has played a major role in the shaping of national consciousness among the Muslims of Central Asia, but this argument calls for an explanation which takes into consideration political ideologies, state authority and power, cultural heritages, individual perceptions and experiences, and regional affinities. The usage of the terms *national identity* and *ethnicity* have little meaning in and of themselves, but rather are social and political indicators.

It may be said that "nationalism" is the most forceful ideology of the postcolonial period. In the case of Central Asia, the terms *nationalist movement* and *nationalism* have become part of the everyday rhetoric of journalists, academics, and politicians alike. In the post Soviet-Afghan war period, and in the wake of dramatic changes which have occurred in the Soviet Union and Eastern Europe, it appears that "nationalist sentiment" has reached epic proportions. But is it valid to apply, in blanket fashion, the nationalist label to outbreaks of ethnic conflict, to a resurgence of Islam, to the revival of past cultural heritages? Does such labeling reveal the social, political, and economic processes of change occurring in such cases?

An excellent case in point is the recent "revival" of Chinggis Khan in Mongolia. According to recent reports, Chinggis Khan is "re-emerging as a national hero" (Kristof, 1990). The fact that, after six centuries, this nomadic tribal leader of the steppes who succeeded in building an empire that reached Hungary in the West, included most of Asia, and lasted over a century, whose rule eventually succeeded in destroying the Russian principalities, remains a figure of such magnitude says a great deal about the strength of cultural traditions and symbols. The fact that the man, the symbols of his power and accomplishments, and the past culture he represents, still hold such powerful meaning in the minds of present-day Mongolians says much about habitus and the conscious heritage of shared values. It also says much about the reconstruction of ethnic history.[14] It has also been reported that Mongolian script is being revived, and that several Buddhist monasteries are being reopened. Six centuries after the fact, Chinggis Khan's legacy remains significant, and has, in fact, been strengthened. Did this heritage have a different cultural and political meaning in the pre-Soviet period, a period in which Chinggis Khan memorabilia would not have been labeled nationalist amulets either by the rulers of Mongolia or by outsiders?[15] In a period of increasingly defiant expressions of national, religious, and ethnic identities, Mongolian pop songs about Chinggis Khan are convincing examples of how identities may be reshaped and revitalized. The process whereby such a revitalization is taking place may be revealed by digging beneath the surface of the nationalist label.

Islam as a Source of Identity

The umma as a world community serves to orient Muslims to a whole set of common traits and values. It is a community which overrides state, regional, and local affinities. So how relevant to Muslims of Central Asia is this broadest community? Where does identification as a member of this world community begin to have meaning, and where does it end, or does it? Such questions have interested scholars studying the Muslim societies of Central Asia of the past as well as the present. Certainly, the Muslim educational network, the international theological discourse, and the diffusion of and interpenetration of philosophical ideas attest to the strength of such overriding identities. However, Islam as a source of identity also may be measured in ways which reflect the fluidity of such shared values as localized Islam (Eickelman, 1982; Waldman, 1985) rather than the steadfast traditions of a unified world community. The relationship between *yāsā* (the traditional law of the steppes) and the Shariʿa is a case in point. Yāsā continued to be a meaningful source of steppe identity at the same time as the Shariʿa was invoked for Islamic legitimacy among the Timurids of Central Asia in the fifteenth century. The values of orthodoxy could be invoked while simultaneously looking to a past Turko-Mongolian, non-Muslim heritage. Both provided identities which were meaningful in different ways to different groups—to the ruling elite (military elite being Turkic/Chaghatay) as well as to the subject Iranian (Tajik) population. Indeed, the historical understanding of legitimacy implicitly involves the understanding of identity (Manz, 1988; Allsen, 1990; Subtelny, 1988; Woods, 1987). Historiography is a literary genre which pays homage to such an idea, whether it be the history of the Mongols written by a Persian court historian, or the history of the Uzbeks written by a Soviet historian.

Islam has been and continues to be a major source of identity among the Muslims of Central Asia. But the manner in which religious identity is shaped and reshaped, the meaning of religious affiliation, the understanding of religiously based identities is only one aspect of a complex of identities which are not closed, unidimensional, unchanging categories. Such an approach may be applied to the argument that Muslims living in non-Muslim states have made sense of their Muslim identity in ways that differ from Muslims living in predominantly Muslim states (Voll, 1985). It has also been suggested that there are different processes at work in the organization of Islamic communities in China and the Soviet Union. The processes of religious identity formation, however, are not intrinsically different among minority populations; rather the sense of identity and the shaping of that identity is particular to the experience of those minorities in those specific regions (Gladney, 1987a, 1987b; Lipman, 1984, 1988).

Conclusion

Yuri Bregel, in his article "The Role of Central Asia in the History of the Muslim East," referred to the neglect shown by scholars to

Central Asian history (Bregel, 1980). He attributed this neglect to its character as a "double periphery," since the region belongs within the sphere of both Inner Asian nomadic civilization and the sedentary Islamic world. In the eleven years since the publication of that article, the field of Central Asian studies has grown considerably. It remains an understudied region, however, since double peripheries often fall between disciplinary cracks. However, more significant to the study of identity in Muslim Central Asian societies is the fact that it is precisely the double periphery character of this region which poses the most critical questions for scholars concerned with understanding the formation of religious, ethnic, and national identities in such societies.

Whether nomadic or sedentary, Turkic or Tajik, Chinese or Mongolian, Central Asian societies were not and are not closed entities. The interrelationship between Muslim and non-Muslim populations, sedentary and nomadic populations, or different ethnic and/or nationality groups has been and continues to be an integral part of the cultural and political expressions of identity. Relationships between non-Muslim Mongols and their subject Muslim populations of thirteenth-century Transoxiana, relationships between conquering Christian tsarists and the Muslim khanates in the nineteenth century, and relationships between the Uzbek and Tajik populations in present-day Soviet Central Asia and Afghanistan are only three of many examples. As these and other examples point out, identity formation may be characterized by shared or opposed social, cultural, and political heritages as well as by the state-fostered creation of ethnic labels or the settlement of ethnic or religious groups.

In this volume it has been shown that the process of ethnogenesis in such a multicultural, multiethnic social world is a fluid one which undergoes transformation, revitalization, and reshaping through time. In considering both the cultural heritage and the way in which this heritage is created, defined, and expressed, these studies provide examples of research which treat identity formation and its social representations and meanings. It has been suggested that theoretical models offered by anthropologists provide a useful framework within which to investigate the subjective perceptions of ethnic identity, and the historical framework within which they are formed, changed, manipulated, or adopted through time. For, as these studies show, ethnic, religious, and national labels or concepts of identity are dynamic, whether in China or Afghanistan, whether formulated in the thirteenth or twentieth century.

The studies in this volume illustrate, finally, the appropriateness of an interdisciplinary dialogue in the development of new approaches to understanding the Muslim societies of Central Asia. Given the dual Turkic/Iranian sociopolitical and cultural environment of the Muslim societies of Central Asia, literary, political, religious, anthropological, and historical understandings of identity provide valuable perspectives. The chapters in this volume should help create an awareness of the common issues and relationships between the Muslim societies of Central Asia and other Muslim societies.

Notes

1. Soviet historians and ethnographers have long been interested in aspects of ethnogenesis and ethnicity. It is beyond the scope of this introductory chapter to review Soviet ethnographic theory or to review in depth the current ethnographic work in Soviet Central Asia. However, in light of the limited access to firsthand knowledge of Soviet Central Asian societies, ethnographic studies by Soviet scholars are an extremely valuable resource to Western scholars. Examples of such works include B. Kh. Karmysheva, 1954; S. M. Demidov, 1990; V. Basilov, 1986, 1989, and 1990. For surveys of theories of "ethnos" and ethnogenesis (in English), see Bromley, 1983 and 1984. See also R. G. Kuzeev, 1978 and K. Shanijazov for articles in English. For a fine example of historical ethnography, see Bregel, 1967. A good introduction to Soviet anthropology is Gellner, 1980.

2. For an excellent study of such a transformation, see Manz, 1989.

3. Robert McChesney's paper "Perceptions of Group Identification: Sixteenth–Seventeenth Century" addressed this problem in his examination of the term *Uzbek*. Workshop on Approaches to Islam in Central and Inner Asian Studies, Columbia University, 4–5 March 1988. Other recent studies are Thomas Barfield, 1981 and Peter Golden, 1990.

4. For Khubilai Khan, see Rossabi, 1988. For the Mongols, see Allsen, 1987; de Rashewiltz, 1973; Morgan, 1986. For the Timurids, see Manz, 1988 and 1989.

5. For two studies that treat the development of printing and education in Central Asia, see Allworth, 1965 and Bennigsen and Lemercier-Quelquejay, 1964. See also Alstadt-Mihradi, 1983 for a treatment of similar issues in Azerbaijan.

6. The only significant difference between the Soviet and Chinese

systems is the fact that the Soviet constitution theoretically permits a republic to secede, while the Chinese constitution does not. This divergence is one which is most apparent in the current movement toward secession taking place today in several of the Soviet republics, Lithuania, Azerbaijan, and Uzbekistan being three examples. Sixteen of the eighteen republics have declared their sovereignty as of early 1991.

7. For a review of the anthropological theories of ethnicity, see Bentley, 1987 and Keyes, 1976.

8. If we accept Smith's position that "modern nations are not as 'modern' as modernists would have us believe" (Smith, 1986:6–18, 212), and that the "origins and genealogy of nations" (Smith, 1986:ix) are to be found in their ethnic roots, the comparative historical study of ethnic groups is not problematic but in fact necessary if we are to understand the relationship between ethnic groups and nations.

9. For a discussion of ethnicity and cultural identity in anthropological theory as it applies to studies of the Middle East, see Eickelman, 1989. See also John Comaroff, 1987.

10. For a comparable discussion of theories on nationalism and the nation, see Smith, 1986:6–18.

11. The examples of ethnic unrest in Central Asia include outbreaks in Kazakhstan in 1986; the Nagorno-Karabagh conflict which first broke out in February 1988; the Uzbek-Meshketian conflicts in June 1989; the outbreak of anti-Armenian sentiment in Dushanbe and Samarkand in February 1990; and the Kirghiz-Uzbek clashes in Osh and Frunze, Kirghizia in June 1990. Numerous examples outside the Soviet Union come to mind, among them the Muslims in Kashmir, the Turks and Greeks in Cyprus; Turks in Bulgaria; Czechs in Czechoslovakia. For an article that provides an analysis of the growth of ethnic conflict in a world historical context, see Tambiah, 1989.

12. For a provocative collection of essays on the subject of Muslim discourse, see Roff, 1987.

13. For further discussion of the question of ethnicity and nationalism, see Smith, 1986. As mentioned above, Smith rejects the modernist position that nationalism is a direct outcome of the birth of the modern nation-state, and adopts a theory that views nationalism as a process rooted in much earlier notions of ethnicity.

14. In his chapter on "Legends and landscapes," Smith discusses the functional aspects of nostalgia in the reconstruction of history, and the two ways in which "historical drama" is acted out: poetic spaces (distinctive territories, historical monuments and/or shrines, etc.), and golden ages (heroes and nationalist mythologies). See Smith, pp. 174–208. His comments on the appeal of "heroes of the golden age" for "embattled communities" are particularly relevant to the case of Mongolia.

15. It should be noted that the Soviet treatment of the history of the Mongols and Chinggis Khan is quite different from that of the Chinese. Whereas the Soviets present Chinggis Khan as a regressive force impeding the development of Russian culture, the Chinese, particularly from the

1960s Sino-Soviet split onwards, portray Chinggis Khan as a progressive force. I am grateful to Thomas Allsen for his comments on this point. For further discussion, see Allsen, 1976:5–8.

References

Ahmed, Akbar (1984), "Emergent Trends in Muslim Tribal Society: The *Wazir* Movement of the Mulla of Wana in North-Western Frontier Province of Pakistan," in Said Arjomand (ed.), *From Nationalism to Revolutionary Islam*. Albany: State University of New York Press, pp. 71–93.

Allsen, Thomas T. (1976), "Mongolian Rule in East Asia, 13th–14th Centuries: An Assessment of Recent Soviet Scholarship," *Mongolian Studies* 3:5–27.

——— (1987), *Mongol Imperialism: The Policies of the Grand Qan Möngke in China, Russia, and the Islamic Lands, 1251–1259*. Berkeley: University of California Press.

——— (1990), "Changing Forms of Legitimation in Mongol Iran," in Gary Seaman (ed.), *Rulers from the Steppe: State Formation on the Eurasian Periphery*. Los Angeles: Ethnographics Press, pp. 186–204.

Allworth, Edward (1965), *Central Asian Publishing and the Rise of Nationalism: An Essay and a List of Publications in the New York Public Library*. New York: New York Public Library.

Alstadt-Mihradi, Ayse (1983), "The Azerbaijani Bourgeoisie and the Cultural-Enlightenment Movement in Baku: First Steps Toward Nationalism," in G. Suny (ed.), *Transcaucasia: Nationalism and Social Change*. Ann Arbor: University of Michigan Press, pp. 197–208.

Arjomand, Said Amir (1984), "Introduction: Social Movements in the Contemporary Near and Middle East," in Said Arjomand (ed.), *From Nationalism to Revolutionary Islam*. Albany: State University of New York Press.

Barfield, Thomas J. (1981), "The Hsiung-nu Imperial Confederation: Organization and Foreign Policy," *Journal of Asian Studies* 42/1.

——— (1989), *The Perilous Frontier: Nomadic Empires and China*. London: Basil Blackwell.

Barth, Fredrik (1969), "Introduction," in Fredrik Barth (ed.), *Ethnic Groups and Boundaries*. Boston: Little, Brown, pp. 9–38.

Basilov, V. (1986), *Drevnie obriady verovanii a i kul'ty narodov Srednei Azii: Istoriko-etnograficheskie ocherki*. Moscow: Nauka.

——— (ed.) (1989), *The Nomads of Eurasia* (trans. Mary Fleming Zirin). Seattle: National History Museum of Los Angeles County in Association with the University of Washington Press.

Bennigsen, A., and Ch. Lemercier-Quelquejay (1964), *La presse et les mouvements nationaux chez les musulmans de Russie avant 1920*. Paris and the Hague: Mouton.

Bennigsen, A., and S. E. Wimbush (1979), *Muslim National Communism in the Soviet Union*. Chicago: University of Chicago Press.

Bentley, G. Carter (1987), "Ethnicity and Practice," *Comparative Studies in Society and History* 29:24–55.

Bourdieu, P. (1977), *Outline of Theory of Practice* (trans. R. Nice). Cambridge/New York: Cambridge University Press.

Bregel, Iu. (1967), *Dokumenty Arkhiva Khivinskikh Khanov po istorii i etnografii Karakalpakov*. Moscow: Nauka.

——— (1980), *The Role of Central Asia in the History of the Muslim East.* New York: Afghanistan Council, the Asia Society, Occasional Paper No. 20.

Bromley, Iu. (1983), "Ethnic Processes," in *Soviet Ethnographic Studies*, no. 3, Moscow.

——— (1984), *Theoretical Ethnography*. Moscow: Nauka.

Cohen, Abner (1974), "Introduction: The Lesson of Ethnicity," in Abner Cohen (ed.), *Urban Ethnicity*. London: Tavistock.

——— (1981), "Variables in Ethnicity," in C. Keyes (ed.), *Ethnic Change.* Seattle: University of Washington Press, pp. 307–31.

Cohen, R. (1978), "Ethnicity: Problem and Focus in Anthropology," *Annual Review of Anthropology* 7:379–403.

Comaroff, John (1987), "Of Totemism and Ethnicity: Consciousness, Practice, and the Signs of Inequity," *Ethnos* 5:301–23.

de Rachewiltz, Igor (1973), "Some Remarks on the Ideological Foundations of Chinggis Khan's Empire," *Papers on Far Eastern History* 7:21–36.

Eickelman, Dale F. (1989), *The Middle East: An Anthropological Approach*, 2nd ed. Englewood Cliffs, N.J.: Prentice-Hall.

——— (1982), "The Study of Islam in Local Contexts," in Richard Martin (ed.), *Islam in Local Contexts*. Leiden, pp. 1–16.

Fletcher, Joseph (1986), "The Mongols: Ecological and Social Perspectives," *Harvard Journal of Asiatic Studies* 6:11–50.

Geertz, Clifford (1963), "The Integrative Revolution: Primordial Sentiments and Civil Politics in the New States," in Clifford Geertz (ed.), *Old Societies and New States*. New York: Free Press, pp. 105–57.

Gellner, Ernest (1980), *Soviet and Western Anthropology*. New York: Columbia University Press.

——— (1983), *Nations and Nationalism*. Ithaca: Cornell University Press.

Gladney, Dru C. (1987a), "Qing Zhen: A Study of Ethnoreligious Identity among Hui Muslim Communities in China." Ph.D. diss., University of Washington, Seattle.

——— (1987b), "Muslim Tombs and Ethnic Folklore: Charters for Hui Identity," *Journal of Asian Studies* 46(3):495–532.

Golden, Peter (1990), "The Qipčaqs of Medieval Eurasia: An Example of Stateless Adaptation in the Steppes," in Gary Seaman (ed.), *Rulers from the Steppe: State Formation on the Eurasian Periphery*. Los Angeles: Ethnographics Press, pp. 186–204.

Hourani, Albert (1983), *Arabic Thought in the Liberal Age, 1798–1939* (first printed 1962). Cambridge: Cambridge University Press.

Jagchid, Sechin, and Van Jay Symons (1989), *Peace, War, and Trade along the Great Wall*. Bloomington: Indiana University Press.

Karmysheva, B. Kh. (1954), *Uzbek-i lokaitsy Iushnogo Tadzhikistana*. Stalinabad, TadzhSSR.

Keddie, Nikki (1972), *Sayyid Jamal al-Din "al-Afghani."* Berkeley: University of California Press.

Keyes, Charles (1976), "Towards a New Formulation of the Concept of Ethnic Group," *Ethnicity* 3:202–13.

—— (1981), "The Dialectic of Ethnic Change," in C. Keyes (ed.), *Ethnic Change*. Seattle: University of Washington Press, pp. 3–30.

Khazanov, A. M. (1984). *Nomads and the Outside World* (trans. Julia Crookenden). Cambridge: Cambridge University Press.

Kristof, Nicholas (1990), "With Genghis Revival, What Will Mongols Do?" *New York Times*, Friday 23 March.

Kuzeev, R. G. (1978), "Historical Stratification of Genetic and Tribal Names and Their Role in the Ethnogenetic Study of Turkic Peoples in Eastern Europe, Kazakhstan, and Central Asia," in Wolfgang Weissleder (ed.), *The Nomadic Alternative: Modes and Models of Interaction and the African-Asian Deserts and Steppes*. The Hague: Mouton, pp. 157–65.

Lattimore, Owen (1951), *Inner Asian Frontiers of China*. New York: American Geographical Society.

—— (1962), "The Geographical Factor in Mongol History," in Owen Lattimore (ed.), *Studies in Frontier History: Collected Papers, 1928–1958*. London: Oxford University Press.

Leach, Edmund (1954), *Political Systems of Highland Burma*. Cambridge: Harvard University Press.

Lipman, Jonathan (1984), "Patchwork Society, Network Society: A Study of Sino-Muslim Communities," in Raphael Israeli and Anthony H. Johns (eds.), *Islam in Asia*. Vol. 2. Boulder, Colo.: Westview Press.

—— (1988), "The Jahriyya of Ma Hualong: Re-evaluation of a Sino-Muslim Oppositional Movement." Paper presented at the workshop "Approaches to Islam in Central and Inner Asian Studies," Columbia University, 4–5 March.

Manz, Beatrice Forbes (1988), "Tamerlane and the Symbolism of Sovereignty," *Iranian Studies* 21(1–2):104–22.

—— (1989), *The Rise and Rule of Tamerlane*. New York: Cambridge University Press.

McChesney, Robert (1991), *Waqf in Central Asia: Four Hundred Years in the History of a Muslim Shrine*. Princeton: Princeton University Press.

Metcalf, Barbara (1982), *Islamic Revival in British India, 1860–1900*. Princeton: Princeton University Press.

Naby, Eden (1980), "The Ethnic Factor in Soviet-Afghan Relations," *Asian Survey* 20(3):237–56.

Nagata, Judith (1981), "In Defense of Ethnic Boundaries: The Changing Myths and Charters of Malay Identity," in Keyes, *Ethnic Change*. Seattle: University of Washington Press, pp. 88–116.

Roff, William R. (ed.) (1987), *Islam and the Political Economy of Meaning: Comparative Studies of Muslim Discourse*. Berkeley: University of California Press.

Rorlich, Azade-Ayse (1986), *The Volga Tatars: A Profile in National Resilience*. Stanford, Calif.: Hoover Institution Press.

Rossabi, Morris (1988), *Khubilai Khan: His Life and Times*. Berkeley: University of California Press.

Roy, Olivier (1986), *Islam and Resistance in Afghanistan* (first published in French, 1985). Cambridge: Cambridge University Press.

Shahrani, M. Nazif (1986), "State Building and Social Fragmentation in Afghanistan: A Historical Perspective," in Ali Banuazizi and Myron Weiner (eds.), *The State, Religion, and Ethnic Politics: Afghanistan, Iran, and Pakistan*. Syracuse University Press, pp. 23–74.

Shalinsky, Audrey (1982), "Islam and Ethnicity: The Northern Afghanistan Perspective," *Central Asian Survey* 1:2–3.

Shanijazov, K. (1978), "Early Elements in the Ethnogenesis of the Uzbeks," in Wolfgang Weissleder (ed.), *The Nomadic Alternative: Modes and Models of Interaction in the African-Asian Deserts and Steppes*. The Hague: Mouton, pp. 147–55.

Shils, Edward (1957), "Primordial, Personal, Sacred and Civil Ties," *British Journal of Sociology* 7:113–45.

Smith, Anthony D. (1986), *The Ethnic Origins of Nations*. London: Basil Blackwell.

Subtelny, Maria (1988), "Centralizing Reform and Its Opponents in the Late Timurid Period," *Iranian Studies* 21(1–2):123–51.

Tambiah, Stanley J. (1989), "Ethnic Conflict in the World Today," *American Ethnologist* 16:1–13.

Voll, John (1982), *Islam: Continuity and Change in the Modern World*. Boulder, Colo.: Westview Press.

——— (1985), "Muslim Minority Alternatives: Implications of Muslim Experiences in China and the Soviet Union," *Journal of the Institute of Muslim Minority Affairs* 6(2):332–55.

Waldman, Marilyn (1985), "Primitive Mind / Modern Mind: New Approaches to an Old Problem Applied to Islam," in Richard Martin (ed.), *Approaches to Islam in Religious Studies*. Tucson: University of Arizona Press, pp. 91–105.

Williams, Brackette F. (1989), "A Class Act: Anthropology and the Race to Nation across Ethnic Terrain," *Annual Review of Anthropology* 18:401–44.

Woods, John (1987), "The Rise of Timurid Historiography," *Journal of Near Eastern Studies* 46(2):81–108.

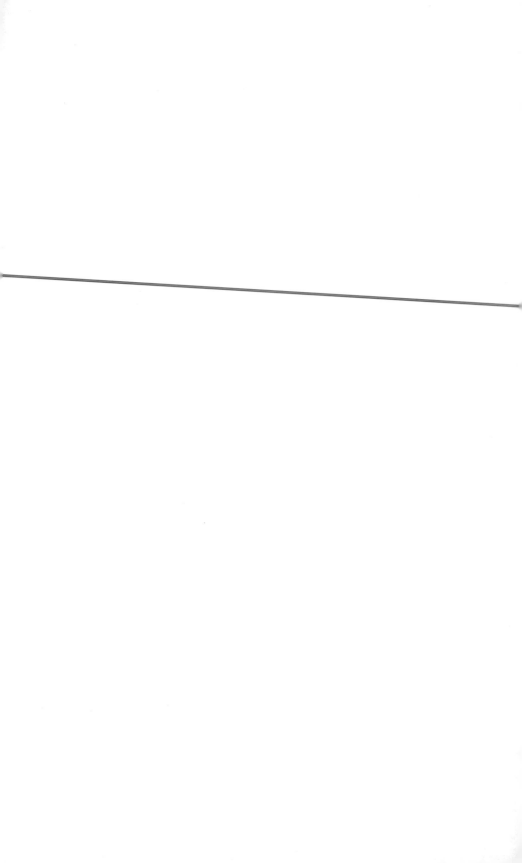

I

The Shaping

and Reshaping

of Identity

1

The Development and Meaning

of Chaghatay Identity

Beatrice Forbes Manz

The process of ethnogenesis has attracted increasing attention in
recent literature, as scholars have noted and studied the formation
of new ethnic groups in the modern world. (See, for example,
Keyes, 1981; Charlesley, 1974; Bromley, 1984; Gladney, 1990).
This chapter is an exploration of a historical case of ethnogenesis:
the development of Turkic Chaghatay (Çağatay) identity under
the Timurid dynasty of the fifteenth century. The Chaghatays
originated as the ruling group first in the Ulus Chaghatay, a nomad
tribal confederation controlling Transoxiana, named after Chinggis Khan's son Chaghatay. It was here that the great conqueror
Tamerlane (1370–1405) rose to power. After Tamerlane's conquest of the Middle East, these Chaghatay nomads became the
ruling group within a large, primarily urban and agricultural realm
covering Iran and present-day Afghanistan. During the rule of
Tamerlane and his successors, they became a defined and self-conscious group of people. They were distinct not only from the members of their subject population, largely Persian speaking and
agricultural, but also from other people of similar life-style and
provenance: the Turkmen nomads of the Middle East and the
Turko-Mongolian ruling elite of neighboring regions, including
Khorezm, the Russian steppe, and the eastern Chaghatayid or Moghul realm to the northeast. The name Chaghatay was used for
this group both by its own members and by outside people, including the Ottomans, Byzantines, and Uzbeks (Eckmann, 1966:
2–4).

The term *ethnic group* is often limited to the modern period in the belief that ethnicity, as a conscious collectivity, emerged in response to nationalism and the nation state. Nonetheless, many concepts connected with ethnicity can be usefully applied to the Chaghatay, who developed and maintained a separate cultural and political identity within a heterogeneous society. The definition of an ethnic group adopted is that of Charles Keyes, who has specified two crucial criteria: the possession of cultural distinctiveness—a set of shared cultural traits—and structural opposition to other groups in society (Keyes, 1979:5). Other scholars add to these criteria that of self-awareness or definition, and common economic or political interests (Hicks and Leis, 1977:2–10; Bromley, 1984:10–14). These criteria can well be applied to the Chaghatay, for whom a distinct group identity, defined both politically and through shared cultural traits, was crucial if they were to continue as a ruling class.

In recent years the concept of ethnicity, and with it that of ethnogenesis, have undergone significant changes. Ethnicity is now portrayed as a fluid and to some extent pragmatic identity, while the process of ethnogenesis is seen not as the gradual development of a primordial cultural group, but as a continuing process, creating a useful but not necessarily unchanging identity. Cultural distinctiveness is not automatic, but acquired, constantly communicated and revalidated through myth, religious ritual, folk history, and other cultural expressions (Keyes, 1979:4). Soviet scholarship, the main forum for the discussion of Central Asian ethnicity, has remained largely outside this movement (Bromley, 1984:93–100; Abramzon, 1971:13–19). Nor have new formulations fully penetrated historical scholarship, where the paucity of sources makes serious inquiry into the process difficult. Much may be learned, then, from a new look at the history of ethnic processes in pre-modern Central Asia. What follows will be a preliminary attempt to trace the process of ethnogenesis for one group; it should be clear that this account presents only the first findings of ongoing research, and its conclusions remain tentative.

In examining the formation of Chaghatay identity, two separate stages may be distinguished, eventually leading to the formation of a definite and self-conscious group which defined its identity in relation to the people around it. This process began with the formation of a large tribal confederation whose elite shared a number of important traits of life-style and cultural and political loyalties, and who were united by common concerns. This confederation came to form a distinct group with boundaries recognized both by its members and by neighboring powers. A second and later process under the Timurid dynasty fixed and developed a separate ethnic identity and status for this group as the ruling class within a large dominion.

The Formation of a Distinct Group

The Chaghatays began as a group of nomads, including an aristocracy and the common nomads making up their armies, organized as a tribal confederation. The Chaghatayid khanate, the domain that Chinggis Khan bestowed on his second son, Chaghatay, split into two parts after the deposition and death of Tarmashirin Khan (Tarmaşirin Ḥan [1326–34]), a controversial figure whose conversion to Islam and acculturation to Islamic and agrarian civilization had cost him the support of part of his nomadic following, unwilling to adapt to settled ways. The eastern section of the realm remained more fully nomadic, and continued under khans descended from Chaghatay, as the eastern Chaghatayid or Moghul khanate. It is the western section, in Transoxiana, which is of concern in this study. This became known as the Ulus Chaghatay; the term *ulus* was used to denote a large group of people, usually several tribes. The nomad population here, while strongly loyal to Mongol traditions, became largely Muslim and lived in close contact with the settled population. The Ulus Chaghatay continued as a separate political entity for about forty years, until in 1381 Tamerlane, or Timur (Temür), began his great career of conquest. During this period the Ulus grew to include much of the territory of northern and eastern Afghanistan.

The Ulus Chaghatay was a confederation of five or six major tribes, controlling smaller nomad populations. As Thomas Barfield has pointed out, a tribal confederation should not be seen as a large tribe; this was a different political entity, in which kinship was not the dominant cohesive force (Barfield, 1989:27). The Ulus Chaghatay had originated as an imperial structure, and it continued to depend on imperial ideology for its political identity. Nonetheless, despite its origins, the Ulus Chaghatay grew and

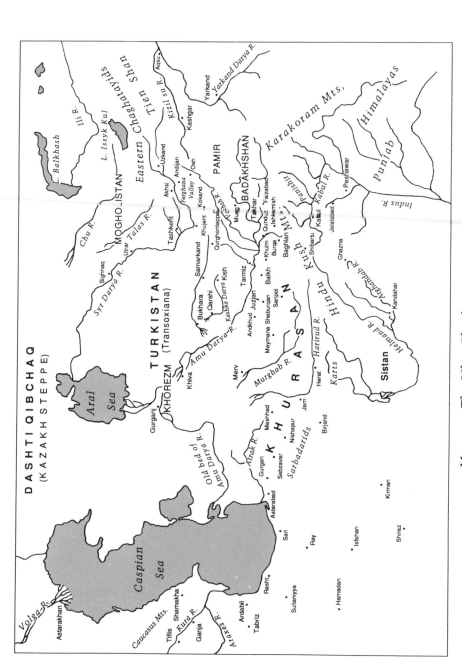

Map 2.   The Ulus Chaghatay in 1360

prospered without strong central leadership; indeed, for much of its existence its leadership was actively contested. This polity was one which was formed largely through the voluntary allegiance of tribes and groups who found an advantage in such adherence and who shared the common life-style of nomadism, along with loyalty both to the Chinggisid dynasty and the religion of Islam (Manz, 1989:22–27). Over a period of thirty or forty years the active members of the confederation remained together and moreover developed a strong identity and sense of cohesion which set them apart from their subjects and neighbors, and which, in the Timurid period which followed, formed the basis of a separate ethnically based identity.

To understand how this process occurred it is necessary to examine the development of both cultural and political bonds within the nomad population of the Ulus Chaghatay which led individuals to transcend tribal identities and to see themselves as members of a supra-tribal entity. The most immediately apparent bonds are the cultural ones, crucial in separating the nomad elite both from its subjects and from other similar nomad groups. First and foremost, this group saw itself as a sharer in the nomad life-style and in the charisma of the Chinggisid dynasty, which still ruled over a large portion of Eurasia. Most tribes traced their origin to tribes or armies which had participated in the Mongol conquest, and their ruling clans usually claimed descent from individual commanders who had served either Chaghatay or Chinggis Khan (Mu'izz al-ansāb, ff. 28b-29a; Manz, 1989:154–65). These nomads continued to speak Turkic, though the tribal aristocracy was largely bilingual in Turkic and Persian. What distinguished this group from other Turko-Mongolian populations was first its willingness to live close to a settled population, directly exploiting its resources, and second, its loyalty to the descendants of Chaghatay. Although actual power lay with tribal leaders, these men ruled through a Chinggisid puppet khan (Manz, 1989:43–44, 50, 57). These traits then served to define what has been called the primordial or charter aspects of Chaghatay identity—the aspects of cultural practice and loyalty. (For the importance of these aspects of identity see Bentley, 1987:24–29; Keyes, 1981:5–10.)

Another important source of cohesion in the Ulus Chaghatay was the dynamics of internal politics, which though based on tribalism nonetheless served to form strong supra-tribal identity and loyalties. The lack of strong central leadership in the Ulus Chaghatay might seem to suggest a segmentary tribal system, in which the existence of a higher collectivity depended not on internal cohesion but on opposition to an outside group (Evans-Pritchard, 1940). This model, however, does not fit the Ulus; tribal leadership was strong, and indeed the leader of the Ulus Chaghatay had considerable strength if he was allowed to maintain his position. The leadership of the Ulus and that of the tribes were constantly contested. The succession to both positions was open to a large number of people, and conflicts were rarely permanently resolved.

The formulation of politics in segmentary tribes—"I against my brother, my brother and I against my cousin, my cousin and I against my neighbor"—likewise does not fit the politics of the Ulus Chaghatay. Here the pattern was reversed. "I and my cousin against my brother, my neighbor and I against my cousin." Members of the same or of rival lineages competed for power within the tribe, and to win this position, they sought alliances outside it. The tribe served as a framework for individual action, but it could not be the only focus for personal loyalty, nor did it confine the relationships of those within it. When Timur first won power within his tribe, the Barlas, for instance, he allied with outside tribal leaders unfriendly to the former tribal chief, men who had recently attacked his tribe. The former chief, setting out to regain power over the Barlas, did not go directly against Timur, but first sought allies for himself among yet other tribal leaders, and attacked Timur's main ally, whom Timur then had to join. When he and his ally were defeated, Timur rejoined his tribe in a subordinate position. The battle over Barlas leadership then was fought not within the tribe itself but among several tribes (Manz, 1989:47).

The struggle for power within the tribes of the Ulus Chaghatay was connected with the struggle over the leadership of the Ulus itself. For someone seeking power within a tribe, the best ally was a claimant for power over the Ulus who, if he won, would install his supporters as chiefs of their tribes. Candidates for central power then usually found it easy to recruit allies among the tribal aristocracy; if one candidate was backed by the chief of a tribe, his rival was likely to find support from another member of the leading tribal lineage, eager to unseat the chief. In many contests for Ulus leadership, therefore, we find members of the same tribe on different sides (Manz, 1989:62–63).

Both the contest for central leadership and the contests within the tribes thus served to create supra-tribal loyalties among the members of the Ulus. As Max Gluckman has shown, conflict over leadership within a confederation can serve to bind it together rather than to divide it, if the validity of the supreme office is not challenged. In describing the relation between immediate family and larger social groups, Gluckman has suggested that larger groups, by claiming individual allegiance, weakened family links and thus strengthened social cohesion at a higher level (Gluckman, 1956:28–29, 44–45, 54–57). In the case of the Ulus Chaghatay, it appears that the relation between smaller and larger groups was a different one. The contest within the smaller group, the tribe, and more specifically within its leading lineage, led to an active search for outside allies. This conflict did not weaken the tribe itself. Although the tribal population could not be counted on for support, as a prize to be fought over, and as a source of wealth and power, the tribe remained central to its members and to the confederation as a whole. However, it could not alone define the loyalty or identity of an ambitious man—politically active individuals operated within the Ulus as a whole. While the individuals whose political activities we can trace were all members of the tribal aristocracy, these men controlled armies of common nomads who followed their leaders in their merry-go-round of alliances and thus fought together habitually with members of different tribes. The personal transactions and relationships whose frequency determine the group to which an individual belongs were bounded not by the tribe but by the Ulus as a whole (Cohen and Middleton, 1970:6, 16).

These constant political contests promoted cohesion in a number of different ways. The fact that the two levels of conflict were interrelated made it difficult to permanently resolve any contest; a tribal chief was always vulnerable to challenge, as was a leader of the Ulus. As leadership of tribes and of the Ulus changed, so did the alliances within it, and because alliances changed so quickly, permanent splits did not develop. In the many battles that Timur fought during his long rise to power, we see an ever changing army, sometimes larger, sometimes smaller, and a different set of alliances for almost every contest. Only his small personal following remained constant.

Some of the political activity of the Ulus must have been carried on in conversation, among the tents of the tribesmen, but most that we know of was carried out on horseback, by armed combatants. If this was to be sustained over a long period without damage to the Ulus, which depended not only on nomad but also on agricultural resources, violence had to be controlled by a set of rules understood by all contestants, and this indeed is what we find. This was a contest carried out among people who knew each other and who followed recognized norms. Rules of tribal vengeance were strongly upheld and usually if a member of the tribal aristocracy was executed, he was handed over to the relative of someone he or his tribe had killed.

Battles on the whole were controlled, and often avoided. We find on one occasion for instance that opposing armies drew up on opposite sides of a river, from which they could observe each other, the weaker side then retreating (ZNY I:45, 62; *Muntakhab*, pp. 209–10). Commanders here were helped by their personal knowledge of their opponents, whose troops were usually very familiar to them; they were likely to have fought together several times within the last years, sometimes on the same side, sometimes on opposing sides. Commanders had also to be aware that they might want many of their opponents as allies in the future, and this was easier to achieve in the absence of serious bloodshed. When in 1367, for instance, the rising star Timur opposed the leader of the Ulus, his former ally Amīr Ḥusayn of the Qara'unas, he faced an army composed of commanders and troops almost all of whom had been his allies within the last two years, and most of whom would fight on his side against Amīr Ḥusayn only one or two years later. These included two of his particular friends, whom his soldiers killed by mistake, failing to recognize them in the heat of battle, to Timur's considerable distress (ZNY I:114–17).

In the formation of the Ulus Chaghatay as a self-conscious group with definite and known boundaries we see that internal structure and political dynamics played a crucial part. The practice of tribal politics required the individual to deal habitually with people outside the tribe. Thus the Ulus as a whole can be defined as a community—a clustered network of interpersonal links (Charlesley, 1974:362–63). Constant political contests both required and created a definite and known set of participants. They further forged a set of norms by which these people acted, including an acceptance of tribal vengeance, of switching alliances, and of minimal killing. These norms then comprised what Bentley and Bourdieu have named a habitus—a set of schemes which produce habitual actions and representations, whose practice reinforces the sense of ethnic belonging (Bentley, 1987:28). The basic units of authority, the tribe on one level and the Ulus Chaghatay on the other, were accepted as given by all participants. The primordial elements—overriding ideologies, nomad superiority, Chingissid charisma, and loyalty to the house of Chaghatay also remained unchallenged, and served to set the Chaghatays apart from the settled population they controlled.

The Ulus Chaghatay did not exist in isolation, and indeed its politics often included its neighbors, the eastern Chaghatayids to the northeast, the Khorezmian dynasty to the northwest, and the Iranian Kart dynasty of Herat to the south. The eastern Chaghatayid khan twice invaded the Ulus Chaghatay and assumed its leadership for short periods, and all adjacent powers served both as refuge for dissidents from the Ulus and as outside allies for contestants for rule over the Ulus and even occasionally for tribal rule. We must ask, then, what distinguished these powers from the members of the Ulus Chaghatay. There were first of all the formal differences which I have described; the eastern Chaghatayids remained directly under Chinggisid rule, while the Khorezmians owed allegiance to a different dynasty, belonging to the sphere of the Ulus Jochi (the Golden Horde), and disputed territory with the house of Chaghatay. The Karts, as Persians, were outside the Turko-Mongolian sphere, and not therefore to be trusted, though they could be used as allies (Aubin, 1976:44, 46–47). When we look at the practice of politics, we find two traits which distinguish these powers from those considered as members of the Ulus Chaghatay. Alliances with powers outside the Ulus Chaghatay were less frequent, and more importantly, the level of violence in conflicts with these powers was notably greater. The Karts, fighting against the southern tribes of the Ulus Chaghatay in the 1340s, massacred large numbers of tribesmen, making minarets of their heads; when the population of Herat rebelled some years after its submission, Timur used a similar level of violence in return, a striking contrast to his very gentle treatment of disloyalty within the Ulus itself (Aubin, 1976:29; ZNS II:49–52). The eastern Chaghatayids, when they took leadership over the Ulus in 1361, executed a large number of tribal chiefs, and soon found the Ulus united against them (Manz, 1989:64). When Timur had achieved leadership over the Ulus Chaghatay, he cemented his position through military activity, and it was these neighbors and occasional participants in local politics whom he first attacked. When they were incorporated into the Timurid realm, their populations remained separate and inferior to the members of the Ulus Chaghatay itself.

The Chaghatay as an Ethnic Group

Before Timur's rule then, the nomad population of the Ulus Chaghatay emerged as a cohesive group of people. This section of the study will describe its evolution into what might be called an ethnic group. After Timur's great conquests these people became the ruling elite within a large dominion, but still maintained a distinct identity as Chaghatay. The *Zafarnāma* of Niẓām al-Dīn Shāmī, written at Timur's orders in 1401–44, used the term *Chaghatay* in a way that suggests self-identification and pride, and that differentiates the Chaghatay from other Turko-Mongolian people. The historian relays a story told to Timur at his court. Two commanders, one Chaghatay and one Uzbek, were sharing an insufficient quantity of water in the desert, and the Chaghatay gave his share to the Uzbek, thus taking the chance of dying of thirst. He explained his action by citing a story told him by Timur, that an Arab in similar circumstances had given his last mouthful of water to a Persian (ʿajamī), to increase the glory of the Arabs. By imitating this action, he was ensuring that the nobility of the Chaghatay name would be preserved. In harking back to the story of the Arab and the Persian, he also emphasized the ruling position held by the Chaghatay. His behavior was approved and rewarded by Timur (ZNS I:140).

While the term *Chaghatay* derives from the name of Chinggis Khan's son, and in the early period probably attached to the dynasty and its close followers, by the beginning of the Timurid period it clearly had a broader meaning. The Spanish ambassador Clavijo, who visited Timur's court at the end of his reign, was an astute observer who gathered his information from conversation with Timur's officials and followers. He defined the Chaghatay as those of the clan or family to which Timur belonged; at the same time he clearly included in this group the officials and envoys who accompanied him, who were certainly not closely related to Timur, just as Timur himself was not closely related to the Chinggisids (Clavijo, trans. Le Strange, 1928:122). Elsewhere Clavijo mentions the Chaghatay nomads of Timur's horde, who camped in Khurasan with their flocks (Clavijo, pp. 186, 190, 196, 214). From the large number of people mentioned as Chaghatay it is clear that the term *Chaghatay* referred to the common nomad soldiers as well as to the tribal aristocracy (Clavijo, p. 214). Shāmī, writing about Transoxiana at the time of Timur's rise, distinguished between the Chaghatay and non-Chaghatay populations; in giving an account of Timur's early career, he mentioned among the small number of men who accompanied Timur outside the Ulus Chaghatay two Khurasanians, one Chaghatay and four Transoxianians, or Māwarānnahrī (ZNS I:20). According to Clavijo, describing the end of Timur's rule, the name Chaghatay belonged properly to the descendants of Chaghatay's followers, but a good number of the population of the Samarkand region had taken on this name, without actually being of Chaghatay descent. Thus, while the term *Chaghatay* retained elements of both dynastic and kin relations, by the end of Timur's life it applied to a large group of people, both aristocrats and commoners, not in fact closely related by blood.

The use of the term *Chaghatay* to designate the ruling group descended from the tribes of the Ulus Chaghatay continued through the Timurid period. Both Sharaf al-Dīn ʿAlī Yazdī and Ḥāfiẓ-i Abrū, writing during the reign of Timur's son and successor Shāhrukh, use this term a number of times, and the Chaghatays are mentioned also in the later *Bāburnāma* and *Tārīkh-i rashīdī* as a separate and identifiable group (ZNY I:25, 452, II:283–84; ZNS II:33, 120). We have mention for instance of "soldiers, peasants, Moghuls and Chaghatays" (*Bāburnāma*, p. 320). Of one of his emirs in India, Bābur remarks that he was "well known among the Turkmens as a Chaghatay." Again, when Bābur wrote about the Uzbek conquest of Transoxiana, he stated sadly that even where Turks and Chaghatays survived in corners and borderlands, all had joined the Uzbeks (*Bāburnāma*, pp. 340, 689). The Chaghatay poet Muḥammad Ṣāliḥ, who after the Uzbek conquest went over to the service of the new rulers, was apparently accused of betraying his Chaghatay loyalties (Eckmann, 1966:4).

Mīrzā Haydar Dughlat, a Moghul writing (in Persian) in the early sixteenth century, likewise used the term *Chaghatay* to refer to the Timurids, with their followers, and distinguished them clearly from the Moghuls, although the Moghuls were themselves followers of Chaghatayid khans. His usage suggests that this term now belonged exclusively to the Timurid population, and was used for them even by the eastern Chaghatayids. He states for instance that in a battle over Kashgar, "the Moghuls started in hot haste after the Chaghatay" (*Tārīkh-i rashīdī*, p. 75). In discussing the four divisions of the Chinggisid realm he stated: "One of the 'four hordes' is that of the Moghul, who are divided into two branches, the Moghul and the Chaghatay." The Moghul and the Chaghatay, often in competition, used derogatory terms for each other, the Chaghatay calling the Moghuls Chete, or robbers, while the Moghuls called the Chaghatay Qaraʾunas, suggesting mixed blood or social status (*Tārīkh-i rashīdī*, p. 148). This usage is attested in sources written during the Timurid period which sometimes use the term Chete to identify emirs of Moghul provenance (ZNY I:342, 441, 463; *Muʿizz*, ff.103a, 137b, 142b).

The Promotion of Chaghatay Identity

The maintenance and development of a separate Chaghatay identity was promoted both by the members of Timurid dynasty and by its nomad followers from the Ulus Chaghatay. Why did this happen? Recent studies of ethnic change and development have shown clearly that minority status and close contact with other groups serves as a spur to the development of a group identity defined in ethnic and cultural terms (Charlesley, 1974:362–65; Schiller, 1977; Trueblood, 1977; Cohen and Middleton, 1970:9). Within the Islamic Middle East this process often occurred in a ruling class coming from outside and needing to keep and develop a prestigious identity, separate from that of the subject population among which it lived. The early history of the Arab caliphate provides an excellent example of this process. In the Umayyad period the Arabs, coming from a peripheral region, developed and promoted a Bedouin identity for themselves. They built their castles on the edge of the desert, sent their sons to Bedouin tribes to learn their ways, and began to preserve and imitate pre-Islamic poetry.

The story of the Arab and Persian, adapted by the Timurids, provides a good example of the way this identity could be used.

From the late Abbasid period onward much of the Middle East was controlled by non-Arab dynasties, often ruling over a number of different ethnic groups, among whom they were a minority. Beginning with the Saljuq invasion of the eleventh century, most of these dynasties were Turks. For the Timurid elite, then, identity as a minority, and particularly as Turks, was rather an asset than a disadvantage, since it associated them with earlier ruling classes. Like the Arabs in the early Islamic period, they came from a civilization with a less formal and developed cultural heritage, but one strongly associated with prowess and success in arms.

The Timurid dynasty, stemming from a tribe that had participated in the Mongol empire, profited directly from the enormous charisma of Chinggis Khan and his successors, who were associated with sovereign rule throughout Eurasia. The members of the dynasty continued through the period of Shāhrukh to stress their Chinggisid connections and their attachment to the Chaghatayid line. Timur maintained a puppet khan of Chinggisid descent. He, and even more strongly Shāhrukh, stressed the fact that his ancestor, Qarachar Barlas, had been an important commander in Chaghatay's armies, and according to court histories and genealogies, had been his personal and extremely powerful advisor (ZNS I:10, 58: *Mu'izz*, ff.81b–82a).

It was not only the dynasty which promoted Chaghatay prestige. For the Timurids' Turkic followers Chaghatay identity likewise remained important, because this was what gave them their status as a ruling group within the Timurid realm. It is clear from the histories of Timur's reign that the nomads who had made up the Ulus Chaghatay remained a separate and privileged stratum within Timur's large and varied army. The Timurid dynasty, like the Mongols before them, used a dual administration; Chaghatays held most military commands and many of the highest court positions, while Persians were almost exclusively in bureaucratic positions dealing with financial administration or official correspondence. Even within these spheres the power they wielded was limited (Manz, 1989:94–96, 100–104, 117–18).

Although local rulers and Persian bureaucrats held a stronger position after Timur's death, the privileged position of the Chaghatay elite did not disappear. This was not due to their loyalty to the Timurid house. During the succession struggle following Timur's death, most of the leading Chaghatay commanders rebelled against the princes they served. A number were executed, but the Chaghatay as a group retained its leading position. This was as true in the courts of Herat and Shiraz as in Samarkand; everywhere we find the descendants of Timur's personal following and the members of the Ulus tribes in prominent positions (*Mu'izz*, ff.102b–150b). The genealogy of the ruling house, the *Mu'izz al-ansāb*, lists offices and their holders for each of the princes who were active politically up to the 1460s. It is notable that almost all the offices listed are ones reserved for Chaghatays. The Persian side of the administration is represented only by two offices: Persian scribes (*navisanda-i tājīk*) under which a rather small number of names are listed without differentiation, and *ṣadr*. The offices on the Chaghatay side, on the contrary, are quite fully represented. There are lengthy lists of *amīrs*, either commanders or members of the Turkic *dīvān* (or both), and many of the court offices developed in the Mongol empire such as cooks (*bukavul*), equerries (*aḥtaçi*), and administrative judges or administrators (*yarguçi*) (*Mu'izz*, ff.102b–151b passim).

The Chaghatay elite also had an interest in maintaining its ties to the past. Tribal identities remain important throughout the Timurid period; indeed, it is notable that whereas Timur had suppressed the power of the tribes, under Shāhrukh some at least seem to have regained their importance (Manz, 1989:78–83; Ando, 1989:370–84). Even though Timur did not rule through his own tribe, the Barlas, his son, Shāhrukh, in 1426–27 commissioned an elaborate tribal and dynastic genealogy, the *Mu'izz al-ansāb*, incorporating and expanding the Ilkhanid historian Rashīd al-Dīn's genealogy of the house of Chinggis Khan. In addition to recording the line of the Chinggisid house and of the Timurid dynasty, the *Mu'izz* gives a full genealogy of the Barlas tribe, beginning with Qarachar. Another work of about the same period, the *Ẓafarnāma* of Sharaf al-Dīn 'Alī Yazdī, which chronicles the career of Timur, likewise includes both a preface on Mongol history and the Timurid connection to the Chinggisid house and significant information on the tribal affiliation of Timur's Chaghatay followers, not found in the earlier *Ẓafarnāma* of Niẓām al-Dīn Shāmī, composed during Timur's life at his orders.

The Timurid dynasty and its Chaghatay followers were from

the very beginning of their rule bilingual in Turkish and Persian, and familiar with much of Persian culture. This acculturation did not lessen their attachment to Turko-Mongolian heritage. It is not entirely clear what defined Chaghatay identity, but some parts of it at least can be discerned. One aspect of considerable importance during this period was language; the Turkic language used by the Chaghatay was purposely preserved and developed. Timur and his successors maintained both Persian chancellery scribes and Turkish scribes (baḫši), who wrote at least some of their productions in the Uighur alphabet. Both the dynasty and its Chaghatay emirs actively promoted literature in Turkic, sometimes written in the Uighur script, but more often in the Arabic. Timur had the history of his campaigns written both in Persian and in Turkish; unfortunately only the Persian histories remain, and indeed we have almost nothing in Turkic from his period. It is from the period of Shāhrukh that the first major extant works date, and it was at this time that the literary language which we now call Chaghatay began to develop as a separate and recognizable literary medium, identified with the Timurid realm though comprehensible to Turkish populations outside their territories. The major centers of patronage for this literature were Samarkand, Herat, and Shiraz, but Chaghatay emirs governing other provinces and cities also patronized it. As examples one can cite Timur's follower Shāhmalik and his son Ibrāhīm, who governed Khorezm and patronized the renowned Sufi Ḥusayn Khwārazmī, writing both in Turkic and Persian (Eckmann, 1964:306–26; Bombaci, 1968:107–18; Deweese, 1985:205, 220, 224). This seems to have been a deliberate promotion of the Turkic language; ʿAlī Shīr Navāʾī, the most famous Chaghatay writer, wrote his *Muḥākamāt al-lughatayn* specifically to encourage the use of literary Turkic. He complained that while most Turks were bilingual, few Persians learned Turkish, and those poorly. This was a proof of the greater difficulty and subtlety of the Turkish language and its superiority to Persian, which lacked many of the shades of meaning which could be found in Turkish (Navāʾī, ed. and trans. Devereux, 1966:5–6).

Despite the competence of the Chaghatay elite in Persian culture, court life in the period of Timur and Shāhrukh retained a Turko-Mongolian character along with its Persian one. Clavijo, describing the protocol and entertainments at Timur's court, shows it to be strikingly similar to the court of the Mongolian Great Khans (Clavijo, pp. 231, 246–47). The popularity of the Turkic *tuyuq* verse form, suitable for singing, suggests that singing in Turkic was part of court life. Descriptions of the Turkic poetry of Shāhrukh's period stress the simplicity of much of the language, the inclusion of proverbs and spoken usage (Bombaci; Eckmann; see above citations).

The Turko-Mongolian code, the *yāsā*, also continued an important part of Chaghatay identity and legitimacy, although its position and use are difficult to discern. While Shāhrukh claimed to adhere strictly to the Islamic Sharī'a, the *Mu'izz al-ansāb* lists among the offices of his realm that of *yarğuchi*, a term which in the Timurid period denoted an investigator or judge following the yasa, with three names under it (Togan, 1949:524, *Mu'izz*, f.133b). This office existed also under many of his sons and grandsons, as mentioned above. The contents of the yasa remain unclear; it is possible that its precepts changed over time, and that they were imperfectly known (Morgan, 1986). It remained nonetheless an important focus for loyalty, and was invoked even at the end of the Timurid period. An example of the way that the yasa was used is Babur's complaint that his sophisticated cousin, Sulṭān Ḥusayn Bāyqarā of Herat, violated the yasa by using gold and silver vessels (Subtelny, 1989:114).

The Chaghatay thus successfully developed and maintained a distinct identity based on separate origins, tradition, and language, and used this to underscore their position as a ruling class. It is hard to tell how long they continued as a distinct group after the fall of the dynasty. They did apparently remain an important and privileged group in the Mughal dynasty of India, since its founder, Bābur, was a member of the Timurid dynasty, and many of his followers were Chaghatay. Here the term continued in use as a name for the Turkic ruling class (*Tārīkh-i rashīdī*, pp. 148, 476–77; *Akbarnāma* III:250, 535). A traveler to Kabul in the nineteenth century was shown the castles attributed to Bābur and told that they were "Chaghatay" castles (*Bāburnāma*, p. 208, note). From the fifteenth to the eighteenth century the term was also used occasionally to denote the Turkic literary language developed under the Timurids (Eckmann, 1959:139–40). It would be instructive to examine the use of the term *Chaghatay* under the Safavids and Uzbeks, who ruled the former heartlands of the Timurid dynasty, but the research required for this is beyond the scope of the present work.

Conclusion

In the case of the Chaghatay the process of ethnogenesis may be traced through different stages, eventually leading to the formation of a definite and self-conscious group, defining its identity in relation to the people around it. This process begins with the formation of a political organization whose ruling class shared a number of important traits: adherence to a nomad life-style, loyalty to the Chinggisid, and particularly the Chaghatayid house, along with the ability to live among and exploit a settled population, whose religion, Islam, they accepted, and whose language they knew. This polity was formed through two processes, neither requiring strong central leadership. The first was the separation of the acculturated nomads of Transoxiana from the nomads of eastern Turkistan and the Altai, and the second was the attraction of the Turko-Mongolian population of east and central Afghanistan to the Chaghatayid house.

This group of people then made up the Ulus Chaghatay by choice rather than by coercion. The political contests over shared objectives, whether leadership of the Ulus, or of the tribes within it, provided an additional source of cohesion. Involvement in this contest and eligibility to hold a position of leadership served to define the membership of the Ulus, and also to forge a set of common political norms necessary to its functioning. Personal relationships and political alliances went well beyond the tribe, forming a network throughout the Ulus.

By the time that Timur began his conquests, the members of the Ulus Chaghatay were a well-defined group, united both by common cultural traits and by a complicated and active political process. After the incorporation of new territory, Chaghatay group identity continued intact and important, serving now to define the ruling class and to separate it from the ruled. Since the Timurid dynasty legitimated its rule through its attachment to the Chaghatayid house, and since the Chaghatay elite held a monopoly on many of the important positions within this realm, both dynasty and elite had a stake in preserving and developing this identity. Separate language, genealogy, and cultural traits were therefore preserved and developed, in an elite which lived closely connected with its Persian subjects and was well versed in their culture.

References Cited

Abramzon, Z. M. (1971), *Kirgizy i ikh etnogeneticheskie i istoriko-kul'turnye sviazi.* Leningrad: Nauka.

Akbarnama. (1939) (trans. H. Beveridge). *The Akbarnama of Abu'l Fazl.* Calcutta: Asiatic Society of Bengal.

Ando, Shiro (1989), "Das Corps der timuridischen Emire unter Šāh-ruḫ," *Zeitschrift der Deutschen Morgenländischen Gesellschaft* 139 (2:3):68–96.

Aubin, Jean (1976), "Le Khanat de Cagatai et le Khorasan (1334–1380)," *Turcica* 8, no. 2.

Bāburnāma (1922), *The Babur-nama in English (Memoirs of Babur),* (trans. A. S. Beveridge). London: Luzak.

Barfield, Thomas J. (1989), *The Perilous Frontier: Nomadic Empires and China.* Cambridge, Mass.: Blackwell.

Bentley, G. Carter (1987), "Ethnicity and Practice," *Comparative Studies in Society and History* 29 (1):24–55.

Bombaci, A. (1968), *Histoire de la litterature turque,* (trans. I. Melikoff). Paris: Klincksieck.

Bromley, Iu. V. (1984), *Theoretical Ethnography.* Moscow: Nauka.

Charlesley, S. R. (1974), "The Formation of Ethnic Groups," in Abner Cohen (ed.), *Urban Ethnicity.* London/New York: Tavistock.

Clavijo, Ruy Gonzalez de (1928), *Narrative of the Spanish Embassy to the Court of Timur at Samarkand in the years 1403–1406* (trans. Guy Le Strange. London: G. Routledge and Sons (Broadway Travellers Series).

Cohen, R., and J. Middleton (eds.) (1970), *From Tribe to Nation in Africa: Studies in Incorporation Processes.* Scranton, Pa.: Chandler.

Deweese, Devin A. (1985), "The Kashf al-hudā of Kamāl ad-Dīn Husayn Khorezmī: A Fifteenth-Century Sufi Commentary on the Qasīdat al-Burdah in Khorezmian Turkic," Ph.D. diss., Indiana University.

Eckmann, János (1966), *Chaghatay Manual.* Bloomington: Indiana University Press.

——— (1959), "Das Tschaghataische," *Philologiae Turcicae Fundamenta,* vol. 1. Wiesbaden: F. Steiner, 139–60.

——— (1964), "Die Tschaghataische Literatur," *Philologiae Turcicae Fundamenta,* vol. 2. Wiesbaden: F. Steiner, 304–402.

Evans-Pritchard, E. E. (1940), *The Nuer.* Oxford: Clarendon.

Gladney, Dru (1990), "The Ethnogenesis of the Uighur," *Central Asian Survey* 9 (1990):1–28.

Gluckman, Max (1956), *Custom and Conflict in Africa*. Oxford: Blackwell.

Hicks, George L. and Philip Leis (1977), *Ethnic Encounters: Identities and Contexts*. North Scituate, Mass.: Duxbury.

Keyes, Charles F. (1979), *Ethnic Adaptation and Identity: The Karen on the Thai Frontier with Burma*. Philadelphia: Institute for the Study of Human Issues.

—— (ed.) (1981), *Ethnic Change*. Seattle: University of Washington Press.

Manz, Beatrice Forbes (1989), *The Rise and Rule of Tamerlane*. Cambridge: Cambridge University Press.

Morgan, D. O. (1986), "The Great *Yāsā* of Chingiz Khān and Mongol Law in the Ilkhānate," *Bulletin of the School of Oriental and African Studies* 49 (1):163–76.

Muʿizz al-ansāb fī shajarat al-ansāb, ms. Paris, Biblioteque Nationale 67.

Muntakhab (Muʿīn al-Dīn Natanzī), *Extraits du Muntakhab al-tavārīkh-i Muʿīnī (Anonym d'Iskandar)* (ed. Jean Aubin). Tehran: Khayyam, 1336/1957.

Navāʾī Mīr ʿAlī Shīr (1966), *Muḥakamat al-lughatayn* (ed. and trans. R. Devereux). Leiden: Brill.

Schiller, Nina Glick (1977), "Ethnic Groups Are Made, not Born: Haitian Migrants and American Politics," in George L. Hicks and Philip Leis (eds.), *Ethnic Encounters: Identities and Contexts*. Duxbury, Mass.: Duxbury Press.

Subtelny, M. (1989), "Babur's Rival Relations," *Der Islam* 66 (1):102–18.

Tārīkh-i rashīdī (Mīrzā Muḥammad Ḥaydar Dughlat), 1898, *A History of the Moghuls of Central Asia, being the Tārīkh-i Rashīdī of Mirza Muhammad Haydar, Dughlat* (trans. E. Denison Ross and ed. N. Elias). London/New York: Curzon, 1972).

Togan, Ahmad Zeki Validi (1949), "Büyük Türk Hükümdari Šahruḫ," *Istanbul Universitesi Edebiyat Facultesi Turk Dili ve Edebiyat Dergisi* 3 (3–4):520–38.

Trueblood, Marilyn A. (1977), "The Melting Pot and Ethnic Revitalization," in Hicks and Leis.

Woods, John E. (1987), "The Rise of Timurid Historiography, *Journal of Near Eastern Studies* 46(2):81–108.

ZNS: Shāmī, Niẓām al-Dīn, *Histoire des conquêtes de Tamerlan intitulée Ẓafarnāma, par Niẓāmuddīn Šāmī* (ed. F. Tauer). Prague, vol. 1, 1937, vol. 2, 1956 (volume 2 contains additions made by Ḥāfiẓ-i Abrū).

ZNY: Yazdī, Sharaf al-Dīn ʿAlī, *Ẓafarnāma*, (ed. Muḥammad ʿAbbāsi). 2 vols. Tehran: Amir Kabir, 1957.

2

Religious, National, and Other

Identities in Central Asia

Muriel Atkin

The link between religious and national identity is an axiom in the study of the peoples of Soviet Central Asia. This viewpoint holds that many members of the major nationalities of that region do not differentiate between being a Muslim and belonging to their particular nationality. The two identities are inextricably intertwined, so that national customs are viewed as Islamic and Islamic practices are viewed as national traditions. Even people who are not religious in a spiritual sense are said to participate in Islamic rituals because these are seen as expressions of membership in the nationality (Ashirov, 1978:54, 65; Bennigsen and Lemercier-Quelquejay, 1968:188; *Islam v SSSR*, 1983:30, 50–51, 117; Saidbaev, 1984:5, 217, 218, 230; Dadabaeva, 1980; Dadabaeva, 1983:258). Yet Central Asians also have other loyalties that do not fit tidily into the equation between religion and nationality.

There is ample reason to believe that the religious-national linkage is indeed strong among the indigenous peoples of Central Asia. It may even have helped legitimate the comparatively recent political emphasis on national identity. For, while people have felt loyalty to groups larger than their nuclear families since time immemorial, there is nothing automatic about associating on the basis of nationality, whether in Central Asia or anywhere else. As Ernest Gellner justly observes, "nations as a natural, God-given way of classifying men, as an inherent though long-delayed political destiny are a myth," which those who advocate nationality-based groupings create by selecting and molding existing cultural traits (Gellner, 1983:48–49). Thus a nationality is not the same as an ethnic group, which does not necessarily have a political program of its own. A nationality is an inherently political form of social organization, whose advocates argue for the primacy of a nationality's interests (as defined by the advocates) in determining the cultural and political goals of the group and, in some cases, the dimensions of the state.

In Central Asia, before the Soviets launched the nation-creating process in the 1920s, the overwhelming majority of indigenous inhabitants considered themselves part of the Muslim community but also saw that community as subdivided into groups which were different and, not infrequently, mutually hostile. Among the criteria for these divisions was ethnicity, though this was rarely linked to the political quest for nation-states. Yet other bases for division at times conflicted with religious or ethnic ties; these included loyalty to dynasties, local political chiefs, tribes or clans, economic interests, geographic subdivisions of the region, and political ideologies.

Nowadays in Central Asia, there are several different ways of defining one's identity in addition to the religious-national synthesis. Each person can choose to stress any of a number of traits to which he or she can lay claim on the basis of background and environment. Many of these have survived since before the revolution, while others became important in the Soviet era. Anya Peterson Royce's observation on the functional nature of ethnicity applies equally well to other kinds of identity, which also reflect people's needs as they deal with society.

Ethnic identity is one of many identities available to people. It is developed, displayed, manipulated, or ignored in accordance with the demands of particular situations. . . . At the level of the individual, ethnic identity is both a mental state and a possible strategy. . . . In a very real sense, ethnic identity is an acquired and used feature of human identity, subject to display, avoidance, manipulation, and exploitation. (Royce, 1982:1, 185)

The strength of the Islamic component of national identity in Central Asia does not always bring with it a strong sense of belonging to a broader, supranational Islamic community, in keeping with the ideals of the faith. Furthermore, Central Asians can draw on their repertoire of traits in ways which do not necessarily emphasize divergence from the avowedly atheist and "internationalist" Soviet system. (Here we will not consider the most extreme option, that of abandoning the ethnic-religious heritage entirely and identifying solely with the values of the Communist Party.) Some ways of defining one's national identity help one gain advantages within the Soviet system or at least withstand better the prejudices of the regime and the larger nationalities. Others reflect more localized identities of the type that were common before the advent of modern nationalism and the centralized state. To illustrate a few of the varieties of group identification in the region, this essay will consider one particular nationality, the largest non-Turkic nationality indigenous to Soviet Central Asia, the Tajiks, primarily those living within the Tajikistan Soviet Socialist Republic (SSR).

All of Central Asia's nationality-defined republics are creations of the Soviet regime for purposes of its own, not least of which was *divide et impera.* Although various Central Asian groups had competing plans for the political structure of the region, the creation of separate states for each nationality was not among them. The area which became Tajikistan had never existed as a single, independent state in its own right. Over the centuries, it had at times been part of large empires and, at other times, had been divided between regional powers based in Central Asia or Afghanistan. Often, local rulers in what are now central and southern Tajikistan profited from the relative inaccessibility of the mountainous terrain to make themselves autonomous or independent. Tajikistan began its existence in 1924, as an autonomous republic within the larger Uzbekistan SSR, and was fashioned out of the easternmost provinces of Bukhara. In 1929 this was enlarged by the addition of territory further north, notably a portion of the populous, agriculturally important Ferghana Valley, and was promoted to an SSR, a "union republic," the highest-ranking administrative division in the Soviet Union.

The ethnography of this division has never been precise, significant numbers of Tajiks having been left outside the republic's borders while significant numbers of others were included.[1] The very notion of who is a Tajik contains ambiguity. The Soviet practice of categorizing Central Asians according to nationality, as defined by the Soviets, was unfamiliar and even threatening to some of the inhabitants of the region, who were not accustomed to describing themselves in those terms and feared being forcibly relocated to ensure that a given nationality would be entirely contained within its "own" republic. Thus some of the self-designations as "Tajik" or "Uzbek" did not reflect that individual's ethnic consciousness but rather his estimate of which answer would enable him to remain in his home.[2] In some cases, members of a single family chose different nationality designations (Bregel', 1983). In addition, there are a number of small ethnic groups in Tajikistan which are studied by ethnographers but are not recognized by the regime as full-fledged nationalities, in the sense that they have no access to education, publications, or broadcasts in their own languages. For official purposes, they are counted as Tajiks, regardless of how they describe themselves or the language they speak as their mother tongue.[3]

Even the very existence of a Tajik nationality, however defined, has caused controversy. The term has been used for centuries to distinguish Persian speakers from speakers of Turkic languages in Iran, Central Asia, and Afghanistan. Heated disputes over the word's origin and how it came to be applied will not be resolved here. What is of concern here is the way members of what is now the Tajik elite use to their own advantage within the Soviet system the debate on whether the Tajiks constitute an ethnic group distinct from either their Turkic neighbors or other Persian speakers beyond the borders of the Soviet Union. In this context, "elite" may be defined very broadly as those people who have some combination of education beyond the middle-school level and access, through party membership, employment, or other means, to privileges not granted by the Soviet system to the vast majority of ordinary citizens. (These privileges can take various forms, among them greater access to desirable goods and services and power over others.)

Whatever resentment Tajiks may feel toward Russians, who are widely perceived as haughty toward others and manipulative of the Soviet system to their own benefit, there is little Tajiks have felt they could do to voice such feelings openly, given the realities of Soviet politics.[4] That many Russians perceive the system as discriminating against them to the benefit of other nationalities is a reminder that there are few "objective" absolutes in nationality relations. However, there is also a regionally powerful nationality which evokes similar resentment among the Tajik elite—the Uzbeks—and a regional climate of Turkic pride, which the Uzbek elite has done much to encourage. These are targets which are vulnerable to Tajik criticism because they are strong only relatively, on a regional level, but not at the center of power. Moscow harbors a deep-seated, although exaggerated, fear of Pan-Turkism inherited from the tsarist empire. Members of the Tajik elite have tried to exploit that fear to their own advantage, making tactical use of the fact that the Tajiks are an Iranian rather than a Turkic people.

Considerable ethnographic evidence supports the argument that, despite the difference of language, there are many cultural similarities between Uzbeks and Tajiks, who have for centuries lived in close contact in cities like Samarkand and Bukhara and settled agricultural communities in what are now Tajikistan and eastern Uzbekistan. However, some Uzbeks carried this much further, denying the existence of a separate Tajik people and arguing that Tajiks are in fact fellow Turks who have forgotten their original language. Thus the 1920 constitution of the short-lived Turkistan Autonomous Soviet Socialist Republic,[5] in which Uzbek and other Turkic Communists had considerable influence, recognized only three "indigenous nationalities," the Uzbeks, Kirghiz, and Turkmens, denying the Tajiks any status apart from Uzbeks (Barthold, 1963:468). Some Uzbek Communists subsequently opposed the creation of the Tajikistan republic and continued to reject the concept of a Tajik nationality for many years thereafter (Rakowska-Harmstone, 1970:19, 240–41).

Nowadays, members of the Tajik elite seek to play on the central leadership's fears of Pan-Turkism by arguing that they have a common interest in opposing it. According to this argument measures which strengthen the Tajik sense of identity in a political or a cultural sense benefit Moscow by undermining the alleged Turkic threat to the Soviet regime. Tajik sources have repeatedly described Pan-Turkism as vehemently anti-Tajik, or, as one writer put it, the Pan-Turkists were the "mortal enemy of our people" (Ghafforov, 1987; see also "Namunai," 1984:89). Furthermore, this argument contends that the creation of the Tajikistan republic in the 1920s dealt a blow to Pan-Turkism (Istoriia, 1983:139; "Panturkizm," 1984:469). Since that time, this argument holds, the publication of studies praising Tajik literature and the spread of Tajik-language instruction have demonstrated the falsehood of Pan-Turkist claims that all the peoples of Central Asia are Turkic and should be united in one greater Turkic state (Ghafforov, 1987; Nabiev, 1986; Kucharov, 1987; S. Aini, 1986:66; "Kalomi navisanda," 1987:1; "Namunai," 1984:89).

In recent years, the Tajik elite has shown signs of resentment of what it sees as Turkic condescension toward Tajiks and has responded with a "counter-condescension" of its own. For example, an article in a mass-circulation teachers' magazine has compared the heritage of the Tajiks and the Kirghiz to the detriment of the latter. According to this article, noted Kirghiz author Chingis Aitmatov is right to worry about what elements of the Kirghiz heritage deserve to be preserved by civilization because the Kirghiz are a formerly backward people with no written language (before the Soviet era). In contrast, Tajik civilization is one of the world's oldest; the masterworks of classical Tajik literature are an integral part of the treasures of world literature (Tursunov, 1984).

One popular way of challenging Turkocentric views is by interpreting negatively themes associated with Turkic pride. The Tajik elite has even inverted the pro-Turkic explanation of the Tajiks' origins (as Turks who no longer speak Turkish) to call the Uzbeks Turkicized Iranians, who still owe much to their Iranian roots. This argument appears in a number of works, perhaps most influentially in those of Bobojon Ghafurov (1908–1977; Russian spelling: Babadzhan Gafurov), First Secretary of the Communist Party of Tajikistan from 1946 to 1956 and the dominant figure in postwar Tajik culture until his death. His argument on this subject was reiterated posthumously in the 1980s by the publication of a Tajik-language edition of his The Tajiks (Tojikon) in a fairly large press run.[6] This work has been hailed in the Tajik press as a "national holy of holies" (Tursunov, 1984).

Ghafurov's account of the origins of the Uzbeks is formally correct, never disparaging them directly but instead asserting that the Tajik and Uzbek masses have much in common, not only in their way of life but also in their joint struggle against oppression. Yet he also portrays the Uzbeks as profoundly indebted to the Iranians genetically as well as culturally. The two people stem, he contends, from a single "race," which is Central Asian Iranian.[7] Uzbeks are racially different from the other main Turkic peoples of

Central Asia, the Kazakhs and Kirghiz, showing far less Mongol influence. As Turkic tribes began moving into Central Asia, from the sixth century A.D., they came into contact with the various Iranian peoples already living there. The Uzbeks evolved from this Turkic-Iranian synthesis by the eleventh century, long before they were called "Uzbeks." According to this view, the Uzbeks, though speaking a Turkic language, are in large part descended from the ancient Iranian inhabitants of the region and are heirs to those ancient Iranian cultures. By the time the Uzbek people had taken shape, the Tajiks were already a fully developed people with a brilliant culture; the Tajiks also accounted for a majority of the population of Central Asia's cities and settled agricultural areas. In later centuries, additional waves of immigration to the region by Turkic peoples made them numerically dominant and also led to the Turkicization of many Tajiks. Thus the Uzbeks remained in essence Turkicized Iranians. The opposite trend, of Uzbeks becoming Tajikicized, was rare, according to Ghafurov. Even the Turkic languages of the new majority derived much of their vocabulary from Persian and another Iranian language (as well as Arabic) and many a Turkic poet wrote in Persian as well (Ghafurov, 1983:3, 494–96; idem, 1985:34–35, 40–45).

A similar revisionism appears in the way Tajiks interpret the centuries of Turkic dominance in Central Asia. Thus the Turkic peoples' military and political strength in the region does not reflect admirable achievements but primitive rapacity. In this view, civilization building in Central Asia was the work of Persian speakers, the Samanids (874–999), who began as provincial governors and eventually established a strong Islamic-Persian state in Central Asia, eastern Iran, and northwestern Afghanistan. They patronized the development of Persian literature, which Soviet Tajik historiography treats as one of the glories of the Tajik heritage. The Samanid realm was replaced by the rule of primitive, Turkic nomadic tribesmen, who reversed Samanid policy by ignoring the very essence of civilization—the development of cities (Musoev, 1985:42).

The attack on Turkic pride in a heritage which esteemed military valor goes much further, contending that Turkic military achievements were of the negative sort—aggressive conquests—and that when martial resolve was most needed, in defense against the Mongol conquerors, the Turkic ruler of Central Asia fled. In contrast, Tajiks protest that their people's military prowess has been unjustly disparaged by some Turks simply because the Tajiks were not aggressive. Yet they fought bravely to defend their homeland against brutal, Nazilike "conquering nomads" and later rebelled twice against the (Uzbek) rulers of Bukhara (S. Aini, 1986:75–76). This argument first appeared in a minor essay by Sadriddin Aini (1878–1954), a Tajik writer who was the dominant figure in Soviet Tajik culture until his death. The argument was revived when the essay was reprinted in the Tajik-language literary magazine in 1986. Aini remains an officially revered figure in Tajikistan, so, in this context, invoking his name to make this anti-Turkic argument is an attempt to declare it above criticism (analogous to the way Marx's and Lenin's names are invoked for polemical purposes in the Soviet Union as a whole). No storm of protest has arisen in response to this contentious declaration.

The Tajik elite's resentment of what it sees as Uzbek condescension stems also from clashes of interest in mundane matters. For example, Uzbekistan dominates the regional electric planning body and uses that authority to ensure that electric generating facilities are built to meet Uzbekistan's needs, while allegedly slighting Tajikistan's (Plotnikov and Atakhanov, 1985). The Tajik elite has also criticized contemporary Uzbekistan's heavy-handedness toward Tajiks and their heritage, including the destruction of various historic sites valued by Tajiks (Osimi, 1988; "Az mavqei," 1988). Tajikistan's government has protested to Uzbekistan about alleged inadequate protection of the Tajik language in the latter republic ("Khabari informatsioni," 1989; see also "Muzokira," 1989). The current political climate in the Soviet Union is favorable for such criticism of Uzbekistan, given the much publicized campaign by the Gorbachev regime against malfeasance by that republic's officials.

Another way the Tajik elite can use its ethnic identity to advantage within the Soviet system is through Soviet style "affirmative action," the policy of representing minority nationalities in the Communist Party, government, professions, and skilled trades. Defects in the process, most prominently tokenism and continued underrepresentation in certain specialties, certainly exist; but these are not necessarily the only important features for people like the Tajiks, who were not their own masters for centuries before the revolution either. In the Soviet Union, the difference between the way of life of those who have any access to privilege, however limited, and those who have none is sufficiently great to give "affirmative action" attractions despite its flaws. Tajiks and other minorities may be more interested in obtaining feasible gains within the system than in holding out for an unattainable ideal. Many Tajiks have availed themselves of the benefits of "affirmative action." The most conspicuous way this system works is in the selection of many, but not all, of the high-ranking party and state personnel in the republics, but it affects a great many more people beyond these select categories at the top.

Tajik speakers have access to higher education in Tajikistan in their own language for the study of a broad range of subjects from some sciences and technical specialties to the humanities (although it is also the case that specialized training in several professions and skilled trades is impossible without a knowledge of Russian). Some departments even weight their offerings to favor Tajiks by maintaining programs in Tajik but not Russian in some fields, such as mathematics, physics, early childhood education, labor economics, and history-pedagogy (Kommunist Tadzhikistana, 1986), although Russians and other nonindigenous peoples comprise a disproportionate number of higher education students and professionals working in the sciences and technology (Sotsial'no, 1986:83–84). Despite ample access to advanced training, educated Tajiks are still not heavily represented in the sciences and technology, but rather in such fields as education, the mass media, culture, and administration (ibid.:66). The mere fact that they are Tajiks, reared to some degree in their own culture, gives them advantages for working in such fields, where a knowledge of "Tajikness" is useful, as opposed to the sciences or technology. The most competitive fields for admission to Tajikistan State University include several which give Tajiks the option to study their own heritage: history, Oriental studies, and Tajik philology ("Dar rohi murod," 1986). Tajiks are also heavily represented on the faculty in these three fields (Nauka, 1983:89–110). (The final highly competitive field is economic planning.)

By 1989, as various nationalities tested the limits of the Gorbachev era's tolerance for reform, the Tajik elite, consciously emulating developments in other republics, pushed through a law to make Tajik the official language of Tajikistan, albeit with certain provisions for the use of Russian and other languages ("Qonuni zaboni Respublikai Sovetii Sotsialistii Tojikiston," 1989; "Mas'u-liyati buzurg meboyad," 1989). There was a strong overtone of defensiveness in the arguments of the law's proponents, who deemed language an essential component of national identity but lamented the shrinking sphere in which Tajik is used in public life and the poor knowledge of the language even among educated Tajiks ("Muzokira," 1989:1; "Kori partiyavi," 1989; Bobojonov, et al., 1989; "Mas'uliyati buzurg meboyad," 1989; "Dar borai loihai qonuni zaboni RSS Tojikiston,"1989.)

The Soviet manipulation of Tajik national identity was intended not only to undermine calls for a unified Turkistan state but also to reduce the affinity Tajiks might feel for fellow Persian speakers in Iran or Afghanistan. However, the Tajik elite commonly asserts that the Tajiks are an integral part of the wider Iranian cultural sphere and full heirs to more than two millennia of Iranian civilization. This claim is used to counter what is perceived as condescension by others, not only Turkic neighbors but also the central party and state, which still routinely remind the Tajiks of how much they, as a so-called formerly backward people, owe the advanced Russians. Ironically, the claim is also used against the tendency of some Iranians to view Tajiks as peripheral beneficiaries of a civilization created on the Iranian plateau. Despite the Soviet regime's apprehensions regarding Tajiks' links to Persian speakers south of the border, there are ways in which it finds such connections useful for its own purposes, which in turn gives the Tajik elite further leeway to develop this claim.

One way Tajiks assert their kinship to Persian speakers elsewhere is to avoid broaching the subject directly. That is, they treat the ancient and medieval history and cultural achievements of Persians and eastern Iranian peoples in Iran, Central Asia, Afghanistan, northern India, and elsewhere as a seamless whole, without divisions according to contemporary definitions of nationalities or states. (Typical of this widespread practice are Ghafurov, 1983; see also K. Aini and Maltsev, 1988.) Great medieval Persian-language authors are simply labeled Tajik, regardless of where they were born or made their careers. This designation avoids the taint of foreign influence and makes these authors' works permissible reading in Soviet Tajikistan. However, the linkage is also explicit. Thus, Sadriddin Aini is invoked to show that after the Arab conquest of Central Asia, the "whole Tajik-

Persian people" remained "one nation" (S. Aini, 1986:77). A Tajik professor, writing in a large-circulation newspaper, has defined "Iran" as not only the name of a particular twentieth-century state but also the much larger area, from the Indus and Syr Darya to the borders of what are now Turkey, Iran, and Syria, that formed the original homeland of all the Iranian peoples, including the Tajiks (Dodkhodoev, 1986). A related argument is that the Tajiks were a large and powerful people in the past, inhabiting northeastern Iran, Afghanistan, Xinjiang, and other areas, in addition to Central Asia (Siddiqov, 1984:14).

Although Soviet policy from the 1920s to the 1940s emphasized that written Tajik was a separate language from, not a dialect of, Persian as written in Iran and elsewhere (Rakowska-Harm-stone, 1970:242–45), contemporary, educated Tajiks commonly stress the kinship between the two, using the compound name "Persian-Tajik" ("forsiu tojiki") to describe the language and literature. The head of Tajikistan's Academy of Sciences until recently, Muhammad Osimi (Russian spelling: Asimov) has stated that Persian, Dari (Kabul Persian, a lingua franca in Afghanistan), and Tajik are essentially a single language despite numerous differences in specialized vocabularies and spoken dialects, adding that, "our classical literature, which was written in the Dari Persian language,[8] is the common property of the Iranians, Afghans, and Tajiks alike" (Rajabi, 1987:4). A similar view has support in the republic's political elite as well, notably the head of the republican government, Ghoibnazar Pallaev ("Dar borai loihai qonuni zaboni RSS Tojikiston," 1989). That fundamental unity is seen as surviving into the present in a linguistic, though not a political sense, for, as one prominent Tajik philologist stated, "we come up against no impenetrable barriers among contemporary Persian, Dari, and Tajik. . . . The concept of a translation from Persian to Tajik or from Tajik to Persian is like talking about black milk or burning snow" (Ikromi, 1984). The 1989 law making Tajik the state language of Tajikistan treats "Persian" and "Tajik" as synonyms ("Qonuni zaboni Respublikai sovetii sotsialistii Tojikiston," 1989).

Not only does the Tajik elite argue for the kinship between Tajiks and Persian speakers beyond the Soviet border, but it also contends that the Tajiks played the pivotal role in the creation of Persian civilization. This was at first a controversial view among

Soviet scholars (Rakowska-Harmstone, 1970:234–35), but has long since become the standard interpretation in Tajikistan. For a generation, Bobojon Ghafurov played a leading role in promoting this interpretation (Mukhtorov, 1984), which has remained in favor since his death in 1977.

Ghafurov contended that the Persian language of the medieval literary masterpieces and high Islamic-Persian civilization originated in Central Asia, among the ancestors of the Tajiks. According to this interpretation, Tajik had already acquired its main characteristics and was spoken in Central Asia, northeastern Iran, and northern Afghanistan before the Arab conquest began in the seventh century, although the language was called "Persian" rather than "Tajik." In the centuries following the Arab conquest, Persian displaced a number of other Iranian languages spoken in Central Asia. These displaced languages had a lasting influence on the vocabulary and pronunciation of the Persian dialects spoken there, making them markedly different from dialects spoken further west. It was only these eastern dialects which first bore the name "Persian." The language of the medieval literary masterpieces was this Persian of the Tajiks, which developed between the ninth and thirteenth centuries. Ghafurov denied western parts of the Iranian world any contribution to its development, contending that they received the language as it eventually spread from its Central Asian birthplace. Its use as a literary language was a progressive development, Ghafurov argued, because it marked a rejection of dominance by the Arab caliphate (Ghafurov, 1983: 496–501, 504–8, 510).

There are ways in which the Tajiks' links to the wider Persian-speaking world are useful to the Soviet regime. Soviet-sponsored publications in Tajikistan, Iran, and Afghanistan have used official interpretations of Tajikistan's history and its transformation under Communist rule to impress kindred peoples outside the Soviet Union (Najmonov, 1985; Mahmadaminov, 1985; "Kitob," 1987). Academic institutions in Tajikistan, such as the Society for the Study of Tajikistan and the Iranian Peoples beyond its Borders (1925–1930) as well as, more recently, the Tajikistan Academy of Sciences and Tajikistan State University, have produced topical as well as historical, literary, and linguistic studies regarding Persian speakers abroad. Some of the people who studied Persian in the Faculty of Oriental Languages at Tajikistan State University were sent to work in Iran in the 1960s and 1970s (*Istoriia*, 1983:64–65; *Nauka*, 1983:83–110; Najmonov, 1985:3; Atkin, 1987:236; Aini and Maltsev, 1988).[9]

The Soviets have used the cultural similarities among peoples living north and south of the Soviet-Afghan border in an attempt to bolster the foundering Communist regime in Afghanistan. This has included such measures as bringing young people from Afghanistan to study in Tajikistan, including at the polytechnic institute and the state university (Mirzoev, 1984; Tabibulloeva, 1982:68; Shukurov, 1980:57; Tasmin, 1987), sending Tajik academics to Afghanistan to teach and help build Afghanistan's Academy of Sciences, and arranging cooperative projects for the study of a range of subjects, from seismology to the shared cultural heritage (Mahkamov, 1986:4; Rajabi, 1987:4; Karimova, 1982:7; Usmonov, 1986). Tajikistan also sends Afghanistan books, newspapers, magazines, films, exhibits, cultural delegations, and troupes of entertainers; it brings in Afghans to see how things are done in Tajikistan (Najmonov, 1984:131, 133; "Kontserthoi," 1985; Karimova, 1982:7–8; Shodiev, 1985; "Safar," 1985; "Dustiro," 1986; "Dusti," 1986; "Mehmoni," 1987; "Kitob," 1987). The authorities even use Tajikistan to impress foreign Muslims with the status of Islam in the Soviet Union ("Vizit," 1986; Sharifov, 1985:77). In a very different sense, the cultural similarities between Tajiks and kindred peoples in Afghanistan have not prevented the Red Army from sending Tajiks to fight there. Contrary to rumors that soldiers from the Central Asian republics were not used in Afghanistan after the initial wave of invasion because their loyalty was suspect, Tajiks continued to be assigned to military postings in Afghanistan until the withdrawal of the Red Army in 1988 (Kiromov, 1987; J. Yusufov, 1987; Yuldoshev, 1988).

The attitudes discussed thus far can only be ascribed with reasonable certainty to members of the Tajik elite, which comprises only a small minority of that nationality. Most Tajiks live in what is nearly a different world and may well perceive their identity in other ways. For this very reason, outside observers cannot know directly how ordinary Tajiks define their group affinities. However, certain things which are known about the conditions under which they live make it probable that smaller-scale kinds of loyalties, well established under pre-modern conditions, such as to neighbors in one's locality, extended families, or patrons, remain at least as strong among them as loyalties to a national or supra-national community defined in either national or religious terms. What a villager means when he describes himself as a Tajik (or a Muslim) is not necessarily what a member of the elite has in mind when he uses the same terms.

The fact that many a Tajik villager is said to know some of the poetry of Firdawsi and other great medieval Persian poets by heart (Procyk, 1973:128–29) does not prove the existence of a modern type of national consciousness, whether called Persian or Tajik, among such villagers. A similar familiarity with classics of Persian high culture is traditional among Persian-speaking villagers in Iran as well. Although that may indicate an orientation of *cultural* identity along certain lines, it does not demonstrate the existence of a *national* consciousness, in a modern political sense among Persian speakers, who for centuries lived in states, some large, some small, but all defined by such criteria as dynasty, tribe, religion, or social protest, but not by the criterion of the nation-state. Indeed, Iranian nationalism, in contrast to appreciation of the Persian cultural heritage, is a recent historical development, arising from a number of sources, some of which have little direct connection with traditional culture (among them, the ambition of rulers, opposition to major powers' involvement in Iranian affairs, and the intellectual and material consequences of modernization).

Several aspects of modernization which have played such an important role in much of the world in supplanting traditional, localized loyalties with broader ones have had comparatively little effect in Tajikistan. Of course decades of Soviet rule have wrought many changes, including the establishment of mass education and the mass media, urbanization, some industrialization, the collectivization of agriculture, a military draft, and an extensive network for political mobilization, indoctrination, and control. Yet Soviet-style modernization has changed Tajikistan, especially its villages, where most Tajiks live, far less than many other parts of the Soviet Union.

The very fact that a majority of Tajiks live in rural rather than urban areas reflects how much more of the traditional way of life has survived in Tajikistan. That republic is the least urbanized of all the Soviet republics. Although the population of the USSR as a whole was only 38 percent rural, according to the 1979 census, the figure for Tajikistan was 65 percent (Tsentral'noe, 1984:9). In fact, the republic has become more, rather than less, rural since 1970. Moreover, the settlement pattern of Tajiks is even more rural than that of the republican population as a whole; 72 percent of the Tajiks live in the countryside; Tajiks account for only 42 percent of the total urban population (*Sotsial'no,* 1986:38, 39, 44, n. 34).

Rural life in Tajikistan is comparatively isolated and inward focused. More than 80 percent of the villagers still live in the place where they were born. The rural population is dispersed among more than three-thousand villages. Since Tajikistan is 93 percent mountainous, the countryside is divided into a host of separate areas, which are linked by roads which are often poor and in many cases are seasonably impassable (Tsentral'noe, 1984:362; "San"a-ti," 1983; Ismailov and Kleandrov, 1983:26). Many villages are inhabited by members of a single nationality. Even where they are officially classed as multiethnic, in practice they may be subdivided into separate, ethnically homogeneous hamlets (Saidbaev, 1984:222; Islomov, 1986). Tajiks are highly endogamous, villagers even more than city dwellers. On the rare occasions when they marry exogamously, they are most likely to marry Uzbeks, rather than Russians or others of nonlocal origins (Vinnikov, 1980:36; *Sotsial'no,* 1986:153, table 19; p. 167, table 27). (However, conclusions about endogamy and exogamy or the ethnic composition of villages should be tempered with caution, given the imprecision of "Uzbek" and "Tajik" as nationality designations.)

Avenues of communications which could help spread the influence of the cities, whether of the political establishment or of any proponents of a consciousness broader than traditional kinds, are weak. Deficiencies of the transportation system make travel itself difficult (Karimov, 1985; Saifulloev, 1985). Rural cultural and entertainment facilities, including libraries, clubs, and movie theaters, are woefully inadequate (Mahkamov, 1986:4; Kuznetsov, 1986; "Kitobkhonai ommavi," 1986; "Ma'qul," 1987). Tajikistan ranks last among the Soviet republics in book reading and among the lowest in subscriptions to newspapers and magazines (Nasrullo, 1987). Education in the countryside is inferior to what is available in the cities (Rosen, 1973:63; Abdulloev, 1984; "Islohoti maktab," 1984; Shoismatulloev, 1984; "Marhalai nav," 1984:14; Rasulzoda, 1985; "Bo rohi," 1987:17). Even though the republic's population is two-thirds rural, only one-third of the

Communist Party members live in the countryside, and the party leadership has voiced concern over the quality of rural Communists ("Nomi baland," 1987).

In many countries, the widespread adoption of a standardized language has been conducive to the victory of national or other broad foci of loyalty over traditional, narrower ones. In Tajikistan, no standardized language as yet plays that role, despite the fact that roughly 99 percent of the Tajiks in the republic claimed fluency in Tajik in the 1979 census (Tsentral'noe, 1984:132–33). Although many members of the elite know literary Tajik (and Russian), ordinary people speak various dialects, broadly divided between north and south, with several further subdivisions (Oranskii, 1983:29–30; Monogarova, 1980:130). Even though public education is universal in Tajikistan, a significant number of Tajiks remain most at home in a dialect of their native tongue and cannot use standard written Tajik. The problem begins in the elementary grades and continues through higher education. As one middle school teacher lamented, "It is a secret to no one that after receiving a primary education students go on to upper grades who not only do not know one excerpt of poetry by heart but also cannot read a book correctly" (Abdulloev, 1987:3).

The problem persists even among people who get a higher education, especially in areas outside the humanities, and who then teach in local schools and perpetuate the use of nonstandard Tajik. The competence of Tajik language and literature teachers has also been called into question ("Mavzu," 1983; Ibrohimov, 1985; Abdulloev, 1984; idem, 1987:3; Samadov, 1985; Abdulhaev and Uzbekov, 1985; "Tahlili," 1983; Saifiev, Aminov, and Naimboev, 1984). "Thus, in school everyone teaches physics, mathematics, chemistry, biology, etc. in his own local dialect" (Lutfulloev and Qalandarov, 1986).

Nor does Russian serve as a lingua franca for the indigenous inhabitants. More than one-third of the Tajiks surveyed in the 1979 census claimed they had a working knowledge of Russian (Tsentral'noe, 1984:71). However, the repeated alarms in Tajikistan about the scant knowledge of Russian among the indigenous population and the poor quality of Russian-language instruction (Mahkamov, 1985:3; "Kadrho," 1987:32; Sultonov, 1987:72–73; "Islohoti maktab," 1986:2; "Mas'uliyati buzurg meboyad," 1989: 1) undermine the credibility of the census data, which here, as in the other republics, are tainted by the self-reporting of language competence and the tendency to make the data fit the regime's goals.

A similar problem exists with ordinary Tajiks' knowledge of their own history. In many countries, the elite's reinterpretation of history along culturally nationalist lines, to prove that their nationality has a distinct identity, a proud heritage, and, in some cases, legitimate grievances against other nationalities, has played a key role in building a national consciousness. The Tajik elite has tried to reinterpret Tajik history in a similar fashion, to the extent permitted by the central authority, but with little effect among the majority of the population. Only a small fraction of Tajikistan's professional historians deal with the history of the Tajiks before 1917. The majority deal with post-1917 topics or other, quite different, subjects, like the history of the Communist Party. Their publications on Tajik history have been few and there is no good textbook on the subject in the Tajik language (Mirboboev, 1987). Tajik history is taught poorly as a rule in Tajikistan and is not even treated as a separate subject in its own right (except at the advanced, specialized level). As a result, "students know the history of Greece and Egypt and Rome and China better than the history of Tajikistan" (ibid., 1987; see also Bobojonov, Botirov, and Mavlaviev, 1989). Many Tajiks have little interest in or knowledge of their own history (Kerimova and Khan, 1985:29; "Bo rohi," 1987:3; Osimi, 1988:4; Rashidov, 1987:2; "Muzokira," 1989:1).

Given the linkage between religious and national identity in Central Asia one may question whether it is Islam which provides the alternative to local foci of loyalty. A definitive answer may be unobtainable, given that so much information about the status of Islam in the Soviet Union is mediated through partisan sources. There are grounds at least for skepticism that Islam exerts its considerable influence in particular as a countervailing force against localism. As an abstraction, the unity of the community of believers has been a deeply held principle among Muslims. In practice, it has been unable for fourteen centuries to prevent wars and uprisings in which fellow believers have shed each other's blood. The spiritual unity of Islam has been riven by worldly rivalries in Central Asia as elsewhere. In the nineteenth century, regional leaders did not forgo their rivalries to cooperate in opposing the

Russian conquest; and the antagonisms which divided them did not disappear after the conquest. For example, in the last quarter of the nineteenth century there were numerous uprisings in what had formerly been the khanate of Kokand but was then part of the Russian governor-gencralship of Turkistan. Many of these uprisings were called holy wars but were directed primarily against indigenous inhabitants of the region, who were fellow Muslims, rather than against the Russians (Manz, 1987:265). The fight of the Basmachi (1918–c. 1925) to prevent the Red Army's conquest of Central Asia was marked by a lack of coordinated efforts and acrimony among coreligionists (Wheeler, 1964:107–11; Pipes, 1964:178, 257).

As the established Soviet constraints on unauthorized mass activity eroded in the Gorbachev era, bitter, sometimes violent clashes erupted between rural Tajiks and neighboring Muslim peoples. This set Tajiks at odds with both the Kirghiz and Uzbeks; there was also a spillover of anti-Meskhetian violence from Uzbekistan. The immediate cause of the strife appears to have been concern over economic interests, including access to land and water (TadzhikTA, 1989a; ibid., 1989b; Kozlov, 1989; Bobojonov, et al., 1989; Popov, 1989). To date, there is insufficient information to indicate the weight of national or other considerations in the participants' attitudes.

Muslim religious figures in contemporary Central Asia lack a broad-based organization which could increase the cohesion of the Islamic community there. The one network which does encompass the entire region is state controlled—the Muslim Spiritual Administration of Central Asia and Kazakhstan, one of four such geographically defined bodies established in 1940 and subject to the central government. The mullas who operate under the aegis of all four Spiritual Administrations are few in number, about two thousand for the entire Muslim population of the Soviet Union, far too few to serve the needs of most Muslims in Central Asia or the rest of the country. The same is true of the legally recognized mosques (Bennigsen and Lemercier-Quelquejay, 1979:151). Many more mullas and other religious figures operate without official sanction. No evidence has yet surfaced to indicate that any of them have established extensive networks over a large geographical area. For example, the most radical Islamic preacher in Central Asia to come to public note in recent years is a Tajik, Abdullo

Saidov, who had been active for years but was finally arrested in the summer of 1986, after calling for the establishment of Islamic rule in Tajikistan. He did not set his sights beyond the frontiers of the republic and advocate the union of all Central Asia under the banner of Islam. If his strongest supporters, who demonstrated briefly for his release (and thus became known to the authorities) are any indication, his horizons may have been far narrower even than this. Fewer than a dozen people, some of them Saidov's relatives, have been identified by name as having demonstrated against his arrest outside the Ministry of Internal Affairs offices in the provincial (*oblast'*) capital of Qurghonteppa. With a single exception, all, like Saidov himself, lived in this southwestern oblast'; the lone exception lived just north of the oblast' border. The press account describes Saidov as having had the use of an automobile, which could have given him the mobility to reach further afield, but he is known to have traveled only within Qurghonteppa oblast' to preach (Rabiev, 1987a; idem, 1987b).

The ways mullas and ordinary believers receive their instruction in Islam is conducive to a localized orientation. Officially recognized mullas have been trained at two madrasas, one in Bukhara, the other in Tashkent. For decades these were the only ones legally empowered to provide such training in the Soviet Union. Both institutions graduate a total of about sixty men a year (Binyon, 1985:250). Additional madrasas have just recently been opened. Men who study to become "unofficial" mullas or Sufi adepts do so in many different villages and cities (I. Yusufov, 1986; Vohid, 1987; "Durdona," 1987:2). Thus the situation contrasts sharply with that in the central Islamic lands, where renowned, centuries-old madrasas in major cities have established normative curricula for the education of students drawn from far beyond the immediate environs. Even under those conditions, the practice of Islam in rural areas has included local variations which differed from the kind of Islam taught at the urban centers of Islamic scholarship. Soviet policy has, no doubt inadvertently, encouraged this divergence further by weakening the urban Islamic leadership, which it can control more readily than the religious figures dispersed throughout the countryside. The religious education of ordinary believers in Central Asia is similarly localized. Since Soviet law bars religious proselytizing among children, most of them learn about their faith from whoever is available in the village to teach them. Foremost among the teachers are the parents themselves and other family members; others include public school teachers who give religious instruction as a sideline, "unofficial" mullas, and anyone else who can claim some knowledge of Islam (Dadabaeva, 1983:257; Davlatov, 1986; Komilov, 1982:12; Rahmatov, 1986; Sattorov, 1987:47; Smirnov, 1988:116, 123). It in no way disparages the religious convictions of Tajiks who learn about Islam in this way to say that the very circumstances of their instruction are far better suited to pass on from generation to generation the local varieties of Islamic practice as these have developed as a living faith among ordinary people rather than the formal, scholarly tradition of the madrasas.

Tajikistan's Muslims have contacts with the wider Islamic world through radio broadcasts, videotapes, and publications produced abroad and transmitted to Central Asia. That does not by itself ensure the strengthening of supranational religious ties in any practical sense. These religious messages come from a number of countries, among them Egypt, Saudi Arabia, Iran, Pakistan, and Afghanistan, which differ in their interpretations of Islam and in some cases are adversaries in the political and religious sphere. Moreover, the fact that Central Asians receive such messages does not reveal how they respond to them. Even those who receive a particular message favorably may respond by feeling encouraged in the beliefs they already hold rather than by transforming those beliefs.

The aspects of identity discussed here by no means exhaust the range of possibilities available to Tajiks. For example, there are some signs that Tajik veterans of the war in Afghanistan at times feel closer bonds to other veterans (or at least other Tajik veterans) than they do to Tajiks who did not serve. Tajik men and women, those who are highly educated and those who are not, those who live in the cities and in the villages are all divided on whether the extremely high birth rate among Tajiks should be reduced through family planning. Other concerns produce yet other realignments within what appears to be simply a single people. Collective identities matter because people live in society and must deal with other people in a host of ways. Therefore, the range of possible identities is potentially as broad as the range of a person's social interactions. The setting of the particular interactions determines which affiliations meet a person's needs in that situation or are pushed to the fore in reaction to the behavior of others. Many forms of group identity, whether of long-standing or transient significance, do not have well-established names to distinguish them from such familiar categories as "nationality" and "religion." Thus, terms like "Tajik" and "Muslim" tend to subsume, and at times conceal, a complex assortment of other loyalties that also exist among the members of those broadly defined communities.

Notes

1. According to the 1979 Soviet census, 22.8 percent of the Tajiks lived outside Tajikistan; almost all of them (594,627) lived in Uzbekistan. Tajiks accounted for 2,237,048 of Tajikistan's 3,801,357 inhabitants. A large number of other regional peoples (as well as nonindigenous peoples) also lived in Tajikistan. Foremost among these was the large Uzbek minority (873,199) (Jamolov, 1984:66–67; Tsentral'noe, 1984:7, 132). Early reports from the 1989 census indicate that the republic's population has risen to 5,112,000 ("Darborai," 1989). A passing remark by Q. M. Mahkamov, First Secretary of the republics' Communist Party, indicates that the Uzbeks now comprise roughly a quarter of Tajikistan's population (Zokirov and Bobjonov, 1989). The current size of Uzbekistan's Tajik population is hotly disputed. Uzbeks contend that the Tajiks number 700,000 out of a total republican population of twenty million. Tajiks contend that there are at least 800,000 Tajiks in Uzbekistan, and that the republic's authorities have for decades misidentified many Tajiks as Uzbeks. Foreign Broadcast Information Service, Soviet Union, *Daily Report*, Nov. 18, 1988, p. 97; B. Firuz, "Didu bodide muborak," *Adabiyat va San"at*, 20 April 1989, p. 4; A. Semerkin, "Drug-zerkalo druga," Komsomolets Tadzhikistana, 14 Oct. 1988, p. 2; Kh. Sharifov, "Tojikiston-Uzbekiston: robitahoi farhangi," *Gazetai muallimon*, 13 Sept. 1988, p. 3.

2. One long-term reflection of this may be the odd fact that, according to the 1979 census, 7,396 Uzbeks living in Tajikistan described themselves as speaking Tajik as their native language, while 5.7 percent of the Tajiks living in Uzbekistan said their native language was Uzbek (Tsentral'noe, 1984, pp. 132–33; *Sotsial'no*, 1986, p. 310).

3. These include speakers of other Iranian languages, such as the Yaghnabs (descended from the Soghdians of antiquity) and seven peoples classed as "Pamiris" (all of whom live in the remote heights of the Pamir Mountains in Gorno-Badakhshan Autonomous Oblast' in southeastern Tajikistan) as well as small numbers of others who moved to Tajikistan from points further south in earlier centuries (Vinnikov, 1980:30; Oranskii, 1983; Monogarova, 1980; Tsentral'noe, 1984, pp. 132–33).

4. In 1989, as many Soviet nationalities became more assertive in voicing their grievances, stories spread of a few incidents in which young

Tajiks berated members of other nationalities living in the republic for not learning Tajik (Istad, 1989).

5. The Turkestan ASSR, which encompassed the territory of what had formerly been the tsarist governor-generalship of Turkistan, existed briefly as the Communists took control of the region during the civil war. Beginning in 1921, Moscow began to redivide Central Asia into nationality based ASSRs and later SSRs, so that by 1924 the Turkestan ASSR ceased to exist.

6. Although *Tojikon* was published under Ghafurov's name alone, it was in fact the work of a number of scholars, not all of whom were Tajik (Tursunov, 1984).

7. Ghafurov used several names interchangeably for this "race": Māwarānnahr (the land between the Amu Darya and the Syr Darya), Ferghana-Pamir, and "European."

8. "Dari" in this context refers to literary Persian, not to the Kabul dialect of Persian.

9. Through the 1950s, a large population of the people engaged in such work were non-Tajiks, mainly Russians and some Jews. Since then, many Tajiks have entered these fields, although they have not acquired a monopoly in them.

References Cited

Abdullhaev, L., and G. Uzbekov (1985), " 'Usuchahoi begunoh,' " *Gazetai muallimon*, 11 June:2.

Abdulloev, Q. (1984), "Darkhosthoi mo," *Gazetai muallimon*, 14 January:1.

———— (1987), "Charo mo zaboni khudro namedonem,?"*Tajikostoni soveti*, 23 August:3, 4.

Aini, K., and Y. S. Maltsev (1988), "Oriental Studies in Tajikistan," *Iranian Studies* 21:18–22.

Aini, S. (1986), "Ma'noi kalimai tojik," *Sadoi Sharq* 8:66–86.

Ashirov, N. (1978), *Musul'manskaia propoved'*. Moscow: Izdatel'stvo politicheskoi literatury.

Atkin, M. (1987), "Iranian Studies in the USSR," *Iranian Studies* 20:223–51.

"Az mavqei kushodadilona" (1988), *Tojikistoni soveti*, 13 March:2.

Barthold. V. V. (1963), "Tadzhiki. Istoricheskii ocherk," in *Sochineniia*. Moscow: Izdatel'stvo Vostochnoi Literatury. Vol. 2, pt. 1:451–68.

Bennigsen, A., and C. Lemercier-Quelquejay (1968), *L'Islam en Union Soviétique*. Paris: Payot.

———— (1979), " 'Official' Islam in the Soviet Union," *Religion in Communist Lands* 7:148–59.

Binyon, M. (1985), *Life in Russia*. New York: Berkeley Books.

Bobojonov, R., H. Botirov, and M. Mavlaviev (1989), "Mo hama farzandi yak oilaem!" *Tojikistoni soveti*, 30 July:3.

"Bo rohi bozsozi, bo rohi islohoti maktab" (1987), *Matkabi soveti* 8 (August):12–30.

Bregel', Iu. (1983), Remarks made at the "Conference on the Study of Central Asia" at the Woodrow Wilson International Center for Scholars. Washington, D.C., 10–11 March.

Dadabaeva, S. Iu. (1980), "Sama saboi ne otomret," *Kommunist Tadzhikistana*, 31 October:2.

——— (1983), "Konkretno-sotsiologicheskie issledovaniia v praktikeateisticheskoi raboty," *Voprosy nauchnogo ateizma*. Vol. 31. *Sovremennyi islam i problemy ateisticheskogo vospitaniia*, 251–60.

"Dar borai loihai qonuni zaboni RSS Tojikiston" (1989), *Tojikistani sovieti*, 12 July:1.

"Dar borai natijahoi peshakii baruikhatgirii umumiittifaqii aholi dar soli 1989" (1989), *Tojikistoni soveti*, 7 May:3.

"Dar rohi murod" (1986), *Tojikistoni soveti*, 1 August:4.

Davlatov, Q. (1986), "Asht," *Gazetai muallimon*, 2 June:2–3.

Dodkhodoev, R. (1986), "Ironu Turon chi ma"ni dorand,?" *Adabiyot va san"at*, 13 November:15.

"Durdona adoshinosi dar'yost" (1987), *Gazetai muallimon*, 2 June:2–3.

"Dusti antiho nadorad" (1986), *Tojikistoni soveti*, 19 July:4.

"Dustiro mustahkam kunem" (1986), *Tojikistoni sovieti*, 10 July:2.

Firuz, B. (1989), "Didu bodide muborak!," *Adabiyot va san"at*, 20 April:4.

Foreign Broadcast Information Service (1988). *Soviet Union. Daily Report*, 18 November:97.

Gellner, E. (1983), *Nations and Nationalism*. Ithaca: Cornell University Press.

Ghafforov, R. (1987), "Nakhustin 'Sarfu nahv'-i zaboni tojiki," *Adabiyot va san"at*, 25 June:11.

Ghafurov, B. (1983), *Tojikon*. Vol. 2. Dushanbe: Irfon.

——— (1985), *Tojikon*. Vol. 2. Dushanbe: Irfon.

Ibrohimov, S. (1985), "Darkhosti zamon," *Gazetai muallimon*, 19 March: 2.

Ikromi, D. (1984), "Paivandi afkor," *Adabiyot va san"at*, 15 March:4.

Islam v SSR (1983), Moscow: Mysl'.

"Islohoti maktab dar muhokimai kollegiya" (1984), *Gazetai muallimon*, 26 May:1.

"Islohoti maktab—kori umumikhalqi" (1986), *Gazetai muallimon*, 13 December:1,2.

Islomov, A. (1986), "Az ki madad juem,?" *Tojikostoni soveti*, 25 March:3.

Ismailov, Sh., and M. Kleandrov (1983), "Roli takomuloti qonunguzori dar ijroi programmai ozuqavori," *Kommunisti Tojikiston*, December: no. 12.

Istad, A. (1989), "Ba ki ta"na mezanem?" *Tojikistoni soveti*, 1 July:3.

Istoriia kul'turnogo stroitel'stva v Tadzhikistane (1917–1977 gg.) (1983). Vol. 2. Dushanbe: Donish.

Jamolov, Q. (1984), "Migratsiyai aholi—omili muhimi ba ham nazdikshavii millatu khalqhoi soveti," *Kommunisti Tojikiston*, June: no. 6.

"Kadrhoro muvofiqi talabhoi van ta"lim dihim" (1987), *Maktabi soveti*, 8 (August):31–36.

"Kalomi navisanda—vositai muhimi tarbiyati internatsionali" (1987), *Adabiyot va san"at*, 11 June:1–4.

Karimov, H. (1985), "Mashruti dushvor," *Tojikistoni soveti*, 16 October:4.

Karimova, O. B. (1982), "Muvaffaqiyathoi maorifi khalqi mo namunai ibrat baroi mamlakathoi Osiyo va Afrika," *Maktabi soveti*, October, no. 10.

Kerimova, O., and V. Khan (1985), "Holat va naqshahoi minba"dai ta"limi ta"rikhi RSS Tojikiston," *Maktabi soveti*, March, no. 3.

"Khabari informatsioni" (1989), Tojikistoni soveti, 23 July:1.

Kiromov, H. (1987), "Ehsosi dilovari," *Tajikistoni soveti*, 14 August:2.

"Kitob—qosidi dusti" (1987), *Tojikistoni soveti*, 3 January:2.

"Kitobkhonahoi ommavi" (1986), *Tojikistoni soveti*, 13 September:1.

Komilov, Ch. (1982), "Ba"ze sababhoi dindorii maktabiyon va rohhoi barhamdodani onho," *Maktabi soveti*, November, no. 11.

Kommunist Tadzhikistana (1986). Announcement of admissions openings for the 1986–1987 academic year at Tajikistan State University (Dushanbe); Tajikistan Politechnic Institute (Dushanbe); the Leninobod branch of Tajikistan Politechnic Institute; the Pedagogical Institute (Dushanbe); the Leninobod Pedagogical Institute; the Kulob Pedagogical Institute; the Dushanbe Qurghonteppa branch of the Pedagogical Institute. 29 April:4.

"Kontserthoi dusti" (1985). *Tojikostoni soveti*, 26 April:3.

"Kori partiyavi fardoro didan ast" (1989), *Tojikistoni soveti*, 30 July:2.

Kozlov, B. (1989), "Asli gap chi bud,?" *Tojikistoni soveti*, 18 June:1.

Kucharov, A. (1987), "Man ham khohari zahmatkashi shumoyam . . . ," *Tojikistoni soveti*, 15 September:4.

Kuznetsov, A. (1986), "Klubhoi dastnoras," *Tojikistoni soveti*, 23 April:4.

Lutfulloev, M., and Q. Qalandarov (1986), "Vazifai asositarin," *Tojikistoni soveti*, 20 June:3.

Mahkamov, Q. M. (1986), Report to the Twentieth Congress of the Communist Party of Tajikistan, *Kommunist Tadzhikistana*, 25 January.

Mahmadaminov, A. (1985), "Vassofi gohyahoi Lenini," *Tojikistoni soveti*, 22 January:4.

Manz, B. F. (1987), "Central Asian Uprisings in the Nineteenth Century: Ferghana under the Russians," *Russian Review* 46:267–81.

"Ma"qul meshumorem" (1987), *Tojikistoni soveti*, 29 July:3.

"Marhalai nav dar inkishofii maktabi soveti" (1984), *Kommunisti Tojikiston*, July, no. 7:12–18.

"Masʿuliyati buzurg meboyad" (1989), *Tojikistoni soveti*, 25 July:1–3.

"Mavzu," imtihonhoi tobistoni va davlati" (1983), *Gazetai muallimon*, 13 September:1.

"Mehmoni Afghonistoni" (1987), *Tojikistoni soveti*, 29 August:1.

Mirboboev, A. (1987), "Ta"rikhdoni khudshinosist," *Tojikistoni soveti*, 18 August:3.

Mirzoeva, G. (1984), "Bazmi dusti," *Adabiyot va san"at*, 6 December:11.

Monogarova, L. F. (1980), "Evolutsiia natsional'nogo samosoznaniia pripamirskikh narodnostei," *Etnicheskie protsessy u natsional'nykh grupp Srednei Azii i Kazakhstana*. Moscow: Nauka, 125–35.

Mukhtorov, A. (1984), "Qadamhoi buzurgi 'Tojikon'," *Adabiyot va san"at*, 29 March:12.

Musoev, O. (1985), "Oinai ta"rikh," *Sadoi Sharq*, No. 9:39–43.

"Muzokira az rui ma"ruzai 'Dar borai loihai qonuni zaboni respublikai soveti sotsialistii Tojikiston" (1989), *Tojikistoni soveti*, 26 July:1, 3.

Nabiev, A. (1986), "Nakhust asari abadiyotshinosii marksistii tojik," *Tojikistoni soveti*, 23 April:3.

Najmonov, G. (1984), "Rahovardi khub," *Sadoi Sharq*, no. 7.

——— (1985), "Vasfi Tojikiston dar sahifahoi Payomi Navin," *Tojikistoni soveti*, 5 January:3.

"Namunai adabiyoti tojik" (1984), *Entsiklopediyai Sovetii Tojik*. Vol. 5:89–90. Dushanbe: Sarredaktsiyai ilmii Entsiklopediyai Sovetii Tojik.

Nasrullo, K. (1987), "Charu be majallai 'Chashma' obuna Kamast?" *Tojikistoni soveti*, 10 October:3.

Nauka v Tadzhikskom gosuniversitete (1983). Vol. 7. Dushanbe: Donish.

"Nomi baland" (1987), *Tojikistoni soveti*, 29 August:1.

Oranskii, I. M. (1983), *Tadzhikoiazychnye etnograficheskie gruppy Gissarskoi doliny (Sredniaia Aziia)*. Moscow: Nauka. Glavnaia redaktsiia Vostochnoi literatury.

Osimi, M. (1988), "Bo taqozoi hayot va amri vijdon," *Tojikistoni soveti*, 29 April:4.

"Panturkizm" (1984), *Entsiklopediyai Sovetii Tojik*. Vol. 5, 468–69. Dushanbe, Sarredaktsiyai ilmii Entsiklopediyai Sovetii Tojik.

Pipes, R. (1964), *The Formation of the Soviet Union*, rev. ed. Cambridge, Mass.: Harvard University Press.

Plotnikov, E. and Kh. Atakhanov (1985), "Muhtoji dar farovoni," *Sadoi Sharq*, no. 9.

Popov, M. (1989), "Janjol metavonist sar nazanad," *Tojikistoni soveti*, 28 June:3.

Procyk, M. (1973), "The Search for a Heritage and the Nationality Question in Central Asia," in E. Allworth (ed.), *The Nationality Question in Soviet Central Asia*. New York: Praeger, 123–33.

"Qonuni zaboni Respublikai Sovetii Sotsialistii Tojikiston" (1989), *Tojikostoni soveti*, p. 1.

Rabiev, V. (1987a), "V klass . . . s koranom?" *Kommunist Tadzhikistana*, 31 January:2.

——— (1987b), "Idushchie v nikuda, *Kommunist Tadzhikistana*, 12 February:3.

Rahmatov, H. (1986), "Aznavsozii jiddi meboyad," *Gazetai muallimon*, 30 September:1.

Rajabi, D. (1987), "Har kasero bozsozi boyado," *Adabiyot va san"at*, 30 July:4–5.

Rakowska-Harmstone, T. (1970), *Russia and Nationalism in Central Asia*. Baltimore: Johns Hopkins University Press.

Rashidov, A. R. (1987), "Ufuqhoi darakhshoni maorif," *Gazetai muallimon*, 4 June:1, 2–3.

Rasulzoda, B. (1985), "Taiyori khubu shefho dar kanor," *Gazetai muallimon*, 25 May:2.

Rosen, B. M. (1973), "An Awareness of Traditional Tajik Identity," in E. Allworth (ed.), *The Nationality Question in Soviet Central Asia*. New York: Praeger, 61–72.

Royce, A. P. (1982), *Ethnic Identity*. Bloomington: Indiana University Press.

"Safar ba kishvari dust" (1985), *Tojikistoni soveti*, 27 October:4.

Saidbaev, T. S. (1984), *Islam i obshchestvo*, rev. ed. Moscow: Nauka. Glavnaia redaktsiia Vostochnoi literatury.

Saifulloev, H. (1985), "Dehae dar oghushi kuhsoron," *Adabiyot va san"at*, 24 January:15.

Samadov, Gh. (1985), "Husni zabon," *Gazetai muallimon*, 2 March:3.

"San"ati yagonai sermillat" (1983), *Madaniyati Tojikiston*, 21 October:2.

Sattorov, A. (1987), "Taftishi hamdigarii kori ideologi," *Kommunisti Tojikiston*, June, no. 6:46–49.

Semerkin, A. (1988), "Drug—zerkalo druga," *Komsomolets Tadzhikistana*. 14 October:2.

Sharifov, Kh. (1988), "Tojikiston—Uzbekiston: robitahoi farhangi," *Gazetai muallimon*, 15 September:3.

Sharifov, U. (1985), "Butoni ideologhoi burzhuazi dar borai vaz"i islom dar SSR," *Kommunisti Tojikiston*, August, no. 8.

Shodiev, A. (1985), "Payomi dusti," *Tojikistoni soveti*, 24 October:4.

Shoismatulloev, Sh. (1984), "Chorsui zindagi," *Adabiyot va san"at*, 26 July:3.

Shukurov, M. R. (1980), *Kul'turnaia zhizn' tadzhikistana v period razvitogo sotsializima*. Dushanbe: Irfon.

Siddiqov, S. (1984), "Zaboni guyo va guvogo," *Adabiyot va san"at*, 12 July:14.

Smirnov, Iu. (1988), "'Strannyi' islam," *Pamir* 2:104–55.

Sotsial'no-kul'turnyi oblik sovetskikh natsii (1986). Moscow: Nauka.

Sultonov, Sh. (1987), "Takozoi boisrori zamon," *Kommunisti Tojikiston*, July, no. 7: 69–76.

Tabibulloeva, M. (1982), "Tashkiloti partiyavi va tarbiyai mutakhassisoni javon," *Kommunisti Tojikiston*, November, no. 11.

TadzhikTA (1989a), "Dar Prezidiumi soveti Olii RSS Tojikiston," *Tojikistoni soveti*, 23 June:2.

TadzhikTA (1989b), "Doir ba voqeahoi raioni Isfara," *Tojikistani soveti*, 15 July:2.

"Tahlili natijahoi imtihonho" (1983), *Gazetai muallimon*, 6 December:1.

Tasmin, M. (1987), "Poyahoi ustuvori rafoqat," *Tojikistoni soveti*, 1 September:2.

Tsentral'noe Statisticheskoe Upravlenie SSSR (1984), *Chislennost' i sostav naseleniia SSSR*. Moscow: Finansy i statistika.

Tursunov, A. (1984), "Mukolamai notamom," *Gazetai muallimon*, 24 November:4.

Usmonov, I. (1986), "Inqilob oftobro monad . . ." *Tojikistoni soveti*, 27 April:3.

Vinnikov, Ia. R. (1980), "Natsional'nye i etnograficheskie gruppy Srednei Azii po dannym etnicheskoi statistiki," *Etnicheskie protsessy u natsional'nykh grupp Srednei Azii i Kazakhstana*. Moscow: Nauka, pp. 11–42.

"Vizit Afganskikh druzei" (1986), *Kommunist Tadzhikistana*, 26 March: 2.

Vohid, Sh. (1987), "Duruyagi," *Tojikistoni soveti*, 21 August:4.

Wheeler, G. (1964), *The Modern History of Soviet Central Asia*. New York: Frederick A. Praeger.

Yuldoshev, A. (1988), "Bozgasht," *Tojikistoni soveti*, 20 May:1, 3.

Yusufov, I. (1986), "Avomfirebon," *Tojikistoni soveti*, 3 December:3.

Yusufov, J. (1987), "Yak lahzai qahramoni," *Tojikistoni soveti*, 17 August:2.

Zokirov, I., and Kh. Bobojonov (1989), "Isfara: konferentsiyai matbuot dar huzuri Q. M. Mahkamov," *Tojikistoni soveti*, 21 July:1.

3

Ethnic Identity and Political Expression

in Northern Afghanistan

Olivier Roy

Historically, geographically, and ethnically, northern Afghanistan
is a part of Central Asia. From the tenth century, northern Afghanistan experienced a slow process of Turkicization which accelerated twice, first during the sixteenth century with the Uzbek
invasion, and again in the early twentieth century when tens of
thousands of Turkmens and Uzbeks from Soviet Central Asia fled
the USSR to settle in northern Afghanistan. The Amu Darya became a political border between Afghanistan and the state of Bukhara only during the nineteenth century. Previously, both sides of
the river were dominated by the Uzbek khanates since the failure
of Babur to recover the land of his Turkic ancestors. Today it is
usual for Afghans to distinguish "Turkistan," referring to the hills
and plains sloping down from the Hindu Kush toward the Amu
Darya, from "Kuhistan," the mountainous areas emerging rather
suddenly from the lowlands which are mainly inhabited by Persian speakers. From the nineteenth century onward, a process of
Pashtunization, triggered by the Afghan central government, has
been under way, producing an objective alliance between the indigenous Persian speakers and the Turkic-speaking population,
both threatened by the new Pashtun settlers. These Pashtuns were
called *nāqil* ("displaced"). Despite this Pashtun migration, one
finds in Soviet and Afghan Turkistan the same traditional ecological repartition between the ethnic groups as before the massive
Pashtun settlements of the twenties in northern Afghanistan. The

irrigated lowlands were cultivated by Uzbeks in Bukhara as in Afghanistan (where they were supplanted by Pashtuns); the loessial uplands (dry farming) were cultivated by Uzbeks in both countries; and the high mountains were cultivated by Tajiks,[1] with other ethnic groups nomadizing from the plains to the mountain pastures.

Ethnic Identities in Northern Afghanistan

Is there any "Central Asian" identity in northern Afghanistan, and if there is, is this identity a "Turkic" one? In fact, ethnic identities in Afghanistan cannot be reduced to linguistic groups. Rather, a slow process of politicization, initiated among the northern intelligentsia in the fifties, has been accelerated by the war against the Communists and the Soviets. Now, "macro-ethnic" affiliations (that is ethnic identity as determined by the spoken language) may play a greater role in northern Afghanistan.

Northern Afghanistan is not ethnically homogeneous, and "ethnic" identities are very difficult to determine because people use different levels of identification which are not always symmetrical. This heterogeneity has some historical causes. In the nineteenth century, northern Afghanistan was largely depopulated due to internecine wars between the Uzbek khanates, raids from Turkmens, malaria in Kunduz, and depopulation of Badakhshan by the Uzbek Amir Murad Beg, who wanted to repopulate the Kunduz area. But the entire picture changed during the twentieth century. The central government in Kabul, traditionally held by representatives of the southern Pashtun tribes, decided to transfer the Pashtun population of nomadic origin (friendly Durrani or unruly Ghilzay tribes) to the north, both to repopulate and to ensure Kabul's power. These Pashtuns became settled, lost their tribal traditions, and instead of contending with central power as they used to do in their former areas, became the best supporters of the Pashtun central administration. A Pashtun governor rehabilitated the Kunduz area in the thirties. Government-sponsored irrigation schemes developed the Baghlan province during the same period. Pashtuns were given most of the newly rehabilitated irrigated areas (in Baghlan province, for example) and were able, by encroachments on the Uzbek former settlers, to obtain most of the best land. At the same time, a migration of Central Asians (not solely due to the Bolshevik revolution) sent tens of thousands of people across the Amu Darya into Afghanistan. In 1970, according to most observers, there was for the first time demographic pressure on the land, enhancing tensions between the various groups.[2] The ethnic map of northern Afghanistan is thus a patchwork; there is no clear-cut territorial basis for the different ethnic groups, whatever the definition of those ethnic groups. Different ethnic and linguistic groups can cohabitate in one village. An Uzbek village can be followed by a Pashtun one and then by an Uzbek one. This partially explains why *all* the ethnic maps of Afghanistan are inaccurate.

How, then, do the various groups living in northern Afghanistan identify themselves? Linguistic identities are obvious and known by everyone. If we use the language criterion, northern Afghanistan is populated by Persian speakers (mainly Sunni Tajiks, but also Aimaqs, Shiʾa Hazaras, and Persian speaking Arabs and Baluchis), Pashtu speakers, and Turkic speakers, the latter being divided into Uzbeks and Turkmens.[3] The remaining Arabs, Baluchis, Kazakhs, Uighurs, Kirghizes, Moghols, and Karakalpaks did not usually retain their original language (except Kirghizes in Pamir). Tajiks seem to constitute the aborigine population. The Uzbeks are divided between *aṣlī* (lit., original, referring to those who came in the sixteenth century) and *muhājir* (lit., immigrant, referring to those who came in the late twenties).[4] Pashtuns, as mentioned, were sent by the rulers of Kabul from 1890 to "Afghanize" a recently conquered area (in two waves—1890 and 1930), even if, according to de Planhol, one finds in Badghis a more ancient Pashtun settlement.[5]

But even this definition of "macro-ethnic" groups based on linguistic criteria is not very relevant as far as primary identities are concerned. Ethnic groups are more a construction in which politicization might play a role. The real level of identification is that of the *qawm*. Qawm is the term used to designate any segment of the society bound by solidarity ties. It could be an extended family, a clan, an occupational group, a village, etc. Qawm is based on kinship and client/patron relationships; before being an ethnic group it is a solidarity group which protects its members from encroachments from the state and other qawm, but which also is the scene of inside competition between contenders for local supremacy.[6] Even if there is a sense of linguistic community, the primary identity is qawm and not ethnic affiliation. Shalinsky makes the following observation about the Uzbek refugees from the USSR: "When asked about qawm, or ethnic identity, muhājir individuals of the immigrant generation identified with relatively small groups such as Namanganis, Kokandis, Andijanis, after towns of origin in the Soviet Union."[7] Our own field research confirms that, for these refugees, the origin supersedes linguistic affiliation, even among the generation born in Afghanistan. Both a Persian speaker and an Uzbek speaker from a family having come from Bukhara use the same term for their qawm, that is "Bukhara'i."[8]

Ethnicity and Political Affiliations

Qawm, and not ethnic affiliations, explain local politics. For example, in the present war, two groups which are very closed as far as ethnicity and language are concerned could be the worst enemies, like the Sunni Persian-speaking Panjshiris and Andarabis, the inhabitants of the neighboring valleys of Andarab and Panjshir. If, at a national level, the Hebz-i Islami of Gulbeddin Hekmatyar is mainly Pashtun and the Jamiat-i Islami, headed by Rabbani, mainly Tajik, the civil war, which has been pitching both parties against each other in the Northeast since 1980, does not systematically oppose the Pashtun-populated pockets and the Tajik majority. Some local Hezb commanders are Tajik (like Nehzatyar in Baghlan) or at least Persian speakers (like the Baluch Abdul Wadud in Keshm, Badakhshan Province), and some local Jamiat are Pashtun (like Arif, member of a nāqil Mohmand clan in Kunduz Province). Qawm affiliations, at the very local level, play a bigger role than ethnic ones. But participation in a nationwide political game induces the local qawm to express themselves in terms of broader ethnic affiliations. This process had been noticed by ethnologists before the war. For example, some Turkic-speaking groups used to retain their names and identities (in the sense of a qawm), like the Qarluq of Rustaq, but will call themselves Uzbeks in front of other people.[9] Other groups such as the Tatars of Doab-i Ruy (Samangan province), although retaining an oral tradition supporting their Turkic origin, speak exclusively Persian and used to be considered Tajiks.[10] The Arabs and Baluchis of Takhar also primarily speak Persian. This ethnic identity can also be bestowed by a dominant group and not necessarily accepted by the people who are thus named. In Juzjan, according to Tapper, the Pashtun Durrani used to call "Parsiwan" ("Persian speakers") the Pashtun that used to have Pashtu as their sole mother-tongue.[11] Although the Persian-speaking Shiʾas in the north are all undoubtedly called "Hazaras," there are some Sunni Hazara groups that used to call themselves Tajiks, but are called Hazaras by the Tajiks. A good demarcation line in these cases is the matrimonial rule: one gives women only to an equal or superior group. It is clear that people try to shape their ethnic identity according to social and political constraints, discarding when possible linguistic, racial, and historical features.

The conclusion of this rapid survey is that ethnic identity is a dynamic process, even if there are clear-cut linguistic groups. The spoken languages do not determine clear-cut ethnic groups with a common sense of identity and a will to express themselves politically. It is not rare to see some families shifting from their original language to a more common one, usually Persian. Strangely enough, there is no recorded example of a group shifting from its native language to the language of the rulers, Pashtu, in order to acquire a more prestigious status. It is probably due to the fact that, for Pashtuns, it is not enough to speak Pashtu to be a Pashtun. A genealogy and a tribal affiliation are a must. It is easier to become a Tajik, and it is at least more fashionable than to be an Uzbek.

Jihād and Ethnic Identities

The Soviet-Afghan war has played a large role in reshaping ethnic identities toward larger entities. But this process did not start suddenly in 1979; its roots are to be found in the creeping politicization of Afghan society. This process was precipitated by state policy and external factors mainly resulting from confrontation with the USSR from the Basmachi period to the present day, but also from both Pakistani and Iranian policies toward Afghanistan. If qawm affiliation is the rule of the political game at the grassroots level, ethnicity might now be the bigger stake in state policy, one greater than the confrontation between Islam and secularism.

In northern Afghanistan, both Turkic and Persian speakers perceived Pashtun settlements as a double threat; first toward their own rights on the land, and then as a tool for tougher state control because the central government was Pashtun. On the other hand, Tajiks and Uzbeks were not opposed to each other because they shared different and complementary places in the ecological system, whereas Pashun settlers and nomads used to take the best of everything. There has generally been an alliance between Uzbeks and Tajiks against Pashtuns. This alliance did not take the shape of a "nationalist" movement that would have split the Uzbeks from the Tajiks, but rather of a fundamentalist movement, opposing Islam and umma against Pashtun nationalism. This trend was reinforced by the Basmachi movement from Soviet Central Asia. The Basmachi used to speak Uzbek or Persian, but not Pashtu, and used to combine the values of Islam with loyalties to qawm affiliations, discarding the construction of a state. That fit well with the political values of northern Afghanistan. The Basmachis resented the good relations between Kabul and Moscow, and were restrained in their activities by the Pashtun monarchs of Kabul. On the other hand, the Basmachis found support among the Persian-speaking ulama of northern Afghanistan, many of whom were members of the Naqshbandi order. When a Tajik, Bacha-ye Saqqao, challenged the Kabul dynasty in 1928, he was supported by the majority of the Tajiks and Uzbeks of the North, and by the fundamentalist clerical networks.[12] The Bacha-ye Saqqao movement was both an anti-Pashtun coalition and a fundamentalist movement.

This pattern of a supra-ethnic alliance in the name of Islam, uniting both Uzbeks and Tajiks against an infidel power, and incidentally, against the Pashtun settlers, is still very vivid in northern Afghanistan. The Jamiat-i Islami party embodies this alliance today. But the degree of Uzbek participation in the actual jihād does not seem to match the level of Tajik involvement. Even if it is more difficult to conduct guerrilla warfare in the plains inhabited mostly by Uzbeks, compared to the hills and mountains where Tajiks are a majority, it is not so much a question of terrain, because the Turkmens, who live in a more difficult area close to the Soviet border, are more involved in the fighting. Most of the Jamiat leaders are in fact Tajiks. Even in Uzbek dominated areas it is not rare to have Tajiks commanding a mixed troop of Tajiks and Uzbeks. There are very few great Uzbek commanders among the Afghan resistance. Damulla Madamin (in Faryab) was arrested in 1987, and Qazi Islamuddin in Kunduz (of Jamiat-i Islami) was assassinated by the Hezb-i Islami party in 1989. This lesser degree of Uzbek involvement in the jihād can be explained by the fact that the Uzbek intelligentsia has been influenced more by secularist and nationalist ideologies than by political Islam. The Uzbeks who joined the Mujahidin tend thus to be less educated and more traditionalist than their Tajik brothers; that is why they mainly joined the moderate Harakat-i Enqelab, whose local leaders are almost always traditional mullas educated in private madrasa or religious schools. Since access to the Bukharan theological schools was closed after the Soviet revolution, these mullas were educated in Afghanistan or even in Pakistan. They are all at least bilingual (Uzbek and Persian, but also sometimes Pashtu and Urdu) and do not promote the issue of "Turkic identity." They are very close to what the Basmachis used to be. By contrast, some of the more fundamentalist groups in northeast Afghanistan are recruited among muhājir Uzbeks. This is the case with the Hezb-i Islami (Hekmatyar) group in Burqa (Baghlan), and with the Wahhabi movement, which recruited among the Uzbeks of Argo (Badakhshan).

To sum up the political affiliations of the Mujahidin Uzbeks in northern Afghanistan, they used to join, by order of importance: the moderate Harakat-i Enqelab, which recruited among Uzbeks in the North and Pashtun in the South; then the Islamist Jamiat-i Islami, which is mainly Persian speaking; then the Azad Beg movement (see below), and, for some muhajir pockets, the Hezb-i Islami of Hekmatyar.

A Pan-Turkic Islamic Movement: Azad Beg's Party

Azad Beg's maternal great grandfather was Nasseruddin, the last amir of Kokand. He was born in British India, is now a Pakistani citizen, and speaks Persian, Urdu, English, and Uzbek. In 1981 he founded in Peshawar, with the help of the Pakistani government, the *Ittiḥādīya-i Islāmī-yi vilāyāt-i samt-i shamāl-i Afghānistān* (the Islamic Union of the Northern Provinces of Afghanistan). Note that the title is in Persian, although the movement is pri-

marily aimed at the Turkic-speaking populations. The aim was to
bring together all the "Turks" of Afghanistan ("*az nizhād-i turk*,"
from "Turkic stock") according to an interview with Azad Beg,[13]
and then to liberate Soviet Turkistan. In fact, although it was not
avowed, the real objective seemed to be to provide an "Islamic"
alternative to the Kabul-regime-sponsored "Turkic" nationalism.
None of the Peshawar-based leaders was Turkmen or Uzbek, and
the Pakistani Services (Inter-Services Intelligence, which were in
charge of the support for Mujahidin) were eager to provide a framework to channel any "Turkic" nationalism against both the Soviets and the Kabul regime. The "Islamic Union" received a great
deal of money and weapons. It endeavored to attract Mujahidin
field commanders by providing them with weapons that were not
easily available through the established Peshawar parties. The criterion entitling one to join Azad Beg's organization was to show
any kind of "Turkic" identity. Of course the linguistic evidence
was of primary importance. All the Turkmens and Uzbeks were
considered to be the primary targets for Azad Beg's pan-Turkism.
But any group that could claim a "Turkic" origin, whatever its
language, was also included in the natural constituency of Azad
Beg. That included any qawm with a Turkic name, such as the
Persian-speaking Tatars from Doab-i Ruy in Samangan province,
but also the Shiʾa Hazaras, who bore some evident physical
Moghol features but spoke Persian. The Aimaqs, who are Sunni
Persian speakers, were also called "Turks" according to the origin
of their name. Any local field commanders able to provide some
loose "Turkic" credentials instantly received a batch of weapons,
with a special permit to carry them through the Pakistani borders.
Of course, most of the field commanders who applied for membership to the Islamic Union of the Northern Provinces did so only
for opportunistic reasons in order to gain access to weapons. They
generally retained their former political affiliation.

Azad Beg was unable to create any "Turkic liberated area"; but
he did establish patron/client relationships with some individual
commanders and fighting groups, in the traditional Afghan manner. If we examine these connections, some general patterns
emerge. The field commanders who joined Azad Beg were generally Uzbeks, previously members of the traditional and clerical
Harakat-i Enqelab party, such as Sauri from Almar (Faryab province), and Mawlawi Quddus from Samangan. But there were also

Uzbek muhājir from Soviet Central Asia, such as Khaluddin of
Kunduz province, said to be the nephew of the Basmachi leader
Ibrahim Beg; and Ait Murad from Burqa (Baghlan province), a former member of the fundamentalist Hezb-i Islami, like many muhājir. A few Turkmens also joined: Ashir Pahlawan of Juzjan,
along with some Persian speakers from "Turkic" qawm such as
the Tatar Mawlawi Islam from Samangan. Generally, the Persian
speakers who joined Azad Beg did so only to obtain weapons; they
retained their former political affiliation. In fact, Azad Beg's party
faced strong opposition from the fundamentalist parties, which
accused him of dividing the umma along the same lines advocated
by government propaganda. Local fighting occurred between Azad
Beg's people and the Mujahidin fundamentalist parties. The Jamiat-i Islami Uzbek field commander from Ishkamish (Takhar),
Qazi Islamuddin, was able to check the progress of Azad Beg in
the Northeast. Far from attracting the "Turkic" people under the
umbrella of the Mujahidin movement, the Azad Beg party seemed,
on the contrary, to be used as a Trojan horse by the Kabul regime
to infiltrate and split the resistance.

The Kabul Regime and the Uzbeks

In Afghanistan, the Marxist movements which developed from
the sixties were divided into pro-Soviet (the PDPA, or People's
Democratic Party of Afghanistan) and Maoist groups. But the
cleavage was less ideological than ethnic. Pashtuns dominated the
PDPA, while the Maoist movements recruited among non-Pash-
tuns, mainly Shi'as, Uzbeks, and Tajiks. Except Abdul Hakim
Shara'i, an Uzbek from Saripul who became minister of justice in
1978, the PDPA had few Uzbek members. The Maoists advocated
a front of non-Pashtun ethnic groups to fight Pashtun hegemony.
The main political party created by them was the Setam-i Melli,
which was not a Turkic nationalist movement, but was recruited
among Uzbeks as well as Tajiks. There has also been a loosely
organized purely "Turk" movement, which originated among Uzbek students more nationalist than Marxist. The Uzbek intelligentsia was frustrated by their lack of access to high positions
under the monarchy and wanted the Uzbek language to be recognized. This movement had no success among the Turkmens,

who are more traditionally oriented and deprived of a modern intelligentsia.

Unable to create a viable liberation movement, the Uzbek Maoists chose to infiltrate the moderate Harakat-i Enqelab, which always suffered from a dearth of intellectuals and educated people. It is very common to have a traditional Uzbek mulla assisted by a *munshī* (secretary) who is a former Maoist. But these former Maoists came under heavy attack from the more fundamentalist parties and led the Harakat in local feuds with both Hezb and Jamiat. They also became a fertile ground for government infiltration, which explains why the government was able to infiltrate the Harakat. In December 1983, for example, the greatest northern commander, the Tajik Zabihullah of Jamiat, was assassinated by followers of the Uzbek local leader of Harakat, Mawlawi Osman. Caught between the pro-Soviet PDPA and the Islamic resistance, the Maoist groups were on the verge of collapse when they were invited by Najibullah (general secretary of the PDPA appointed in May 1986) to join the Kabul regime, under the policy of "National Reconciliation" launched in December 1986. They accepted the offer.

Another tool with which the Kabul regime penetrated the Uzbek Mujahidin has been a pro-regime group called Guruh-i Kar, which was founded by non-Pashtun leftists headed by the Tajik Dastagir Panjshiri. This group tried to capitalize on the growing rift between some Uzbek field commanders of Harakat or Azad Beg's Union and the Jamiat. The official PDPA party is seen as too Pashtun to attract Turkic speakers. The Guruh-i Kar used to present itself as an Uzbek nationalist movement, attempting to join together Uzbek secular nationalists and traditional religious leaders. Incidentally, it is among Uzbek mullas that the Islamic policy of the regime had the best success: the minister of Islamic affairs appointed by Najibullah in October 1986 is Mawlawi Abdul Jamil, an Uzbek from Balkh and a former ghazi of Harakat-e Enqelab, for example.[14] This group has infiltrated most of the Azad Beg field commanders and is in charge of avowed pro-regime militias such as the one headed by the Uzbek Pahlawan Ghaffur in Juzjan province. Thus the traditional alliance between Tajiks and Uzbeks, under the banner of Islam, has been shaken, the Tajiks perceiving the Uzbeks as more prone to collaboration with the Communist regime of Kabul.

But these government successes among the Uzbeks were not only due to manipulation through the secret service (the *khad*). The government has tried to promote a "nationalities" policy that is identical with the Stalinist policy of nationalities.[15] A new word has been coined to translate "nationality"—*mellīyat*. Officially there are eight "nationalities" in Afghanistan: Pashtuns, Tajiks, Hazaras, Uzbeks, Turkmens, Baluchis, Nuristanis, and Pasha'is. The criterion for the Uzbeks and Turkmens is purely linguistic. As in the USSR, there is no attempt in Afghanistan to design a broad "Turkic" nationality; on the contrary, everything is designed to separate Turkmens and Uzbeks. Radio broadcasts are made in Uzbek. An Uzbek newspaper (*Yulduz*) was being published in Arabic script. Soviet Uzbek experts have played a big role in the cultural sphere. ʿAlī Shīr Navāʾī, the renowned Uzbek poet, was promoted as the symbol of Uzbek culture, and incidentally, of the identity shared on both sides of the Amu Darya. But in fact, despite the creation in 1987 of a new province, Saripol, which is exclusively Uzbek, there has been no real endeavor to create an autonomous Afghan Uzbek Socialist Republic. The mainly Pashtun Kabul regime is surely reluctant to promote "nationalities" that could contest the Pashtun hegemony, apply for an independent state, or even join Soviet Uzbekistan. In fact, notwithstanding rhetorical speeches about the rights of the Uzbek nationality, the government in Kabul plays on infra-ethnic fragmentation, at the qawm level, pitting local groups against each other and taking advantage of the weaker jihād spirit among Uzbeks to enroll them into well paid militia groups which could be used against other ethnic groups. A famous group of Uzbek militiamen, the Juzjani, has been fighting from 1986 on the government side in such remote areas as Kandahar and Jalalabad. Money seems to play a bigger role than any commitment to Marxism or Uzbek nationalism. If any sense of an Uzbek identity could have developed it would have been due more to the proximity of Soviet Uzbekistan than the "nationalities policy" promoted by Kabul.[16]

In fact there is no political expression of any pan-Turkic national identity in Afghanistan. Uzbek nationalism, where it worked, did so only in favor of the Kabul regime. Turkmens remained on the side of the Mujahidin. To counter the effect of government propaganda in favor of Uzbek identity, the Mujahidin had to reinforce the Islamic identity of the movement while making some concessions to Uzbek identity. For example, Jamiat-i Islami is encouraging Uzbek mullas to preach in Uzbek.

In conclusion, two trends are noticeable among the Uzbeks in a process of polarization between Uzbek identity and fundamentalism. The moderates and nationalists tend to be infiltrated by the Kabul regime (the traditional Harakat-i Enqelab, for example), while the fundamentalists tend to become more radical. Nowhere have the Uzbeks been able to create a viable ethnic Uzbek political movement. The contradictory tendencies of nationalism and fundamentalism have resulted in splitting the Uzbek population and making it politically amorphous. This situation is reflected in the fact that there is almost no well known Uzbek leader both in the government (except Shara'i) and in the resistance (except the late Qazi Islamuddin).

Notes

1. For Bukhara see Barfield, 1981:9; for Afghanistan, see Centlivres, 1976:12.

2. See Tapper, 1979:237. On the complexity of the population settlements in Badghis Province, see de Planhol, 1973, no. 1–2:1–16; and 1976, vol. 5, fasc. 2.

3. Shahrani observes that both Uzbek and Turkmen speakers refer to their language as *turkī* or *turk telī*, (Shahrani, 1979:178).

4. According to Shalinsky, only the urban refugees, who came after 1928, used the term *muhājir* to identify themselves. Shalinsky, 1982:75.

5. de Planhol, 1976.

6. For the definition of *qawm*, see Centlivres, 1972:158–59; Azoy, 1982:31–32; Roy, 1986, ch. 1.

7. Shalinsky, 1982:78. This remark also shows that qawm is not taken to mean "ethnic identity" by Afghans.

8. Research made in Baghlan province in the summer of 1987 by Olivier Roy and Chantal Lobato. For example, one local commander of the Jamiat-i Islami, Mulla Shams, is a Persian-speaking "Bukhara'i."

9. See Centlivres, 1975. This paper is one of the more informative on Uzbek ethnic identity in Afghanistan.

10. Personal observation, August 1987.

11. Tapper, 1979:241.

12. On the support given by the Uzbeks to the Tajik Bacha-ye Saqqao, see Tapper, 1979:242. In Saripol district in 1930, a coalition of Uzbeks and Persian-speaking Aimaqs expelled the Pashtun settlers, who were reinstalled by the government after the defeat of Bacha-ye Saqqao. On the

coalition between Uzbeks and Tajiks against the Pashtuns, see Azoy, 1982:12.

13. Personal interview with Azad Beg in Peshawar, February 1986.

14. Chantal Lobato, 1988.

15. A special bimonthly journal, *Melliat-hā-ye Barādār* ("The Brother Nationalities") has been published since 1984 by the Ministry of Tribes and Nationalities. The borrowing of the Soviet nationalities policy is obvious from theoretical articles such as "Ḥall-i masʿala-yi milli dar ittiḥād-i shūravī va ahammīyat-i bayn al-milalī-yi ān" ("The Solution of the Nationality Problem in the Soviet Union and Its International Importance"), in *Saur*, April 1986.

16. A typical indication of the reluctance of Kabul to put the words into reality is that I did not find any article in the issues in my possession of *Millīyat-hā-yi Barādār* that dealt with the social bases of the Uzbek and Turkmen nationalities. There are, however, a dozen articles on this topic for the Nuristani and Pasha'i nationalities, whose coming into being is not seen as a threat by the Pashtuns.

References

Azoy, Whitney (1982), *Buzkashi, Game and Power in Afghanistan*. University of Pennsylvania Press.

Barfield, Thomas (1981), *The Central Asian Arabs from Afghanistan*. University of Texas Press.

Centlivres, Pierre (1976), "Problèmes d'identité ethnique dans le Nord de l'Afghanistan," in *Actes du XVIème Congrès des Orientalistes, L'Iran Modern*, L'Asiathèque, Paris.

—— (1975), "Les Ouzbeks du Qataghan," *Afghanistan Journal* 2, no.1.

—— (1972), *Un Bazar d'Asie Centrale: Forme et organisation du bazar de Tashqurghan* [Afghanistan]. Weisbaden: Dr. Ludwig Reichert Verlag.

de Planhol, Xavier (1973), "Sur la Frontière turkmene de l'Afghanistan," *Révue Géographique de l'Est*. Vol. 13, n.1–22:1–16.

—— (1976), "Le Repeuplement de la basse vallee afghane du Murghab," *Studia Iranica*. 5:fasc. 2.

"Ḥall-i masʿala-yi milli dar ittiḥād-i shūravi va ahammīyat-i bayn al-milalī-yi ān" (1986), in *Milliat-hā-ye Barādār* ("The Brother Nationalities"), April 1986.

Lobato, Chantal (1988), "Kabul 1978–1988: Communists and Islam," in *Religions in Communist Lands*. Keston College.

Roy, Olivier (1986), *Islam and Resistance in Afghanistan*. Cambridge: Cambridge University Press.

Shahrani, M. Nazif (1979), "Ethnic Relations under Closed Frontier Conditions: Northern Badakhshan," in W. O. MacCagg, Jr., and B. D. Silver (eds.), *Soviet Asian Ethnic Frontiers*. New York: Pergamon Press.

Shalinsky, Audrey (1982), "Islam and Ethnicity: The Northern Afghanistan Perspective," *Central Asian Survey* 1, no. 2–3.
Tapper, Richard (1979), "Ethnicity and Class: Dimensions of Conflict,"
in M. Nazif Shahrani and Robert Canfield (eds.), *Revolutions and Rebellions in Afghanistan*, Institute of International Studies, University
of California, Berkeley, 230–46.

II

Islam

as a Source

of Identity

4

The Hui, Islam, and the State

A Sufi Community in China's

Northwest Corner

Dru C. Gladney

While living in the Ningxia Hui Autonomous Region, I was surprised on several occasions when Communist Party officials complained to me of a "new problem."[1] This was the "problem of party members who believe in religion" (*danguan xinjiaode wenti*). In one particular Hui Muslim village where I engaged in participant observation, there were a total of sixty-three party members, representing only 1.7 percent of the total population. Of those sixty-three party members, twenty-two publicly worshipped at the mosque and said they believed in Islam. Three of those believers went to mosque five times daily and one officially quit his party membership in order to become an *ahong* (imam).[2] Many of these Muslim party members have at one time been a team-level chairman, and four have been brigade vice party secretaries in the past. When I asked one Hui state cadre who openly prayed at the mosque in another city about this apparent contradiction, he rationalized, "I believe in Marxism in my head, but I believe in Islam in my heart." At the end of the last century, Isaac Mason, a Western Protestant missionary to Chinese Muslims, remarkably reported a similar explanation offered to him by Muslim Confucian officials in the Qing dynasty:

It may be added that military officials in the Manchu times were not altogether exempt from certain ceremonies of worship at temples; but Moslems seem to have made a compromise with conscience and went with the rest; one said to me long ago in Szechwan that though his bodily presence was there, and he shared in the prostrations, his heart was not there, so it didn't matter! (Mason, 1929:7)

Local cadres gave many reasons for religious behavior among Hui party officials. In this particular village, it was rationalized that 80 percent entered the party in the 1950s and were too old and uninvolved with party affairs (Wang, 1985:9). As they grow older, these veteran party members are becoming more interested in religion. Yet we may also note that no one has been admitted to the party in the village since October 1976.

Involvement of party members in religious activities, state support of mosque reconstruction, and recent visits by foreign Muslims and guests to the village mosque have been interpreted by some Hui as the party's encouragement of religion. Hui villagers have been quoted in official documents as saying: "Whoever does not believe in religion, does not do good works (xingshan) and does not carry out the policy of the Communist Party" (in Wang, 1985:9). Acceptance of the party's position on atheism has been declining in religious minority nationality areas, to the extent that some youths accept Islamic doctrines such as the creation of the world in place of scientific materialism. These trends have led many local cadres to argue that there has been a revival of Islam among the Hui to the point of fundamentalist "fanaticism" (kuanre or zongjiao re, lit., "religious heat," see Zhang, 1985:11).

As several Western visitors and reporters to other northwestern Muslim communities have noted, since 1979 Islamic conservatism has become more pronounced among the Hui (Burns, 1986:4; Mann, 1985:10; Parks, 1983:3). A potential radicalized Islam worries local government cadres: is this really a fundamentalistic Islamic revival, or is it merely the expression of latent ethnic customs? Has the private responsibility system gone too far by engendering too much personal and religious freedom in rural areas? Studies by local government research academies in Muslim areas have attempted to quell these rising concerns by arguing that, while ethnic customs are maintained, religious belief is not necessarily strong. Reflecting traditional Chinese policy toward nationality religions, the policy encourages the expression of traditional nationality customs and culture, while depicting religion as extraneous to ethnicity (see Connor, 1984:67–100).

In this chapter it will be argued that Hui ethnic identity in

China's Northwest is inseparably identified with an Islamic tradition handed down to them by their Muslim ancestors. Hui identity in the Northwest is more than an ethnic identity; it is ethnoreligious, in that Islam is intimately tied to their self-understanding. Recent reemergence of the meaningfulness of Islam and stress upon the requirements of a decidedly Islamic life-style represent a return to northwestern Hui ethnoreligious roots in interaction with changing socioeconomic contexts and state policies.

This study is based on three years of fieldwork in China among the Hui between 1983 and 1986. Work in Na Homestead (Na Jiahu), upon which this particular study is based, was primarily conducted during one year of fieldwork in Ningxia, the only Autonomous Region for China's Hui Muslims located along the upper reaches of the Yellow River in northwest China. Numbering over eight million, the Hui are the largest group of almost twenty million Muslims in China—divided somewhat arbitrarily by the state into ten Muslim minorities. Distinguished by their speaking the Chinese dialects wherever they live, the Hui differ markedly from the other nine Muslim groups in China who speak Turko-Altaic and Indo-European languages. These other nine Central Asian Muslim peoples are almost entirely concentrated in the northwestern provinces of Xinjiang, Qinghai, and Gansu, while the Hui are spread thinly throughout China, in small isolated, what Jonathan Lipman (1984) calls "patchwork" communities that may be 100 percent Hui ensconced in a sea of the Han majority.[3] The 1982 census revealed for the first time that the Hui inhabit 97 percent of China's 2,372 counties; only 64 counties in all of China do not have Hui residents, and only one-sixth of the Hui are concentrated in Ningxia. (Population Census Office, 1987: xvi, 27–30.) The third largest concentration of the Hui is in Henan, in central China. Given the wide diversity and distribution of the Hui, our understanding of Hui identity must come not from generalized abstractions about "Islam in China," as Raphael Israeli (1978) in his numerous writings has attempted to do, but from particularized studies of these unique, patchwork communities.

Religious Revitalization in Na Homestead

Na Homestead is in many respects typical of other Hui Muslim communities throughout the Northwest.[4] A collection of adobe-

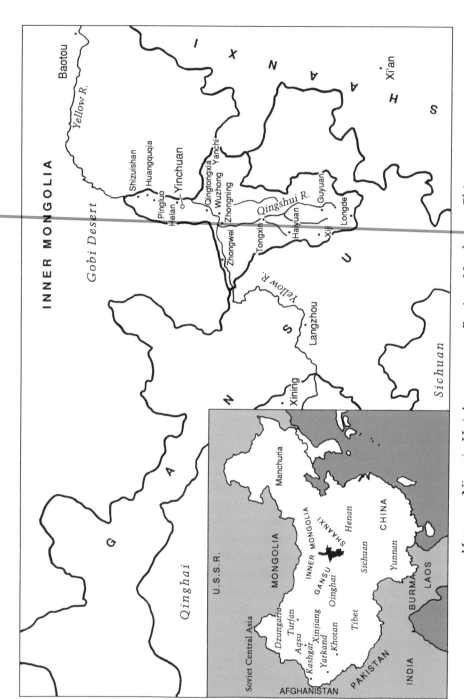

Map 3. Ningxia Hui Autonomous Region, Northwest China

INNER MONGOLIA

Gobi Desert

Baotou

Yellow R.

Shizuishan
Huangquqia
Pingluo
Helan
Yinchuan
Qingtongxia
Wuzhong
Zhongning
Yanchi
Zhongwei
Tongxin
Haiyuan
Xiji
Guyuan
Longde

Qingshui R.

Yellow R.

Langzhou

Xining

Xi'an

NINGXIA

SHAANXI

GANSU

QINGHAI

Sichuan

Qinghai

Soviet Central Asia

U.S.S.R.

MONGOLIA

Manchuria

Dzungaria
Turfan
Aqsu
Kashgar
Yarkand
Khotan
Xinjiang

Tibet

INNER MONGOLIA

GANSU
Qinghai

SHAANXI

Henan

CHINA

Sichuan

Yunnan

BURMA

LAOS

INDIA

PAKISTAN

AFGHANISTAN

mud houses clustered around a central mosque, Na Homestead has been the site of Islamic resurgence in recent years. An isolated, formerly walled community of adobe houses clustered around a central mosque, Na Homestead is a Hui village located fifteen kilometers south of Yinchuan City in Yongning county, central Ningxia. This compact collection of households is comprised of nine teams that are almost 100 percent Muslim. Yongning county is only 12.9 percent Hui, a relatively small minority in contrast to neighboring Lingwu county in the southeast, which is 47 percent Hui, and southern Jingyuan county, which is 97 percent Hui (the highest concentration of Hui in one county in China). Hence, the Hui in Na village, though they live in the Ningxia Hui Autonomous Region, are still surrounded by predominantly Han villages.

Just north of the all-Hui community in Na Homestead, separated by about two kilometers of fields, is another collection of households belonging to the village administratively and containing two teams (numbers one and eleven) of mixed Han and Hui. All twenty-two households (264 people) of the Han families belonging to Na Homestead are located in this smaller community, separate from the nine all-Hui teams. Based on 1984 statistics, Na Homestead is comprised of 767 households, with a total population of 3,871. Hui households total 745, amounting to more than 95 percent of the population. Over 60 percent of the Hui in the village are surnamed Na.[5]

I first became aware of the changing Hui-Han social dynamics in the village from a discussion with one of the Han villagers in team number one. She explained:

Since 1979, we have had less and less social contact with the Hui in the other teams. There are no problems between us, but the Hui are more devout (qiancheng) now and less willing to come to our homes and visit or borrow tools. We raise pigs in our yards and eat pork, so they are afraid it will influence their religion (yingxiang tamende jiaomen).

Like many conservative northwest Hui, most Na villagers have become more conscientious to Islamic purity through attention to dietary restrictions. In order to preserve one's Islamic "qing zhen" life-style, conservative Hui who visit Han homes at the most accept sunflower seeds or fruit when offered by their host.[6] When Han come to their homes, Hui offer them tea from a separate set of cups that the family itself does not use, lest the family utensils become contaminated. Hui are also free to offer Han prepared dishes of lamb and beef, but the Han cannot reciprocate. Gradually this imbalance of obligation leads to less and less contact. Increasingly scrupulous attention to the culturally defined notions of Islamic purity—especially in a culture that traditionally places high priority on extending social courtesies—has begun to increasingly limit Hui-Han social interaction.

The rise in religious activity and conservativism in Na Homestead stands in stark contrast to the closed mosques and restricted religious behavior that became common in China since the 1958 Religious System Reform Campaigns. Mosque attendance has risen dramatically since 1979, with over five hundred individuals worshiping on Friday (out of a total 764 households), and an average of two hundred attending mosque every day of the week. During Ramadan, every household has at least one member who fasts.

Mosque income (sifei) derived from offerings (nietie) has also risen dramatically. According to the mosque's own careful accounting records, in the last two years it averaged 20,000 yuan ($6,700 U.S.) annual income from offerings. Based on an outside study, over a four-month period during 1984 and 1985, offerings of grain produce, goods, or money totaled 8,997.23 yuan (about $3,000 U.S.). An economic survey of expenditures of 113 Hui households in Na Homestead revealed that the average donation to the mosque was 47 yuan per household, or 8.40 yuan per person in 1984 (Wang, 1985:7; Gong, 1987:38). If this average is applied to the entire Hui community of the village, then the mosque's total income last year was well over 32,500 yuan ($10,833 U.S.). The money supports the staff of seven ahong, including one "teaching" or head ahong (kaixue ahong or jiaozhang), and four student ahong (halifat from khalīfa, "successor," or manla, from mullā), and the daily upkeep of the mosque.[7] Offerings are given during the three main religious holidays and to individual ahong when they read the Qur'an at weddings, funerals, and naming ceremonies. Giving at funerals by the family to guests and to the mosque ranges from 100 to 1,000 yuan. As much as 2,500 yuan has been reported when the status of the deceased was extremely high.

On one holiday celebrated in Na Homestead, the "Prophet's

Day" or "Muhammad's Birthday" (Shengji) on December 7, 1984, I witnessed offerings brought by children and adults in bags of flour or rice and in fists full of money. A group of mosque officials dutifully registered each offering according to amount, name, and team number. Gifts totaled 3,000 kilograms of wheat, 2,500 kilograms of rice, and 300 yuan ($100 U.S.), equal to approximately 3,313 yuan ($1,100 U.S.). None of the donated money is required for the restoration of the mosque building (qianliang). The mosque has received over 90,000 yuan ($30,000 U.S.) from the State Nationalities Affairs Commission since it was identified as a national monument in 1981. Dating from the Ming dynasty's Jia Jing period (1522–1567), it is the oldest remaining mosque in Ningxia.[8]

Donations to the mosque come from a village considered fairly poor by neighboring village standards, with an average annual income of 300 yuan (about $100 U.S.) per household.[9] The 1982 average per capita annual income in Yongning county was substantially higher, 539 yuan according to the Population Census Office (1987:206). Poor households (pinkun-hu) occupy 2 percent of the village (Zhu, 1985:6). Mosque income, however, does not necessarily reflect total giving per household. A study of seventeen households from three different villages belonging to different Islamic orders found that out of an annual average income of 96.67 yuan, 8.96 (9.26 percent) was given to religious concerns in 1980.

A decrease in public school enrollment, and an increase in children studying the Qur'an in private madrasas attached to local mosques is another recent phenomenon that has local cadres concerned. In Na village, ten school-age children were not attending public school in 1985; they were studying the Qur'an at home privately or in the mosque. In more heavily populated Hui areas, however, there are even more Hui children who choose the mosque over the public school. In another Hui village just south of Na Homestead, only 12 out of 104 school-age children are attending school, and 27 of those not in school are studying the Qur'an in the mosque. In Hezhou, Gansu, the "little Mecca of Chinese Islam," enrollment has decreased from 78 percent to less than 50 percent in 1982.

When asked about their reluctance to send their children to school, Na Homestead parents expressed doubts about "the value of learning Chinese and mathematics." "It would be much more useful," I was told, "for our children to work in the fields and family business or to learn the Qur'an, Arabic, and Persian." If a child excelled, he or she might become a manla, and eventually perhaps an ahong. Their status in the village would be much higher than the average middle school or even high school graduate, as would their income (estimated at about 100 to 500 yuan a month for a well-known teaching ahong).

Smoking and drinking, once popular during the Cultural Revolution, are now prohibited in the village for the simple reason that "the elders are against it." When asked why, the elders invariably refer to the requirements of a pure Islamic life-style. Young men who want to drink or smoke go outside the village to the Yongning County Seat or Yinchuan City.

While only the older women wear the head-covering associated with the Muslim custom of purdah, younger Hui admit that male-female interaction has become much more restricted than in neighboring Han villages. Men and women rarely work together in the fields anymore, and the majority of marriages are arranged through introductions. In a survey of fifty newly married young couples, only eight (16 percent) met their partners on their own, without an intermediary. The average courtship period was less than five months for 76 percent of the couples surveyed. While some younger Hui complain about this conservativism, change in the near future appears unlikely. Intermarriage with Han is strongly restricted, and I knew only of one case within the village in the last six years. When it does occur, it is along the traditional pattern of bringing in non-Muslim women, who convert to Islam at marriage. This is the only conversion of Han to Islam that I can trace in China, with the growth of the Muslim population being based primarily on migration and intermarriage, not conversion.[10]

The response of local party cadres to this rising conservatism has been marked by ambivalence. On the one hand they are reluctant to return to the repressions of the Gang of Four period. They are impressed by Muslim villages which, compared to many Han villages, have a lower crime rate; a better compliance to central policies in birth planning, health, and education; and a higher tax income generated from a successful responsibility program in agriculture and the free market economy—all of which have been supported by the Muslim elders. At the same time they are concerned about religious fanaticism and are shocked to witness the disintegration of thirty years of Communist Party work in just a few short years. They attempt to resolve this contradiction through appeal to a policy of distinction between minority custom and religious belief. As one cadre in Yinchuan explained to me: "The Hui are allowed to maintain their ethnic customs that are influenced by Islamic traditions, but religion and ethnicity are two separate matters and should not be confused."

The Re-rooting of Ethnoreligious Identity in Na Homestead

The antinomian distinction between ethnicity and religion in this northwestern Muslim area may be somewhat appropriate to urban situations like Beijing and Shanghai, where many Hui no longer practice Islam but continue to maintain Islamic dietary restrictions and celebrate traditional Islamic holidays. It does not, however, make sense for the majority of Hui in the Northwest. The distinction between Hui ethnicity and Islam was an important corrective to the traditional Chinese idea that Islam was the "Hui religion" (Hui jiao), rather than a world religion in which most Hui believe. The ethnicity versus religion policy arises from a Chinese Marxist approach to nationality that views ethnic consciousness, customs, and religion as circumstantial, epiphenomenal traits that are class based, and assume importance only in the competition for scarce resources.

Frederick Barth's (1969) popular "situational" boundary-maintenance approach to ethnicity has been used by Western anthropologists in a similar way to account for the role of sociopolitical factors in ethnic change and identity. According to both of these approaches, ethnic identity should lose its relevance when socioeconomic conditions change, and eventually will disappear with the erosion of class or interest-based differences. While these approaches have shed light on the manipulation and use of ethnicity, they are flawed by a perspective that understands religion and ethnic identity primarily in instrumentalist terms. Such an explanatory model fails to account for the meaningfulness of ethnoreligious identity to the Hui actors in Na village themselves. Nor does a "situational" model adequately deal with the nature of ethnic identity itself in terms of its power and endurance, which is critical for understanding Hui identity in Na Homestead and other areas of the Northwest.

The Cultural Roots of Na Ethnoreligious Identity

The Hui in Na Homestead frequently repeat an "origin myth" to inquisitive outsiders. They say that their ancestor was none other than a son of Nasreddin, the son of Sayyid Edjell, the Central Asian Muslim governor of Yunnan, Sichuan, and Shanxi under the Yuan Dynasty (r. 1271–1368; see Armijo-Hussein, 1987). Nasreddin's four sons, they say, changed their names to "Na, Su, La, Ding" when all foreigners were required to adopt Chinese surnames during the Chinese Ming dynasty. The son surnamed Na moved to this place and had five sons, of which there are still five Na leading lineages in the village. Based partly on historical records and oral traditions, they may or may not be accurate; the story is nevertheless critical for Na self-understanding. The cultural reckoning of their descent from an ancestor not only foreign but Muslim is vital to Na self-identity.

The Na maintained this cohesive identity over centuries of interaction with Han neighbors in the face of prolonged oppressive local government policies and socioeconomic instability. Na villagers are proud of their ancestors' participation in Ma Hualong's Northwest Hui rebellion.[11] During the twenty years of increased religious repression from the Religious Reform Campaign of 1958 to the end of the Cultural Revolution in 1978, the Hui maintained their ethnoreligious identity, albeit in often subordinated, secretive ways.

Hui suffered many degradations during this period: the closure and destruction of mosques, the requirement of the imam to do physical labor, the demand to raise pigs, the devastation of cemeteries, tombs, holy sites, and so on. Throughout this period, I could find no instance where Hui renounced or rejected their ethnic identity and ancestry. While antireligion policies may have mainly afflicted the more devout Hui Muslims, all Hui villagers reacted vehemently, sometimes violently, against the pig raising policy. Mao regarded swine as the "perfect fertilizer factory" and China's "greatest natural resource." Hui who refused to raise them were criticized as backward and feudalistic. Despite resistance by some local cadres who were later accused of "local ethnic chauvinism" (difang minzu zhuyi), by 1966 at least ten Hui households in Na Homestead were raising pigs. Most of these were cadre activists who volunteered. Some ahong in other villages also volunteered to show their support for the party. These were later disparagingly called "policy ahong" (zhengce ahong) and recently have been rejected by many Hui as unqualified to be religious leaders. Many of the Hui who consented did not take care of the animals well, and many of them died prematurely. One Hui villager recounted a familiar story of the dilemma of having to feed the pig, or face criticism. He would look at the animal and say: "Oh, you black bug (a Hui euphemism for pig), if you get fat, you will die. If you get thin, then I will die!"

By 1966, during the Cultural Revolution's "smash four olds" (posijiu) campaign, the mosque was closed and the ahong worked in the fields with the production teams. Other local ahong often returned to their original homes. Na Youxi, head ahong of the neighboring Xinzhaizi ("new stockade") mosque, left to join his relatives in northern Ningxia, where he worked in a store.[12] I was told that no local youth took part in the Red Guard activity of that time. The mosque was converted to a county ballbearing factory, and although it was reopened for prayer in 1979, the factory was not relocated until 1981. By 1982, open participation in mosque affairs had resumed.[13] Throughout this stormy period, the Hui in Na Homestead maintained their ethnic identity and there were no cases that I could find of people attempting to deny or conceal their Hui heritage.[14]

The Recurring Texts of Na Ethnoreligious Identity

Since the 1978 reforms and liberalized policies have taken effect there has been a resurgence of those rituals and texts that, to follow Paul Ricoeur (1981), are most salient to Hui ethnoreligious identity. For the Hui, these texts are intricately tied to rites of passage infused with Islamic content, including birth, adulthood, marriage, death, and Muslim festival days.

On the third day after the birth of each child, every Na villager invites the local ahong to come to the home, read the scriptures, and give the child a Qur'anic name—Muḥammad, Yūsuf, Dāwūd,

Salīma, and Fāṭima. Every Hui household, including the party chairman's, invites the ahong to perform the wedding ceremony, which centers on a series of questions put to the father of the groom, interestingly enough, and not to the groom himself. "Are you the father of this boy?" "Do you agree to the marriage with this girl?" "Do you guarantee that their children will be raised as Muslims?" Only after the father's affirmations, the ahong then turns to the groom and asks him to quote the *shahāda*. In fluid Arabic, the groom loudly proclaims the monotheistic formula. The symbolic import of reinforcing group corporate identity through rites of passage is illuminated by Pierre Bourdieu (1977: 137–38), who states that the "objective intention of marriage rites and ploughing rites is the union of contraries, the resurrection of the grain and the reproduction of the group."

Funerals are a significant part of Na community life, insuring that ethnoreligious identity is crucial in death as well as life. Membership in the community does not end with the cessation of breath. Death ceremonies do not terminate after the funeral; that must take place within three days after death. Important commemoration rituals take place on days 7, 14, 21, 40, 100, and years 1 and 3 after the death date, which follows the traditional Chinese Buddhist commemoration calendar. At one 21 day com-memoration ritual (*jinqi* or *sanqi*) for a ninety-two-year-old man, there were separate prayers and banquets at the older and younger sons' homes. The prayer began when the ahong sat down on the *kang* in the front of the younger son's house. A semicircle of other ahong and village elders was formed around him facing the gath-ered men. The women packed into the back room of the house or stood outside and participated in the prayer. Several people who could not fit into the small room, crowded with over one hundred men, knelt on the ground in the freezing weather outside. The prayer began with a loud chanting of the shahāda in unison, then a recitation by the assistant head ahong (whose voice was stronger than the seventy-seven-year-old head ahong) of several passages of scripture with others joining, and a final chanting of the shahāda by all present, including women.

Although the Na villages are members of a Khufiya Sufi order, they do not practice the silent *dhikr* traditionally associated with the Khufiya. When the Khufiya order was first introduced to China it was known for promoting the silent dhikr, as opposed to the later Jahriya order, known for the vocal use of the *jahr* in remembrance. However, like many Khufiya members in north and central Ningxia, the Na villagers practice an oral dhikr. Local historians suggest that the interesting combination of Jahriya and Khufiya ritual practices among the Na may result from their participation in Ma Hualong's Jahriya uprising (1862–1876), after they had already been Khufiya for many generations.[15] As a result, when they pray in unison at certain rituals, the dhikr is vocally expressed aloud.[16]

At this ritual, they chanted the shahāda in a rhythmic cadence unique to their Khufiya order. The last syllable of the shahāda receives special stress while participants raise their voice and sway their bodies rhythmically from side to side. It is from this movement among Sufi Hui that their religion became known in earlier accounts as the "shaking head religion" or "shakers."[17] As I sat in the rear wedged between several older men, I had no choice but to be swayed back and forth with them. I tried to accustom my ears to the loud chanting that went on for fifteen to thirty minutes. It was always under the control of the lead ahong, and occasionally "primed" by worshipers when the reciting began to die down in intensity. After some duration, the lead ahong intoned a sort of "mm" sound and the service ended. As the men departed, each received a small donation (*dajiawangren*) of about two to four *mao* (seven to thirteen cents), while several stayed for a nine-course banquet. Following the meal, the entire ceremony was repeated in a more elaborate and lengthy fashion at the older brother's home. Mourners also chant the dhikr at funeral ceremonies (*zhenazi*). There, men remove their shoes and kneel in orderly rows behind the deceased, whose body is placed upon a mat on the ground and wrapped in a white shroud.[18]

I subsequently learned that the prayer and funeral ceremony for this ninety-two-year-old man were more elaborate due to his venerable age and standing in the community. Well over 1,000 yuan in offerings were distributed to those attending.[19] By contrast, another man was given a very simple funeral while I was there. One older man complained: "Only 250 yuan was distributed to guests." He explained that this particular individual was not well cared for by his family, nor very religious. He was often left alone in a room and died at the comparatively young age of sixty. "No wonder he died young," one villager told me. "It's like repairing old pants. If you just keep patching them rather than caring for them or getting new ones, when winter comes they won't last." Consequently, fewer than a hundred villagers attended his funeral, the others displaying their disapproval by lack of attendance.

Hui often say that longevity is the result of Allah's blessing (zhenzhu baoyou) for a devout "pure and true" (qing zhen) life. They attribute their good health to their maintaining Islamic dietary restrictions and attention to personal hygiene. Hui say they are cleaner than Han because they must engage in the "small wash" (xiao jin) five times a day before prayer, and the "complete wash" (da jin) every Friday. Hui are proud to note that, though the Hui are only one-third of Ningxia's population, the 1982 census revealed twenty-one of the twenty-three centarians in Ningxia Region were Hui (Ningxia Pictorial 1984)—veritable proof of the benefits of living a true Islamic life.

Wang Zixiao is held up by the Na villagers as an example of God's blessing. At 101 years old, Lao Wang still regularly prays at home even though his legs are too weak for him to go to the mosque. The walls surrounding his warm kang are covered with Arabic texts and flowery Islamic paintings containing Qur'anic verses arranged in traditional Chinese duilian style. His wife lived to 113 years old, and his eldest son is 86. His mother was a Han woman who converted to Islam at marriage and the children were raised in a strict Muslim household. When I asked Lao Wang what his secret was for longevity, he responded: "good religion" (jia-omende hao). This substantiates the Hui belief that Allah rewards a devout qing zhen life-style with health and longevity.

Along with rituals that take place at important stages of the Hui life cycle, Islamic holidays punctuate the normal course of the agricultural year. In addition to the Ramadan and Qurban festivals, Na village Hui celebrate the Prophet's Day, or Muhammad's Birthday, as well as Fatima's Birthday. During these ceremonies, the ahong, elders, and several young manla sit at the front of the mosque and simultaneously read the entire Qur'an divided up into thirty chapters. The ahong explained that this "great reading" benefits the entire village whose majority cannot read the Qur'an in Arabic. Young manla who learn to read the Qur'an are often employed by villagers to read portions of it at the graves of their ancestors. They are thus accorded high status in the village, and are also able to earn a profitable side-income.

In addition to these regularly repeated texts, Hui ethnoreligious identity is expressed and reaffirmed through the distinctive cultural organization of the community: uniquely decorated Muslim homes, the central Mosque and graveyard within the village, and the role of the ahong in adjudicating daily affairs—setting the social world of this Hui community markedly apart from neighboring Han villages.

The Socioeconomic Context of Na Identity

Shared ideas and rituals illustrate the solidarity of the Hui community and the important role the texts of their faith play in defining ethnic identity. The texts become particularly meaningful during periods of intense socioeconomic change. Important shifts in the involvement of the local labor force since the private responsibility system was introduced in 1979, however, reveal significant socioeconomic change. In 1978, only 28 percent of the village population was involved in the labor force. However, by 1984 that figure had grown to 50 percent of the village, reflecting similar pre-1950 levels. This increase was due primarily to a jump in involvement in private enterprise that went from 2 percent in 1978 to 16 percent in 1984.

The Hui operate 70 percent of the new restaurants, food stands, and private sales stalls in the nearby Yongning County Seat market area, even though they constitute only 13 percent of the population. They also participate in the central free market in Wuzhond City, thirty kilometers south. There, Hui merchants make up over 90 percent of those doing business, in a city that is 95 percent Han. Hui from Ningxia are among the twenty to thirty thousand Hui trading and living temporarily in Tibet.

Entrepreneurial activity is an important aspect of Hui ethnoreligious identity. As one Han peasant from Na Homestead remarked, "The Hui are good at doing business; the Han are too honest and can't turn a profit. Han are good at planting, Hui at trade." This propensity has led to typical ethnic derogatory slurs, such as the "larcenous, cheating Hui." Under the Communists, Hui entrepreneurialism has been generally criticized as feudalistic. Yet, significantly, in a recent *China Daily* (1987:4) interview, the eminent Chinese anthropologist Fei Ziaotong, after a brief tour of the Northwest, suggested that these "native business talents" be encouraged in the free market economy for purposes of development.

Only 2 percent of households in Na Homestead are *wanyuan hu*, reporting an annual income of over 10,000 yuan. While not a large percentage compared to some areas in China, it is unusual in a fairly poor Hui area. The prestige and influence of these wanyuan hu is significant. Na Jingling, the most successful of Na Homestead's new entrepreneurs, made his fortune through setting up a popsicle (*binggun*) factory in 1982. A former mechanic for the commune, he and his brother have now moved into the transportation and construction business. They have recently entered into a contract with two other investors to build an "Islamic" hotel in Yinchuan City at a cost of 1.4 million yuan. The hotel will feature a restaurant and shopping facilities with "Arabic" architecture. "We want a real Hui hotel," his brother said, "not like other Hui restaurants in town where you aren't sure if its *qing zhen*."

Recent economic prosperity among rural Hui as a result of favorable government policy and Hui entrepreneurial abilities has led to increased support for religious affairs. Na Jingling, for example, wants to use his profits to help the Hui in Ningxia, support the Mosque, and build a "really qing zhen" Islamic hotel. Other Hui wanyuan hu have told me that because Allah is responsible for their new-found wealth under the new government policies, they should devote some of their profits to promoting Islam and mosque construction. Red posters on the walls in every mosque clearly list by name and amount those who have given to the construction projects, with names of the wanyuan hu and their donations writ large. More wealthy Hui sometimes complained to me of the pressures brought to bear on them to contribute to the mosque.

Local Government Policies and Na Identity

The promotion of more liberal minority policies throughout China is having an important effect on this village. Greater religious freedom since 1979 is evident throughout the region in the rapid state-sponsored rebuilding of mosques that were either closed or destroyed during the "smash four olds" campaign of the

Cultural Revolution. The government has spent large sums of money to rebuild and restore famous mosques in Na Homestead (90,000 yuan), Tongxin (800,000 yuan), and Yinchuan's Southgate Great Mosque (over one million yuan). There are more mosques in Ningxia than before 1949.

In terms of birth planning, the Hui minority are allowed two children in the countryside, and three in mountainous or desert areas, while the Han are permitted only one. In areas where population is sparse, Hui have been known to have more children and infractions tend to be judged more lightly than among the Han.

The Ningxia government is interested in promoting closer ties with foreign Muslim countries to foster economic development. The government has sponsored several economic and "Muslim Friendship" delegations to the Middle East to correspond with the Hajj, with the delegations including important religious leaders and well-known ahong fluent in Arabic. Delegations of foreign Muslim government and religious leaders have been hosted by Ningxia and escorted to visit historic mosques in Yinchuan, Na Homestead, and Tongxin. Hui "Muslim Construction Teams" formed by collectives and encouraged by the government have been sent to third world Muslim nations on state development projects. While many of the workers are Han, several leaders are Hui and some translators are Hui trained in the Islamic schools.

The Ethnoreligious Expression of Na Identity

The influence of recent shifts in government policy and changing socioeconomic conditions illustrate the importance of Islam in the ethnoreligious identity of the Hui in Na Homestead. To be separated from Islam would mean to be cut off from their ancestry. When I asked young Hui why they believed in Islam, the vast majority responded simply: "Because we are Hui." "The Han believe in Buddhism, we Hui believe in Islam"—an assertion made in a state that has promoted atheism for thirty-five years.

State-sponsored interaction with foreign Muslims, in the interest of encouraging economic investment, has led Hui villagers to gain a more international perspective on their faith, and has furthered Islamic renewal. Liberalized economic and nationality policies have fostered a reexamination of the relation of Islam to

Hui identity and economic action by local cadres. At the same time, this reevaluation has allowed the expression of an ethnoreligious identity re-rooted in an Islamic heritage and adapted to the local context. The Hui are actively taking advantage of these favorable policies. In the process, their identity and the policies themselves become reformulated, and reevaluated Islam is an integral part of the identity of Na villagers—one not easily distinguished from their ethnic identity. Policies that make a radical distinction between religious and ethnic identity will only serve to alienate northwestern Hui from participation in the broader society. While the renewed meaningfulness of Islam to the Hui might represent for some a fundamentalist revival of fanatical proportions, or a mere situationalist manipulation of identity for temporary benefits, the revitalized ethnoreligious identity of these Hui communities reflects a return to ethnoreligious roots—a re-rooting, rather than a fanatic revival of Islam.

Notes

1. Funding for three years of field research among Muslims in the People's Republic of China was provided by the Fulbright-Hayes Foundation, the Committee on Scholarly Communication with the People's Republic of China, and the Wenner-Gren Foundation for Anthropological Research. My hosts during this time were the Central Institute for Nationalities, the Ningxia Academy of Social Sciences, and the Xinjiang Academy of Social Sciences. I would like to express my appreciation to the agencies and individuals who made this study possible. This paper was prepared under the generous support of the Harvard Academy for International and Area Studies. This chapter is an adaptation of Chapter 3, *Muslim Chinese: Ethnic Nationalism in the People's Republic*, by Dru C. Gladney (Cambridge, Council on East Asian Studies, Harvard University, 1991), by permission of the Council on East Asian Studies.

2. I learned of at least three other cases of elderly party members becoming ahong in Pingluo, north of Yinchuan.

3. For excellent introductions to the early history of Islam in China, see especially Leslie, 1986; Lipman, 1981:288–99; Ma Qicheng, 1983; Nakada, 1971.

4. Na Jiahu, which I translate "Na Homestead," is a brigade (*dadui*) belonging to Yanghe Commune (*gongshe*). Now that Yanghe has become a township (*xiang*), Na Homestead can be considered a large village, comprised of eleven teams (*xiaodui*).

5. Same-surname villages are common in China, where the growth

of the village may often be traced to the dominance of one central lineage (see Watson, 1975). While a strict observance of same-surname exogamy is maintained among the Han (see Baker, 1968:174–75), Hui often prefer to marry within their lineage, and even take spouses with the same surname, thought immoral and unfilial by the Han. Government officials believe that Hui propensity for intrafamily marriage has led to a higher degree of birth defects among the Han. This has led to special campaigns among the Hui by the government to enforce the marriage law proscribing close-relative marriage within five generations (see Gladney, 1988).

6. For a discussion of the varied meanings of the technical term "*Qing Zhen*" ("*ḥalāl*," lit., "pure and true"), the significance of the early use of "*Qing Zhen jiao*" for Islam in China, and its wide interpretations among the Hui, see Gladney and Ma, 1989; Ma Shouqian, 1979.

7. As elsewhere in Central Asia, in Hui villages any elder who possesses advanced Islamic knowledge (*ahlin*) or who can read the Qur'an is generally recognized as an ahong (*imam*). Among the traditional non-*menhuan* Gedimu or Khufiya, the "teaching" (*kaixue*) ahong is recognized as the preacher (*woerzu*) and is responsible for delivering the main Friday sermon (*hutubai*). The mosque is generally administered by a committee (*siguan weiyuanhui*) that replaced the traditional "three leader system" (*sandaozhi* or zhangjiao zhidu) in 1958, after the Democratic Reform campaign (*minzhu gaige*)—among the Jahriya, the term *zhandjiao* ahong, for the teaching ahong, is preserved. The assistant to the teaching ahong is now known as the *zhangxue* ahong; the mosque administrator in charge of daily affairs is the *si shifu* or *si guan zhuren*. The teaching ahong among the Gedimu and Yihewani is often transferred (*sanxue*) to another mosque after an average of three years. An elder with minimal Islamic knowledge is known as a "second ahong" (*er ahong*) or even "primary school ahong" (*xiaoxue* ahong).

8. The largest mosque in Ningxia, located in Tongxin, dates from the late sixteenth century. It was spared destruction by Red Guards during the Cultural Revolution because it was the site where Mao Zehong declared the first Hui Autonomous County on December 20, 1936. Weizhou was the site of the oldest and largest mosque in Ningxia, but it was destroyed in 1966. It was under reconstruction in 1985, but the former Islamic architecture is not being restored.

9. The only available figures on Ningxia for the average wage of workers in state-owned units was 936 yuan per year and in collective owned units was 646 yuan per year in 1982 (State Statistical Bureau, 1983:488). This does not reflect rural income, which averaged about 400 yuan according to most areas I surveyed.

10. Officially, Han conversion to Islam at the time of intermarriage with a Hui should not involve a change in ethnic registration. However, all Han men I knew of who had intermarried with Hui women before the 1982 census were registered as Hui. Since the census, these spouses are no longer allowed to change their ethnicity whether they convert or not. They should be known as Muslim Han (*xinyang yisilanjiao de Hanzu* or

Hanzu Musilin). I often asked throughout China whether a Han who believes in Islam could become a Hui. Hui workers and farmers always agreed this was possible. Only cadres and intellectuals were inclined to deny this possibility. On the contrary, when I asked if Hui could lose their ethnicity through atheism or violation of the Islamic life-style restrictions, not one Hui said that it would be possible. Such a person would merely be known as a bad Hui, never a Han. This reveals that Hui rarely make the distinction between ethnicity and religion, and according to most Hui, ethnic change is unidimensional: Han can become Hui, but Hui cannot become Han.

11. For the nineteenth century Hui rebellions in the Northwest and Southwest, see Chu, 1955; Gladney, unpublished manuscript; Lipman, 1988; Yang, 1981.

12. Xinzhaizi mosque was torn down during the Cultural Revolution and rebuilt in 1983–84 with 50,000 yuan donated by local Hui. It belongs to the traditional Gedimu Islamic faction, with two hundred households in the village within the mosque's *jiaofang* (religious or teaching area). Visible from the road, we often called it the "Mexican Mosque" because of its bright colors and tall twin minarets (*wangyue lou*, literally, "watching the moon tower"), which resemble the bell towers of Catholic cathedrals in Meso-America.

13. Other important concessions include instructions to local governments to no longer encourage Muslims to raise pigs, and the publication of the Qur'an in 1979 by the Chinese Islamic Society (Ma Weiliang, 1980:78).

14. Reactions to oppressive policies in Na Homestead were considerably milder than in other parts of China. There were reported Hui uprisings in Ningxia shortly after 1949 and during the Great Leap Forward. In 1953, an "independent Islamic kingdom" was declared during an uprising by a Hui group in Henan. During the Cultural Revolution, Hui organized a protest in Beijing, and in 1973 a major uprising took place in Shadian, southwestern Yunnan, where People's Liberation Army regiments reportedly killed between one and nine thousand Hui (see Banister, 1987:316–17; Dreyer, 1976:154,171; Pillsbury, 1981:113). The "Shadian incident" is mentioned in *Asiaweek* 1979(50):35. The village destroyed in the uprising has now been completely rebuilt by government funds.

15. Yang Huaizhong interview; see also Yang, 1981.

16. Fletcher (1977:115–16) also found this inconsistency among the early Central Asian Naqshbandiya, as the following quote from the famous sixteenth-century Naqshbandi Khoja Aḥmad Kāsānī reveals:

The lords of the Naqshbandiyya have preferred the silent *khufi* remembrance, but some of them, if necessary, also perform the vocal (*jahri*) remembrance, just as when Khoja Ahmad Yasawi was appointed to set out for Turkestan, he saw that the inhabitants of that place did not take to the silent remembrance; so he immediately took up the way of the vocal remembrance, and thus the *dhikr-i arra* was created.

17. Note Pillsbury's (1973:174) interview with an elderly Hui woman from Yunnan who also referred to Sufism as the "shaking head religion" (*yaotou jiao*).

18. For more on Naqshbandi Sufism among the Hui, see Fletcher, 1977; Gladney, 1987b:501–13; Lipman, 1981:288–99; Ma Tong, 1983; Yang Huaizong (in press).

19. The family of a well-known Hui elder in Yinchuan distributed over 3,000 yuan ($1,000 U.S.) at his funeral in 1985.

References

Armijo-Hussein, Jacqueline (1987), "A Bukharan Governor of Yunnan and the Origins of the Hui." Paper presented at the Middle Eastern Studies Association Twenty-First Annual Meeting, Baltimore, 15 November.

Baker, Hugh D. R. (1968), *Sheung Shui: A Chinese Lineage Village*. Palo Alto: Stanford University Press.

Banister, Judith (1987), *China's Changing Population*. Palo Alto: Stanford University Press.

Barth, Fredrik (1969), "Introduction," in Frederik Barth (ed.), *Ethnic Groups and Boundaries: The Social Organization of Cultural Difference*. Boston: Little, Brown, 1–38.

Bourdieu, Pierre (1977), *Outline of a Theory of Practice*. Cambridge: Cambridge University Press.

Burns, John F. (1986), "Chinese City Is True to Moslem Self." *Los Angeles Times*, Section Y:4. Friday, 14 June.

China Daily (1987), "Minorities hold key to own prosperity." April 28:4.

Chu Wen-djang (1955), "Ch'ing Policy Towards the Muslims in the Northwest." Ph.D. diss., University of Washington, Seattle.

Connor, Walker (1984), *The National Question in Marxist-Leninist Theory and Strategy*. Princeton: Princeton University Press.

Dreyer, June (1976), *China's Forty Million: Minority Nationalities and National Integration in the People's Republic of China*. Cambridge: Harvard University Press.

Fletcher, Joseph (1977), "Brief History of the Naqshbandiyya in China." Unpublished manuscript, Harvard University.

Gladney, Dru C. (1987a), *Qing Zhen: A Study of Ethnoreligious Identity among Hui Muslim Communities in China*. Ph.D. diss., University of Washington, Seattle.

—— (1987b), "Muslim Tombs and Ethnic Folklore: Charters for Hui Identity," *Journal of Asian Studies* 46(3):495–532.

—— (1988), "Muslim Marriage Endogamy in China: A Strategy for Preserving Muslim Minority Identity?" Presented at the Middle Eastern Studies Association Annual Meeting, Los Angeles, 3–5 November.

——, "Ethno-religious Factionalism and the Panthay Muslim Rebellion in Yunnan, 1855–1873," unpublished manuscript.

Gladney, Dru C. and Ma Shouquian (1989), "Interpretations of Islam in China: A Hui Scholar's Perspective," *Journal. Institute for Muslim Minority Affairs* 9/2:15–26.

Gong Weiduan (1987), "Yongning Xian Na Jiahu Cun Shi Diaocha" [Yong Ning County Na Homestead History Investigation] *Ningxia Shizhi Yanjiu,* 1:34–40.

Israeli, Raphael (1978), *Muslims in China.* London & Atlantic Highlands: Curzon & Humanities Press.

Jin Yijiu (1985), "Sufeipai yu Zhongguo menhuan" [Sufism and China's Menhuan], in *Xibei Yisilanjiao Yanjiu* [Northwest Islam Research], ed. Gansu Provincial Ethnology Department. Lanzhou: Gansu Nationality Publishing Society.

Keyes, Charles F. (1981), "The Dialectics of Ethnic Change," in Charles Keyes (ed.), *Ethnic Change.* Seattle: University of Washington Press.

Leslie, Donald Daniel (1986), *Islam in Traditional China: A Short History to 1800.* Canberra: CCAE.

Lipman, Jonathan (1981), "The Border World of Gansu, 1895–1935." Ph.D. diss., Stanford University.

———— (1984), "Patchwork Society, Network Society: A Study of Sino-Muslim Communities," in Raphael Israeli and Anthony H. Johns (eds.), *Islam in Asia.* Vol. 2. Boulder, Col.: Westview Press.

———— (1988), "The Jahriyya of Ma Hualong: Re-evaluation of a Sino-Muslim Oppositional Movement." Paper presented at the workshop, "Approaches to Islam in Central and Inner Asian Studies," Columbia University, 4–5 March.

Ma Qicheng (1983), "A Brief Account of the Early Spread of Islam in China," *Social Sciences in China* 4:97–113.

Ma Shouqian (1979), "Yisilanjiao zai zhongguo weishenme you chengwei Huijiao huo qingzhenjiao" [Why Islam in China is called Hui religion or pure and true religion]. *Guangming Daily,* October 9. Reprinted in *Huizu shilun ji 1949–1979* [Hui History Collection 1949–1979], 1984. Chinese Academy of Social Sciences Ethnology Department and Central Nationalities Institute Ethnology Department, Hui History Team (eds.). Yinchuan: Ningxia People's Publishing Co.

Ma Tong (1983), *Zhongguo Yisilan Jiaopai yu Menhuan Zhidu Shilue* [A history of Muslim factions and the menhuan system in China]. 1st edition, 1981. Yinchuan: Ningxia People's Publishing Society.

Ma Weiliang (1980), "Various Aspects of Nationality Question, Situation Discussed." U.S. Joint Publications Research Service 76883 (25 Nov.):78.

Mann, Jim (1985), "China's Uighurs—a Minority Seeks Equality." *Los Angeles Times,* 13 July, pt. 1:1, 10–11.

Mason, Issac (1929), "The Mohammedans of China: When, and How, They First Came," *Journal of the North China Branch of the Royal Asiatic Society* 60:42–47.

Nakada, Yoshinobu (1971), *Kaikai minzoku no shomondai* [Studies on the Hui People]. Tokyo: Ajia keizai kenkyujo.

Parks, Michael (1983), "China's Minorities Enjoy New Freedom." *Los Angeles Times.* Thursday, 1 December, pt. 1-A:1–3.

Pillsbury, Barbara L. K. (1973), *Cohesion and Cleavage in a Chinese Muslim Minority.* Ph.D. diss., Columbia University.

——— (1978), "Factionalism Observed: Behind the 'Face' of Harmony in a Chinese Community," *China Quarterly.* June.

——— (1981), "Islam 'Even unto China,'" in Philip H. Stoddard, David C. Cuthell, and Margaret W. Sullivan (eds.), *Change and the Muslim World.* New York: Syracuse University Press.

Population Census Office of the State Council of the People's Republic of China and the Institute of Geography of the Chinese Academy of Sciences. 1987, The Population Atlas of China. Hong Kong, New York, Tokyo, Oxford: Oxford University Press.

Ricoeur, Paul (1971), "The Model of the Text: Meaningful Action Considered as Text," *Social Research* 338:529–62.

Schwartz, Henry G. (1984), *The Minorities of Northern China: A Survey.* Bellingham: Western Washington University Press.

State Statistical Bureau (1983), *Statistical Yearbook of China—1983.* English edition published by Economic Information & Agency, Hong Kong.

Wang Yiping (1985), "Najiahucun de zongjiao zhuangkuang" [The Religious situation in Najiahu village]. Ningxia Shehui kexue 9:7–9.

Watson, James L. (1975), *Emigration and the Chinese Lineage.* Berkeley: University of California Press.

Yang, Mohammed Usiar Huaizhong (1981), "Lun shiba shiji Zhehlinye Musilin di qiyi" [On the 18th century Jahriya Muslim uprisings]. In *Qingdai Zhongguo Yisilan jiao Lunji* [Essays on Islam in China During the Qing Period], Ningxia Philosophy and Social Science Institute (ed.). Yinchuan: Ningxia People's Publishing Society.

——— (in press), "Sufism of the Muslims in Gansu, Ningxia, and Qinghai," in Charles Li and Dru C. Gladney (eds.), *Minority Nationalities of China: Language and Culture.* Amsterdam: Mouton Press.

Zhang Tongji (1985), "Najiahucun de Huizu zhishi qingnian sixiang zhuangkuang" [Najiahu Village Hui Intellectual Youth Situation], *Ningxia Shehui kexue* 9:10–12.

Zhu Yuntao (1985), "Najiahucun chanye jiegou de diaocha" [Najiahu village industrial production structure research]. *Ningxia Shehui kexue* 9:1–6.

5

Shaykh Zaynullah Rasulev

The Last Great Naqshbandi Shaykh

of the Volga-Urals Region

Hamid Algar

Sufism has an ancient if largely unexamined history among the Muslims of the Volga-Urals region. Sufi shaykhs already made their appearance in the period of the Bulgar khanate, and no fewer than a hundred of them are said to have been active during the reign of Yādigār Khan.[1] In the eighth/fourteenth century, there is record of a certain Ḥusayn Bek, a disciple of the celebrated Aḥmad Yasavī, spreading Islam not only along the Danube but also in the Urals, especially among the Bashkirs; his tomb near Ufa was still an object of pilgrimage in the nineteenth century.[2] Sufis also played a role of significance in the Islamization of the Golden Horde. Berke Khan, the fourth ruler of the Golden Horde, was either converted to Islam or confirmed in its practice by a Kubravi shaykh of Bukhara, Sayf ad-Dīn Bākharzī,[3] and Uzbek Khan, under whose rule Islam became more firmly established in this branch of the Chinggisid line, was associated with a Yasavi shaykh by the name of Sayyid Atā.[4]

The Kubraviya disappeared completely from the Volga-Urals region, and the presence of the Yasaviya was marginal although prolonged. It was the Naqshbandi order that was destined to become supreme among the Tatars and Bashkirs, as was the case almost universally among the Turkic peoples. The first Naqshbandi initiate from the Volga-Urals region was probably Khoja Muḥammad Amīn Bulghārī, a disciple of the great Naqshbandi master Khoja ʿUbaydullah Aḥrār. He died in Tabriz in 902/1496 and does not appear to have been active in disseminating the Naqshbandi order in his homeland.[5]

The names of those responsible for ensuring the first implantation of the Naqshbandiya in the Volga-Urals region are not yet known to research, but it can be assumed that they emanated from Bukhara, which—together with Samarkand—was at once the chief center of the Naqshbandi order in Central Asia and a point of authoritative reference in all matters religious for the Muslims of the Volga-Urals region. The evolution of the order in Bukhara and other Central Asian centers was at all times swiftly reflected among them. Thus when the Mujaddidi branch of the Naqshbandiya, established in India by Shaykh Aḥmad Sirhindī, extended its spiritual dominance northward into Central Asia, Mujaddidi influence soon spread across the steppes to the towns of the Volga basin. We find, for example, record of ʿAbd al-Karīm b. Bāltāy (d. 1171/1757–58), the Tatar disciple of Shaykh Muḥammad Ḥabīb-Allāh Balkhī, a Bukharan successor to Khwāja Muḥammad Maʿṣūm, the son of Sirhindī; he propagated the Naqshbandi-Mujaddidi path in the town of Saʿīd (Qargaly).[6]

Thanks to the intensive literary activity that unfolded among the Tatars and Bashkirs in the nineteenth and early twentieth centuries, which included the composition of a number of biographical dictionaries, there is much information available concerning the eminent Naqshbandis who flourished in the region in the late eighteenth and nineteenth centuries. So numerous were they that we can in fact conclude that the Naqshbandiya fully dominated the religious and intellectual life of the period in question.

Two groups of Naqshbandis can be singled out for special mention. The first consisted of Tatars who traveled beyond Bukhara to Kabul, becoming there the *murīds* of a Mujaddidi shaykh by the name of Fayz Khan.[7] We are accustomed, perhaps, to thinking of Kabul as an intellectually insignificant backwater, but Sayf ad-Dīn Shinkārī, one of the Tatar murīds of Fayz Khan, praised its madrasas as superior to those of Bukhara, offering instruction in philosophy, logic, and medicine as well as the religious sciences.[8] This general excellence of Kabul must have been one factor in drawing Tatars to study there and at the same time to join the following of Fayz Khan Mujaddidi.

Perhaps the best known, if not the most erudite, of Fayz Khan's Tatar followers was Muḥammad Jān b. al-Ḥusayn, appointed in

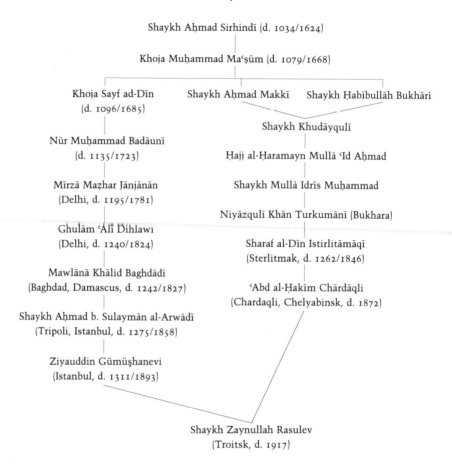

Figure 1   The Naqshbandi Lineages of Shaykh Zaynullah Rasulev

1789 as the first head of the *Dukhovnoe Sobranie,* the religious administration established for the Tatars under Russian auspices. Muḥammad Jān is said to have been an arrogant, dishonest, and not particularly learned person, and he was widely distrusted for excessive loyalty to the Russians.[9] The same reproaches could not be addressed to all his successors, but many of them had in common with him a Naqshbandi affiliation. Naqshbandi influence on the official religious apparatus, down to the Bolshevik revolution and beyond, was at all times considerable.[10]

The second significant group of Tatar Naqshbandis consisted

of the followers of a Bukharan shaykh, Niyāzqulī Khān Turkamānī, a figure whose prestige in Bukhara was such that the ruler
Amīr Ḥaydar—who himself had pretensions to religious emi-
nence—would attend his gatherings. Foremost among the Tatar
murīds of Niyāzqulī Khān was the celebrated Abū Naṣr al-Qūrsāvī
(known as Kursavī; d. 1812), possibly the greatest Islamic scholar
in the history of the Tatars. He is generally presented as having
been a rationalist questioner of theological dogma, one whose
writings prepared the way for the emergence of secular thought
among the Tatars at the turn of the century.[11] His works are for
the most part regrettably inaccessible, but, based on reliable secondary sources (notably the *Asar* of Rizaeddin b. Fakhreddin), the
characterization of al-Qūrsāvī as a proto-modernizer may be rejected. His concern was, on the contrary, to reject the recourse to
rational thought he discerned in the Ashʿarī *kalām* that was still
dominant in Bukhara, regarding it as a form of philosophy in dis-
guise, and to return to what he regarded as having been the creed
of the first generation of Muslims. Particularly controversial in
Bukhara was his rejection of the hypostatic reality of the divine
names, which earned him unjustified condemnation as a neo-
Muʿtazilite.[12]

Al-Qūrsāvī barely escaped from Bukhara with his life,[13] and
even his native land proved inhospitable; he died in Istanbul in
1812, while en route to exile in the Hijaz. Although many of al-
Qūrsāvī's opponents also had Naqshbandi affiliations, his Naqshbandi identity was significant, for his thought became a source of
inspiration to all the eminent representatives of the order in the
Volga-Urals region down to the early twentieth century.[14]

The ties of Tatar dependence on Bukhara had begun to loosen
as early as the mid-eighteenth century when contact was established with centers of Islamic learning in the Middle East. This
process was accelerated in the nineteenth century as Tatars and
Bashkirs began to study, in considerable numbers, in Istanbul,
Cairo, and the Hijaz. One consequence of this partial reorientation
was that Naqshbandi affiliations were sought and obtained from
centers of the order that displayed, perhaps, greater intellectual
and organizational vitality than Bukhara. Numerous Tatars were,
for example, drawn to a variegated circle of devotees grouped
around shaykhs of a branch of the Mujaddidi line that, deriving

from Shāh Ghulām ʿAlī of Delhi, had established itself in Medina. When these Tatars returned to their homeland to function as imams and teachers, they also propagated the branch of the Naqshbandiya to which they were affiliated. Thus towns such as Ufa, Tashbilge, Birjan, and Semipalatinsk became the northern outposts of a Naqshbandi network that also stretched out from the Hijaz across the Indian Ocean to Sumatra and Java.[15]

The Tatar disciples of the Mujaddidi shaykhs of Medina were, however, thoroughly overshadowed by shaykhs of the Khalidi branch of the Naqshbandiya, itself an offshoot of the Mujaddidi tradition and perhaps the most vital and influential of all Sufi groups in the nineteenth century. The Khalidiya was first implanted among the Tatars by a *khalīfa* of ʿAbdullāh Makkı, the representative in Mecca of Mawlānā Khālid Baghdādī. This was Fatḥullāh b. Safar ʿAlī al-Mīnavuzī, who died in 1852 at the age of eighty in a village near Kazan.[16] Another vigorous propagator of the Khalidiya was Shaykh Muḥammad Ẕākir Efendi of Chistav, concerning whom it was said, "There is no region in the lands of Kazan the ulama of which have not submitted to him."[17]

However, the undisputed leader among all the Khalidi shaykhs of the region was a Bashkir, Shaykh Zaynullah Rasulev. Eulogized at his death by the Orenburg biweekly journal *Vakit* as "the spiritual king of his people,"[18] Rasulev has been unjustly neglected by most historians of the nineteenth century Tatar intellectual renaissance, who have consistently shown a predilection for figures identified as secularizing rationalists. In the extent and depth of his influence Rasulev outweighed many of those figures, and his career bears witness to the continuing centrality of the Naqshbandi order among the Tatars and Bashkirs down to the outbreak of the Bolshevik revolution.

Zaynullāh b. Ḥabībullāh b. Rasūl—known later as Shaykh Zaynullāh al-Khālidī, Zaynullah Ishan, and Zaynullah Rasulev— was born, auspiciously enough, on the Festival of Sacrifice in the year 1250 (April 9, 1835) in Sharif, a Bashkir *aul* in the Zlatoustʾ district of Orenburg province. He began his education at the age of ten in the village of Muynaq under a certain Damulla Muḥammad Bukhārī. When this Bukharan teacher died, Zaynullah studied for two further years in Muynaq with Yaʿqūb b. Aḥmad al-Ākhūndī before receiving his permission, in 1851, to move to Troitsk in order to benefit from the more ample resources available there. Among his instructors in Troitsk was Muḥammad Shāh b. Mīrās, imam at the second Stone Mosque, who was highly regarded for his skill in Qurʾanic recitation, having studied the subject in Cairo.[19] But his principal teacher in Troitsk was Aḥmad b. Khālid al-Minkārī, imam at the first Stone Mosque and a graduate of the celebrated Kokeltash madrasa in Bukhara. A rigorous teacher, he insisted on his students' performing the five prayers in congregation behind him. Zaynullah evidently became his preferred pupil, for he has been described as "the foremost and most learned successor of Aḥmad b. Khālid in exoteric learning."[20] He appears in fact to have completed his formal studies with Aḥmad b. Khālid, although he also spent some time studying Arabic grammar with a certain Ḥasan al-Dīn b. Shams al-Dīn in the village of Isterlibash.[21]

After seven years of study in Troitsk, Zaynullah was appointed imam at the village of Aqkhoja in the district of Verkhneuralʾsk, where he also established his own madrasa and began teaching. In conformity with the classical pattern of joining the practice of Sufism to the cultivation of the religious sciences—a pattern followed almost universally in the Volga-Urals region—Zaynullah traveled in 1859 to Chardaqli, a village near Chelyabinsk, for initiation into the Naqshbandi order at the hands of ʿAbd al-Ḥakīm b. Qurbān ʿAlī Chārdāqli (d. 1872).[22] ʿAbd al-Ḥakīm was the chief successor to Sharaf al-Dīn b. Zayn al-Dīn Istirlitāmāqī (d. 1846), who had in turn been one of the Tatar and Bashkir khalīfas of Nīyāzqulī Khān Turkamānī. Nīyāzqulī Khān's silsila (genealogical chain) reached back to Shaykh Aḥmad Sirhindī, and he thus belonged to the Mujaddidi branch of the order. Zaynullah was by no means ʿAbd al-Ḥakīm's only prominent murīd, for he appointed at least five khalīfas, some of whom became important teachers in the Volga-Urals region.[23]

In 1870, about ten years after his initiation by ʿAbd al-Ḥakīm Chārdāqlī, Zaynullah left to perform the hajj, stopping in Istanbul en route in order to see the sights of the great Islamic metropolis and to visit its learned men, as was customary for pilgrims coming from Russia and Central Asia. Among the ulama he met was Shaykh Aḥmad Ziyauddin Gümüşhanevi (d. 1893), the most prominent Naqshbandi shaykh of Istanbul and an adherent of the Khalidi branch of the order. Such was the impact Gümüşhanevi made on Zaynullah that he sought and obtained from him not only a license to transmit hadith—a subject of particular interest to Gümüşhanevi—but also a second initiation into the Naqshbandiya, one which clearly came to override his earlier affiliation to Chārdāqlī. Before proceeding to the Hijaz, he spent several periods of forty-day retreat with Gümüşhanevi, thereby consolidating the initiatic relationship with his new preceptor and fully mastering the techniques of the Khalidi Naqshbandi path.[24]

The Khalidiya was not, in its essence, markedly different from the Mujaddidi branch of the Naqshbandiya from which it had sprung; it, too, emphasized sobriety and anonymity in spiritual practice and close adherence to the Sharīʿa. New only was the vigor with which Mawlānā Khalid Baghdādī propagated the path, together with an attempt to create a centralized and disciplined order focused on his own person. The unified leadership of the Khalidiya did not survive the death of its founder in 1827, but it spread rapidly throughout Anatolia, Kurdistan, the Balkans, Syria, Iraq, Daghistan, and the Malay-Indonesian world, inculcating its message of Shariʿa-oriented militancy almost everywhere it went.

Ziyauddin Gümüşhanevi had been initiated into the Khalidiya in 1847 by Shaykh Aḥmad b. Sulaimān al-Arwādī, who had been Mawlana Khālid's khalīfa in Tripoli (Syria) before coming to teach at Aya Sofya in Istanbul. After his initiation Gümüşhanevi acquired a steadily expanding following which met under his guidance at the Fatma Sultan mosque in the Cağaloğlu section of Istanbul. Numerous members of the Ottoman bureaucracy became his followers, and the *tekke* (religious lodge) he established in 1875 was visited several times by Sultan Abdülhamid II. In addition to activities conventionally associated with Sufi shaykhs, Gümüşhanevi was remarkable for enlisting with his murīds to fight on the eastern front in the Russo-Ottoman War of 1877; for establishing a printing press to produce works written by himself and others; and for setting up public libraries in Trabzon, Rize, and Of.[25] This example of varied and innovative activity was no doubt of influence on Zaynullah, inspiring some of his cultural and educational ventures.

Gümüşhanevi gave Zaynullah "complete khilāfa," or unrestricted authority, to bestow initiation into the Khalidi Naqshbandi path. Returning to Aqkhoja, Zaynullah accordingly set about gathering murīds with a speed and success that was disconcerting to some of the established shaykhs and their followers.

Hostile rumors began to circulate, including one to the effect that the method of *dhikr* practiced by Zaynullah and his adepts was vocal, in violation of Naqshbandi tradition. In an obituary written in 1917, Barthold reflected these rumors by describing Zaynullah as "the first to introduce loud dhikr in Bashkiria."[26]

It is highly unlikely that Zaynullah did indeed practice vocal dhikr. Mawlana Khālid had reaffirmed for his branch of the order the traditional insistence on silent dhikr, and Zaynullah himself prescribed it in *al-Fawāʾid al-Muhimma*, a pamphlet he wrote outlining essential Naqshbandi practice.[27] However, Zaynullah's countryman, Muḥammad Murād Menzilevī writes that "in the circle of Zaynullah, cries could be heard that were previously unknown in that region, cries that are a feature of the Khalidi path and arise from dhikr performed in the station of the heart."[28] Audible cries arising from the performance of silent dhikr might have aroused the impression that loud dhikr was under way.

The competing merits of silent and vocal dhikr have been a frequently recurring controversy in Naqshbandi history.[29] The Naqshbandis had early distinguished themselves from the cognate Yasavi order by insisting on silent dhikr, and although the Yasaviya was not entirely unknown in late nineteenth-century Kazan, there was a clear and universal preference for the silent dhikr of the Naqshbandis. We find, for example, that when in 1861 a dervish from Kokand came to a village near Saratov and began popularizing the vocal dhikr among its inhabitants, the event was promptly reported to the Spiritual Directorate in Orenburg as a scandal.[30]

In any event, the accusations raised against Zaynullah went far beyond the simple question of dhikr. Menzilevī writes allusively that his enemies "attributed to him what should not be attributed to any Muslim and accused him of a monstrosity."[31] He was also accused, Barthold reports, of having performed the hajj without securing permission and of bringing back with him various unspecified innovations.[32] This last suggests that Zaynullah had already aroused in some way the hostility of traditionalist circles loyal to Bukharan models of religiosity and learning and suspicious of the influences that were emanating from Turkey and the Hijaz. The Muslims of the Volga-Urals region seem in general to have been highly disputatious people in religious matters, with their sense of orthodoxy easily outraged, at least in the eighteenth

and nineteenth centuries; Rizaeddin b. Fakhreddin records in his
Asar numerous denunciations of alleged deviance that were made
to the Spiritual Directorate. It might be added, too, that Mawlana
Khālid himself had faced considerable hostility in Sulaymaniya
and Baghdad, and that his first representatives in Istanbul had met
with profound suspicion on the part of established shaykhs; it
seems that the vigor and ambition of the Khalidiya were universally experienced as threatening.

Zaynullah never formally repudiated his affiliation to ʿAbd al-
Ḥakīm Chārdāqlī, and he even mentions it before his Khalidi
affiliation in *al-Fawāʾid al-Muhimma*;[33] dual affiliation, even
within a single order, is by no means a rarity in Sufism. But it was
precisely from the circle of ʿAbd al-Ḥakīm's followers that the accusations against Zaynullah seem first to have arisen.[34] A preliminary interrogation of Zaynullah took place at the house of a
certain Iskandar b. Ḥabīb al-Raḥmān in the village of Elmet; numerous ulama participated, including Ishnīyāz b. Shīrnīyāz, a
scholar from Urgench of whom it was remarked that he used to
issue some very questionable fatwas.[35] It seems that the meeting
failed to satisfy Zaynullah's detractors, for in 1872, joined by certain of the ulama of Isterlibash, they denounced Zaynullah to the
Spiritual Directorate in Orenburg for "heresy and distortion of Islam."[36] Summoned to appear before the court of the directorate,
Zaynullah was interrogated again about his views, and according
to Barthold gave a written undertaking of unspecified content,
which cleared him of the charges against him.[37]

Now, however, the Russian authorities had decided to inter-
vene in the matter; Zaynullah was arrested while returning from
Orenburg to Aqkhoja. He was first imprisoned in Zlatoust' for a
period of eight months, and then a decree of the minister of internal affairs condemned him to a period of exile in Nikol'sk (No-
kolaiskii Gorodok) in the province of Vologda. As Menzilevī
points out, this was a particularly harsh measure, given that Vologda was an area "in which not a single Muslim soul lived."[38]
However, while being transported to Nikol'sk, Zaynullah found
himself one night the cellmate of a certain ʿAbd al-Raḥīm b. ʿUs-
mān who was being deported to Siberia, and he took advantage of the opportunity to initiate him into the Khalidiya.[39] Three
years after his arrival in Nikol'sk, Zaynullah was transferred to
the fortress of Kostroma, and five years later to a Tatar village

nearby. In 1881, the restrictions on him were finally lifted, and he was permitted to return to Aqkhoja.

The hostile interest shown in Zaynullah by the Russian authorities can hardly be explained in terms of the charges his fellow Muslims had brought against him, unless it be that they discerned in the controversy a source of dangerous disorder in the Volga-Urals region. Lyutsian Klimovich, author of a well-known if scurrilous history of Islam in tsarist Russia, suggests that the reason for Zaynullah's travails was that "the autocracy did not wish, in this particular case, to tolerate internal dissension in the Muslim clergy or to put in the position of agent-shaykh [sic] a person who had not been adequately tested. When he had been tested, he was appointed imam."[40] The suggestion that Zaynullah was either tamed or recruited as a government agent during his period of imprisonment and banishment seems wholly unwarranted. It is far more likely that, on the contrary, the Russians discerned in Zaynullah a potential for political trouble, either because of the size of his following or because of his international connections; his *murshid* Ziyauddin Gümüşhanevi was after all engaged in battle with Russian forces while Zaynullah was living in banishment. It is true that after his release neither Zaynullah himself nor his followers had any important clash with the tsarist authorities, but some of his murīds did participate in political activities during the first decade of the twentieth century, and—more importantly— the educational and cultural activities of Zaynullah definitely and effectively ran counter to the main emphases of Russian policy.

The year after he was set free, Zaynullah went again on the hajj, taking advantage of the opportunity to visit Gümüşhanevi once more. Shortly after his return, he settled in Troitsk as imam at a newly constructed mosque on Amur Street, and it became swiftly apparent, as Menzilevī approvingly remarks, that "the envious had not been able to decrease his standing in the slightest."[41] He soon gained such influence among the Muslims of the city that he was able to have the name of Amur Street informally Islamicized and changed to Ma'mūrīya.[42] More important was the fact that thanks to Zaynullah, Troitsk now became a principal center of learning for the Muslims of the Russian empire as well as a base for the further diffusion of the Khalidi Naqshbandi order.

Next to the mosque where he officiated as imam, Zaynullah Rasulev established a madrasa, known after him as the Rasuliya, which drawing Tatars, Bashkirs, and Kazakhs alike, quickly acquired a reputation as one of the foremost institutes of Muslim learning in the Russian-ruled lands; the late Alexandre Bennigsen even goes so far as to describe it as having been "among the best academic institutions in the Muslim world."[43] It enjoyed the material support of a certain Altynsaryn, a rich Kazakh merchant who was disturbed by the progress of the Russian language and culture among Muslims who sought a more varied and modern education than the traditional madrasa was able to provide.[44]

The success of the Rasuliya was indeed assured in part by its adoption of new pedagogical methods. A subject of particular controversy among Tatars and Bashkirs at the turn of the century was the teaching of Kazan Turkic by means of a new phonetical method instead of the traditional but ineffective syllabic method; the proponents of the former came to be known as the jadidists, and the defenders of the latter as the qadimists, as if this one issue encapsulated all the differences between innovators and conservatives.[45] Early in 1908, the Tatar press printed articles attributing to the ulama of Troitsk—including Zaynullah Rasulev—the view that the phonetic method was contrary to religious precept. But in February of the same year, Zaynullah, together with three other scholars of Troitsk, published a denial, pointing out that the phonetic method had been applied in the Rasuliya, as well as the other madrasas of Troitsk, since 1893. He went on to say that the ulama of Troitsk had no objections to broadening the madrasa program to include secular sciences, on condition that the sciences of the Qur'an and the Sunna remained the foundation of the curriculum. The brochure in which the *fatwa* of Zaynullah and his colleagues was printed was continually republished, and was decisive in assuring the near-universal acceptance of the phonetic method by the end of the first decade of the twentieth century.[46]

Despite his espousal of the phonetic method, and the fact that he was one of the few Sufi shaykhs to be respected by the jadidists, it should not be imagined that Zaynullah could himself be classified as a jadidist. The Rasuliya has, in fact, been described as a madrasa of mixed or intermediate (*polovinchatyi*) type,[47] and it served—in matters other than the teaching of the alphabet—to bridge the gap between jadidists and qadimists. Zaynullah seems indeed to have had a remarkable ability to fuse the traditional and the modern. Thus in order to cure the maladies of his followers, he would not only provide them with amulets, a traditional function of the Sufi shaykh, but also prescribe medicines that he provided from his own dispensary. Zaynullah enjoyed a general reputation for "foreign knowledge," presumably acquired autodidactically from the manuals of scientific popularization that were beginning to proliferate in Kazan Turkic.[48]

A contemporary of Shaykh Zaynullah Rasulev, ʿAbd al-Raḥmān al-Maʿāzī, has left an instructive account of his daily regimen at the Rasuliya. His public activity would begin at eight o'clock in the morning with visits from murīds and others who were in need of advice, charity, or practical help. The samovar would be kept on the boil to supply them with tea. At eleven, he would go to teach, giving instruction on basic texts such as *Ṣaḥīḥ al-Bukhārī* and *Tafsīr al-Jalālayn* until it was time for the midday prayer. In the afternoon he would go to any meeting or appointment outside the madrasa that might have been planned, meet again with visitors and petitioners, and then rest until the afternoon prayer. He would then stay in the mosque until the evening prayer, meeting with his murīds and reciting with them the *khatm-i khwājagān*, the distinctive litany of the Naqshbandi order. On Fridays and other days when the afflux of murīds was particularly large *khatm-i khwājagān* would be recited twice in succession. Ramadan would see certain adjustments to this schedule: then Shaykh Zaynullah would teach in the afternoons instead of the mornings, and he would make *iʿtikāf* (retreat in the mosque) for the last ten days of the month.[49]

To understand fully the significance of the Rasuliya, it should be recalled that the Tatars of Kazan and the Bashkirs had been neighbors of the Kazakhs and, more distantly, the other steppe peoples since the sixteenth century. With the expansion of the Tatar mercantile class in the nineteenth century, Tatar merchants traveled ever more frequently in the Kazakh steppes and western Siberia, acting as agents of Islamization wherever they went. However, the cultural and religious influence of the merchants was inevitably limited, and it was through bringing Kazakhs to study in the Tatar and Bashkir madrasas that a deeper implantation of Islamic religion, culture, and literacy was made possible.

The phenomenon of Kazakhs studying in Tatar madrasas appears to have begun in the late eighteenth century when Fāṭima, the daughter of Muḥammad Jān, first head of the *Dukhovnoe Sobranie*, married a khan of the Kazakhs and persuaded him to send a number of young Kazakhs to study in the madrasas of Isterli-tamaq and Isterlibash at his expense.[50] By the mid-nineteenth century, the influence of the Tatars on the Kazakhs had reached proportions that alarmed Russian and Russophile observers who saw in it a clear danger to the policies of Russification. Thus Chokan Valikhanov, the Kazakh who served Russian policy in numerous ways, thought it appropriate to propose in a secret memorandum, drawn up in late 1863 or early 1864, that the Kazakh steppes be withdrawn from the authority of the Orenburg Spiritual Administration, that a separate spiritual administration be established for the Kazakhs, "as a people distinct from the Tatars with respect to the faith they profess"; that *ishans* and *khojas* from the Tatar madrasas not be permitted to dwell among the Kazakh nomads "for no clear purpose"; and above all, that they be kept under strict observation "to prevent them from establishing dervish and mystic communities as they are now doing in the districts of Bayan-Aul and Karkaralinsk."[51]

Some twenty years later, the celebrated lexicographer Wilhelm Radloff noted with similar anxiety, in his work *Aus Sibirien*, that thanks to the activity of the Tatar merchants, "the influence of Islam on the western steppe has become so strong that hundreds of young Kirghiz [= Kazakhs] who have received an elementary education at home now go to the Tatar madrasas in north Russia and there study thoroughly the Islamic sciences."[52] He noted that the village of Isterlibash in particular had for several decades been receiving up to 150 Kazakhs annually who spent at least ten years studying there. Isterlibash, it may be remarked, was also a Naqshbandi center: its madrasa was presided over by Ishān Niʿmatullāh, another khalīfa of Nīyāzqulī Khān Turkamānī.[53]

Troitsk had been founded in 1743 as a fortress town on the edge of Russian-held territory, and being situated thus close to the Kazakh steppes, it was an ideal location for a madrasa to attract students from among the Tatars, Bashkirs, and Kazakhs. The number of students that passed through the Rasuliya is unknown, although al-Maʿāẓī gives a figure of 311 for the time he was writing, probably in the early twentieth century.[54] The proportions of various ethnic groups in the student body is also unknown, but all accounts of Zaynullah's career attribute to him a diverse as well as a large following. Dzhamalyutdin Validov writes, for example, of "tens of thousands of murīds, most of them Kirghiz [= Kazakhs] and Bashkirs."[55] Not all these murīds had necessarily studied with Zaynullah at the Rasuliya, for he would send his students out into the steppe to propagate Islam and raise the level of religious knowledge among the Kazakhs. According to one account, Zaynullah had, by the beginning of the twentieth century, "brought under his influence hundreds of mullas in many towns and villages of the Lower Volga, the Urals, and Siberia."[56]

The extension of Zaynullah's influence and thereby that of the Khalidi branch of the Naqshbandi order into Siberia is of particular interest, for the earliest spread of Islam in the lands once ruled by the Siberian khanate had also been associated with the Naqshbandi order. According to a legend once widespread in western Siberia, Khoja Bahā' al-Dīn Naqshband dispatched some of his companions, in the year 1366, to propagate Islam among the shamanists along the Irtysh river, reinforced in their efforts by 1,700 warriors sent by Shaybān Khān, ruler of the Qipchaq steppes.[57] This legend probably derived from vague memories of the efforts undertaken by Közüm Khan, ruler of the Siberian khanate from roughly 1570 to 1598, to propagate Islam in his realm, with the aid of Naqhsbandi shaykhs sent by ʿAbdullāh Khān, the Shaybanid ruler of Bukhara.[58]

Zaynullah's educational activities, helping as they did to enhance Islamic consciousness among Kazakhs and in Siberia and to reinforce Tatar and Bashkir influence at the expense of Russian control, were clearly inimical to Russian policy, and in 1906 measures were officially taken to limit the Tatar presence in Kazakhstan, to what effect is unknown.[59] Zaynullah also aroused the dislike of the religious arm of Russian authority, for it is said that the missionaries of the Russian Orthodox church, hoping to Christianize Kazakhstan, regarded him "with particular abhorrence."[60]

Both church and state felt affronted by a certain publishing venture undertaken by Zaynullah. In 1908, he provided for the publication in Orenburg of a history of the Volga Bulgars, the Bashkirs, the Kazan Tatars, the Kazakhs, and the Uzbeks, under the title *Talfīq al-Akhbār*. It was written in Arabic by Shaykh Murād Ramzī, a Bashkir who had studied in Bukhara but settled in the Hijaz, revisiting his homeland every summer. Marked by a strong nationalist tone, the book consistently referred to the Russians as Gog and Magog and called for unity of the Turkic Muslim peoples.[61] Soon after its appearance, it was banned by the censorship as insulting to the emperor, Alexander III, and the Orthodox church and as "incitement of Muslims against Russians in general."[62] It is interesting that Zaynullah patronized the publication of this book with its Pan-Turkic as well as Islamic emphases. He doubtless shared the view of its author that the aim of the Russian authorities was "to close off to the Muslims all paths to science and knowledge except the Russian path, for the sake of the well-known goal of conversion to Christianity."[63]

Zaynullah's methods in combatting Russian policy appear to have been exclusively religious, educational, and cultural; there is no record of overt political activity on his part. Nonetheless, he regarded with favor the aspirations of those Tatars and other Muslims of the Russian empire who sought, for a time, an alliance with the Russian liberal bourgeoisie in order to ameliorate the lot of the Muslims. He thus sent a message of good wishes to the Third All-Russian Muslim Congress that met at Nizhnii Novgorod between August 16 and 20, 1906.[64] ʿĀlimjān Barūdī, leader of the Ittifāq al-Muslimīn, a Muslim association that was transformed into a political party at this congress, was a prominent follower of Shaykh Zaynullah. From 1908 onward, it became apparent that the Russians were unwilling to accommodate Muslim demands, and the moderate policies of the Ittifāq al-Muslimīn declined, to the benefit of more radical elements. With these, Zaynullah had no contact.

While Zaynullah's following was extremely large by all accounts, relatively few of his prominent murīds are known by name. ʿĀlimjān Barūdī, in addition to his political activities, was the director of the Muḥammadiya madrasa in Kazan, an institution that followed the new pedagogical methods and with its 300 to 400 students was the largest madrasa in the Russian empire. In May 1917, he became mufti of Ufa and the following year chairman of the Religious Department of the Muslim National Administration based in the same city. After a brief spell as mufti of Orenburg, he died in Moscow in 1921. He is said to have been not merely a murīd of Shaykh Zaynullah but also his initiatic successor in the Khalidi Naqshbandi order.[65]

Another prominent follower of Zaynullah was Ṣābir Jān Ḥasanī, mufti of Ufa for many years. He enjoyed a high reputation for religious learning among all Russian Muslims. In 1910, Ismail Bey Gaspirali (Gasprinskii) received a query from a certain Austrian baroness who was contemplating conversion to Islam but hesitating because of the necessity of veiling herself. Gaspirali forwarded her query to Ṣābir Jān Ḥasanī, who replied that veiling, in the sense of completely veiling the female body and excluding women from all social activity, had no basis in the Sharīʿa and was in any event unknown in many regions of Russia.[66] He also gave proof of broad vision and interests by collecting money in 1901 to aid in the construction of the Hijaz railroad.[67] The date of Ṣābir Jān Ḥasanī's death is unknown.

Another prominent follower of Shaykh Zaynullah was Rizaeddin b. Fakhreddin, the prominent author and pedagogue who abandoned his career as qadi of Orenburg in order to devote himself to scholarship. The most important of his numerous writings is *Asar*, a biographical dictionary primarily of Tatar and Bashkir scholars and men of religion, as well as some Daghistanis and Central Asians. Rizaeddin's respect for Shaykh Zaynullah is evident at many places in this work, and some entries are based entirely on the information he supplied. Rizaeddin returned to official life in December 1917 when he was named deputy mufti of Ufa, and he became mufti at the beginning of 1922 following the death of ʿĀlimjān Barūdī. In the same year, he headed the Soviet delegation to the international Islamic conference in Mecca. In 1931, he was invited by the Soviet authorities to attest publicly that religious freedom prevailed in the Soviet Union. His refusal earned him harassment and hardship for the rest of his life, and he died in April 1936, in conditions of great neediness and poverty.[68] A posthumous rehabilitation was implied by the publication of a laudatory biographical sketch in 1984 in *Les Musulmans de l'Orient Soviétique*.[69]

Another individual known to have been a murīd and khalīfa of Shaykh Zaynullah was the father of the celebrated Turcologist and historian Zeki Velidi Togan, a religious teacher who gave instruction in his madrasa to about two hundred Bashkirs. Father and son would regularly visit Shaykh Zaynullah in Troitsk, and despite his general distaste for Sufis, whom he regarded as hypocrites, Zeki Velidi respected Zaynullah (together with a handful of other shaykhs) as "sincere men, models of morality and virtue."[70] Zeki

Velidi's father received an *ijāza* from Zaynullah to give initiation into the Khalidi Naqshbandi path, but he made use of this authorization only once, remarking—according to his son—that "this is no longer the time for Sufism."[71]

Shaykh Zaynullah died on February 2, 1917, just as tsarist rule was coming to an end. He was eighty-four years of age, and although he had ceased teaching for some years, he was still vigorous enough to continue administering his vast following.[72] Whether he made any comment on the momentous changes then under way is unknown, but one measure of the influence he had wielded was the prominence of his associates such as Barūdī and Rizaeddin in the affairs of the Muslim National Board that on July 22, 1917, proclaimed the autonomy of the Muslims of Inner Russia and Siberia.

The six sons of Shaykh Zaynullah followed quite varied destinies. One of them, Mulla Hibatullāh, predeceased him, apparently in 1903.[73] Another, Khayrullāh Efendi, studied in Medina with three successive masters from the Mujaddidi branch of the Naqshbandi order. He was initiated into the *ṭarīqa* by the last of these, Muḥammad Ṣālih al-Zawāwī, and returning to his homeland became imam and mudarris at Qargaly. He refrained from initiating his own murīds, presumably because of the standing of his father.[74] What became of him, as well as two other sons, ʿAbdullāh and ʿAbd al-Ṣabūr, after the Bolshevik revolution, is unknown. A fifth son, ʿAbd al-Qadīr, went to study in Istanbul and on his return to Russia became imam at a mosque in Astrakhan. In 1959, however, at the advanced age of seventy, he published an article in the antireligious journal *Nauka i Religiya* entitled "Ne khochu byt' mulloi" ("I don't want to be a mulla"), thus breaking entirely with the legacy of his father.[75] The possibility of his having acted under duress is not to be excluded.

Among Zaynullah's sons it was the eldest, ʿAbd al-Raḥmān Rasulev, who played the most visible role in the postrevolutionary period. He had been active politically in the years before the Bolshevik revolution, having served, for example, as member of a fifteen-man commission set up at the Third All-Russian Muslim Congress in 1906 to examine the reorganization of the administration of Muslim religious affairs.[76] In 1941, under the pressure of the German attack on the Soviet Union, Stalin conceded anew to the Soviet Muslims some organized form of religious activity, and ʿAbd al-Raḥmān Rasulev was appointed mufti and director of the newly established Spiritual Directorate of the Muslims of European Russia and Siberia, with its seat in Ufa. Rasulev responded to this small measure of tolerance with a call for Muslims to support the war against Germany.[77] He remained mufti and head of the Ufa directorate until his death in 1952.[78] ʿAbd al-Raḥmān Rasulev appears to have been his father's khalīfa in the Khalidi Naqshbandi order.

His successor as head of the directorate, Mufti Shakir Khiyalettinov, whose tenure lasted until 1974, was also a former student of Shaykh Zaynullah; whether he was in addition his khalīfa is unknown. In an article published in a propaganda volume that appeared in Moscow in 1971, Khiyalettinov evoked his years of study with Zaynullah in Troitsk and recalled a prophecy his teacher had allegedly made in 1909. Commenting on the injustice to which the Muslims were subject in tsarist Russia, Zaynullah reportedly said: "The patience of our people is as unbounded as our faith. But God is just and will compensate us for our sufferings. I will not live to see the day, but you, Shakir, will see a time when nothing can stamp out the light of the truth."[79]

If Zaynullah had indeed made such a hopeful prediction, it is doubtful that he would have seen its fulfillment in Soviet rule. It cannot in any way be presumed that the successive tenures of ʿAbd al-Raḥmān Rasulev and Shakir Khiyalettinov were a natural continuation of Shaykh Zaynullah's legacy, comparable to the activities of ʿAlimjān Barūdī and Rizaeddin b. Fakhreddin in the immediate postrevolutionary years. Nonetheless, the fact that from 1941 to 1974 the Ufa directorate was headed by persons who had once been close to Shaykh Zaynullah suggests they enjoyed a general prominence in the Muslim community which impelled the Soviet authorities to select them for the position.

Basing himself on an examination of Soviet sources, the late Alexandre Bennigsen more than once expressed the opinion that Sufism has effectively died out among the Tatars and Bashkirs, and it is indeed obvious that the Naqshbandiya has not displayed among them the same manifest vitality it has had in Daghistan and Chechenia.[80] It appears *prima facie* unlikely, however, that a tradition going back five centuries should have disappeared in a mere seventy years, however intense the repression may at times

have been. Moreover, a number of recent Soviet publications dealing with the history of Sufism among the Tatars suggest that the
subject has some contemporary relevance.[81]
Irrespective of the postrevolutionary fate of the Khalidi Naqshbandi order in the Volga-Urals region, which cannot for the mo-
ment be measured, the career of Shaykh Zaynullah Rasulev is of
lasting interest in several respects. It demonstrates the continuing
importance of the Sufi orders in the diffusion of Islamic knowledge and practice among the Turkic peoples of Central Asia. Further, it shows how the Khalidiya, in the person of Shaykh
Zaynullah, found much in common with the jadidists, escaping
the opprobrium that was attached to many traditional Bukhara-
oriented shaykhs and contributing thereby to the cultural renaissance of the Tatar people. Finally, it demonstrates how leading
Tatar scholars and men of religion belonged to an informal trans-
national network of their peers, actively sharing the general concerns of the Muslim world before the darkness and isolation of
Bolshevik rule descended on the Muslims of Russia.

Notes

1. Muḥammad Ḥusayn Zarīfoghlū, *Tavārīkh-i Bulghārīya* (Kazan,
1883), 32–33.
2. Rizaeddin b. Fakhreddin, *Asar* (Orenburg, 1901) 1:22–24. Thanks
to Edward Lazzerini for lending me his photocopy of this valuable work.
3. Jean Richard, "La conversion de Berke et les débuts de l'islami-
sation de la Horde d'Or," *Revue des Études Islamiques* 35 (1967):173–78.
4. Wilhelm Barthold, *Zwölf Vorlesungen über die Geschichte der
Türken Mittelasiens* (rpt. Hildesheim, 1962), 177.
5. Muḥammad b. Ḥusain Qazvīnī, *Silsila-nāma-yi Khwājagān-i
Naqshband*, ms. Bibliothèque Nationale, supplément persan 1418, f. 18a.
6. *Asar*, 1:41.
7. Abū 'Abd al-Raḥmān al-Ma'āzī, *al-Qaṭra min biḥār al-ḥaqā'iq fī
tarjamāt aḥwāl mashāyikh at-ṭarā'iq* (Orenburg, n.d.), 63; Muḥammad
Ibrāhīm Khalīl, *Mazārāt-i Kābul* (1339 sh./1960), 92–93.
8. *Asar*, 1:210–11.
9. Ibid., 181–86.
10. Z. A. Ishmukhametov, *Sotsial'naya rol' i evolyutsiya Islama v
Tatarii* (Kazan, 1979), 53; Alexandre Bennigsen and Chantal Lemercier-
Quelquejay, *Le soufi et le commissaire: Les confréries musulmanes en
URSS* (Paris, 1986), 97.
11. See, for example, A. N. Khayrullin, "Mesto G. Kursavi v istorii

obshchestvennoi mysli," in *Iz istorii tatarskoi obshchestvennoi mysli* (Kazan, 1979), 72–78, and Maḥmūd Ṭāhir, "Abunnasir Kursavi, 1776–1812," *Central Asian Survey* 8 (1989):155–58.

12. *Asar*, 1:127.

13. Sadriddin Ayni, "Ta'rikhi amironi manghitiyai Bukhoro," in *Kulliyot*, X (Dushanbe, 1966), 125–26.

14. Shaikh Zaynullah Rasulev was, for example, an admirer of al-Qursavī; see *Asar*, 1:124.

15. Muhammad Murad al-Menzilevī, *Dhayl rashaḥāt ʿayn al-ḥayāt*, in the margins of his Arabic translation of Fakhr al-Dīn ʿAlī Ṣāfī, *Rashaḥāt ʿayn al-ḥayāt* (Mecca, 1300/1883), 186–89.

16. *Asar*, 2:222–3.

17. al-Menzilevī, *Dhayl*, 182–83.

18. Quoted by V. V. Bartol'd, "Sheikh Zaynullah Rasulev, 1833–1917," *Musul'manskii Mir* (Petrograd), 1:1 (1917):73. This article, together with the account given by al-Maʿāzī in *al-Qaṭra* (pp. 48–51), constitutes the chief source for the outlines of Zaynullah's biography.

19. *Asar*, 1:452–53; 2:213.

20. Ibid., 2:511–14.

21. Ibid., 479–81.

22. al-Maʿāzī, *al-Qaṭra*, 49.

23. *Asar*, 2:542.

24. Menzilevī, *Dhayl*, 184.

25. For a complete account of Gümüşhanevi see İrfan Gündüz, *Gümüşhanevi, Ahmed Ziyaüdden* (Ankara, 1984).

26. "Sheikh Zaynullah Rasulev," 73.

27. *al-Fawā'id al-Muhimma li'l-Murīdīn an-Naqshabandīya* (St. Petersburg, 1900), 3.

28. Menzilevī, *Dhayl*, 184.

29. Hamid Algar, "Silent and vocal *dhikr* in the Naqshbandi order," *Abhandlungen der Akademie der Wissenschaften in Göttingen, Philologisch-Historische Klasse*, 3rd ser., 98 (1976): 39–46.

30. *Asar*, 2:385.

31. Menzilevī, *Dhayl*, 184.

32. "Sheikh Zaynullah Rasulev," 73.

33. *al-Fawā'id al-Muhimma*, 9.

34. Menzilevī, *Dhayl*, 184.

35. *Asar*, 1:59.

36. "Sheikh Zaynullah Rasulev," 73.

37. Ibid.

38. Menzilevī, *Dhayl*, 184–85.

39. *Asar*, 1:301.

40. Klimovich, *Islam v tsarskoi Rossii* (Moscow, 1936), 169–70.

41. Menzilevī, *Dhayl*, 185.

42. "Sheikh Zaynullah Rasulev," 74.

43. *L'Islam en Union Soviétique*, with C. Lemercier-Quelquejay (Paris, 1968), 47.

44. "Sheikh Zaynullah Rasulev," 74. It may be noted that another bearer of this name, Ibray Altynsaryn, espoused cultural policies diametrically opposed to those of Zaynullah. He favored the propagation of Russian culture in the steppes and proposed a Cyrillic-based alphabet for the Kazakh language. It would be interesting to know if he was related to the patron of Shaykh Zaynullah. See Thomas G. Winner, *The Oral Art and Literature of the Kazakhs of Russian Central Asia* (Durham, N.C., 1958), 107–10.

45. See Azade-Ayşe Rorlich, *The Volga Tatars: A Profile in National Resilience* (Stanford, 1986), 88–89; Dzhamalyutdin Validov, *Ocherk istorii obrazovannosti i literatury tatar* (rpt., Oxford, 1986), 74–81.

46. "Sheikh Zaynullah Rasulev," 74; Validov, *Ocherk*, 89.

47. Ibid.

48. "Sheikh Zaynullah Rasulev," 74; Validov, *Ocherk*, 89.

49. al-Maʿāzī, *al-Qaṭra*, 50–51.

50. *Asar*, 1:186.

51. Valikhanov, "O musul'manstve v stepi," in *Sobranie sochinenii* (Alma Ata, 1961), 1:528.

52. Radloff, *Aus Sibirien* (Leipzig, 1893), 472.

53. *Asar*, 1:77–84.

54. *al-Qaṭra*, 50.

55. *Ocherk*, 89. A similar figure is given by Emanuel Sarkisyanz in *Geschichte der orientalischen Völker Russlands bis 1917* (Munich, 1961), 297.

56. Ishmukhametov, *Sotsial'naya rol'*, 54.

57. N. Katanov, *O religioznykh voinakh uchenikov Sheikha Bagauddina protiv inorodtsev zapadnoi Sibiri* (Kazan, 1904).

58. See Abdulkadir İnan, "Sibirya'da İslamiyetin Yayılışı," in *Necati Lugal Armağanı* (Ankara, 1968), 335–36.

59. Rorlich, *The Volga Tatars*, 233.

60. "Sheikh Zaynullah Rasulev," 74.

61. Zeki Velidi Togan, *Bugünkü Türkili (Türkistan) ve Yakın Tarihi*, 2nd ed. (Istanbul, 1981), 541–42; Togan, *Hatıralar* (Istanbul, 1969), 44.

62. A. G. Karimullin, *Tatarskaya kniga nachala XX veka* (Kazan, 1974), 145.

63. Ibid.

64. *Politicheskaya zhizn' russkikh musul'man do fevral'skoi revolyutsii* (a collection of documents) (Oxford, 1987), 47.

65. On Barūdī, see Validov, *Ocherk*, 87–92, Rorlich, *The Volga Tatars*, 81, 93, 116, and Abdullah Battal-Taymas, *Kazan Türkleri* (Ankara, 1966), 163–66.

66. See "La presse musulmane," *Revue du Monde Musulman* 12 (1910): 459–60.

67. Reported in *Thamarāt al-Funūn* (Beirut), March 4, 1901, p. 2.

68. On Rizaeddin, see Tamurbek Davletshin, *Sovietskii Tatarstan* (London, 1974), 57, n. 5; Maḥmūd Ṭāhir, "Rizaeddin Fahreddin," *Central Asian Survey* 8 (1989):111–15; Validov, *Ocherk*, 109–12; A. Battal-

Taymas, "La Littérature des Tatars de Kazan," in *Philologiae Turcicae Fundamenta*, vol. 2, ed. Pertev Naili Boratav (Wiesbaden, 1964), 767, 773–74; and Bertold Spuler, "Zum Tode des obersten Geistlichen der Mohammedaner in der UdSSR," *Osteuropa*, 11 (1935/36):782–83. The assertion of Bennigsen & Quelquejay (*Le soufi et le comissaire*, 98) that Rizaeddin died in prison appears to be unfounded.

69. Talgat Tadjouddin, "La fierté et la gloire des peuples tatar et bachkir," *Les Musulmans de l'Orient Soviétique*, 61 (1404/1984):18–19.

70. Togan, *Hatïralar*, 36–37.

71. Ibid, 39.

72. Validov, 89.

73. See *Monla Hibatullah b. eş-Şeyh Zaynullah en-Nakşibendi Hazretlerinin Mersiyesi* (St. Petersburg, 1903).

74. Menzilevī, *Dhayl*, 188–89.

75. Quoted in Bennigsen & Quelquejay, *Le soufi et le comissaire*, 98.

76. Rorlich, *The Volga Tatars*, 238, n. 40.

77. Bennigsen & Quelquejay, *Le soufi et le comissaire*, 43. According to Bertold Spuler ("Die Lage der Muslime in Russland seit 1942," *Der Islam* 29 (1950):297, Rasulev had already been the effective leader of the Volga Muslims since the death of Rizaeddin.

78. Azade-Ayşe Rorlich, "Islam under Communist Rule: Volga-Ural Muslims," *Central Asian Survey* 1 (1982):28. Spuler suggests ("Die Lage," 299–300) that Rasulev exercised general authority over all Soviet Muslims from 1941 until the foundation of the Spiritual Directorate for Central Asia and Kazakhstan in December 1948.

79. *Les musulmans en Union Soviétique: Vers une vie nouvelle* (Moscow, 1971), 31.

80. *Le soufi et le commissaire*, 99; *Muslims of the Soviet Empire*, with S. Enders Wimbush (Bloomington, Ind., 1986), 22.

81. See Rorlich, *The Volga Tatars*, 165–66, and the same author's "Sufism in Tatarstan: Deep Roots and New Concerns," *Central Asian Survey* 2:4 (December, 1983):37–44.

6

Islam in a Changing Society

The Khojas of Eastern Turkistan

Isenbike Togan

The focus of this chapter is the role of Islam in Eastern Turkistan between the seventeenth and early eighteenth centuries, during which time two major changes occurred: principles of rule based on steppe values changed into a rule based on Islamic faith, and the right of legitimate rule shifted from the descendants of Chinggis Khan[1] to the descendants of the Prophet, Muhammad.[2] In sixteenth-century eastern Turkistan, Islam emerged as a unifying factor both sociologically and culturally under a political rule which became increasingly identified with religion. This rule is generally referred to as "the Rule of the Khojas (or Khwājagān) in Eastern Turkistan." It was the late Joseph F. Fletcher who first observed that Khoja rule in eastern Turkistan was but one of many religious revival, missionary movements which emerged in Asia between the sixteenth and eighteenth centuries. In various articles he has explored the interconnections and horizontal continuities between different movements to provide an integrative macrohistory (Fletcher, 1985:37–57). In this chapter, the rule of the Khojas will be approached on a microlevel with the same understanding that interconnections are a key to understanding Inner Asian history. Changes in concepts of legitimacy will be examined in relationship to social changes such as sedentarization and the adoption of Islam.

During this period, which lasted for eighty years (1679–1759),[3] the nature of political rule and concepts of legitimacy of rule changed drastically. Earlier in this region neither Islam, nor for that matter any religion, played a dominant role either in rule or legitimacy. Assigning a separate but secondary place to religion vis-à-vis political rule *(töre* or *törü)* was one of the leading characteristics of the societies that had emerged in the post-Mongolian era, and eastern Turkistan was no exception.[4] The place assigned to religion did not imply subordination. However, the role of Islamic law and the ulama in government was limited.[5] Law was defined by steppe values formulated in the form of *yasak* or *jasagh*.[6] Consequently, this region had been loyal to the principle by which only the Chinggisid line was regarded as the legitimate ruler, as it had become the Turko-Mongolian concept of legitimacy after the Mongolian conquests.

In the period under discussion, legitimacy shifted from the Chinggisid to the line of the Khojas who claimed to be *sayyids* (descendants of the Prophet Muhammad). Earlier principles of rule (töre or törü) , which were based primarily on the values of the steppe, were either replaced by or subsumed under Islamic principles. However, such principles, although called Islamic, were not necessarily always recognized as such.[7]

Historically, this period of rule did not result in a long lasting "state power"; on the contrary, eastern Turkistan came under colonial rule in 1759. Legitimacy, however, was pursued by the line of the Khojas in a series of rebellions. The colonial power, the Chinese Empire of the Manchus, variously punished the rebellious leaders (a new, active line of political legitimacy) and honored the Chinggisid line with princely titles and residences in Peking.[8]

The process of change that took place during this period will be the focus of discussion in this chapter. It will be argued that the geographical and ecological conditions of the region, coupled with a continuous change in population, rendered a rule based on steppe values impractical at a time when the polities of the region were confined to the more sedentary domains south of the Tien Shan. When steppe values proved no longer practical, the available religious and cultural values of Islam provided support for political rule, thus replacing the earlier balance between nomad and sedentary leadership with a new balance between secular (begs) and religious (khojas) leadership. In order to become a partner in the polity, the new emerging leadership had to assert itself, in the

initial stages, quite forcefully. This new rule, which as a consequence assumed a theocratic form and showed centralizing tendencies, did not develop into a strong centralized state. It was an
unstable and short-lived period of rule (1679–1759). This failure
can be ascribed to the lack of an institutionalized central political
organization and the accompanying agencies of enforcement.
Thus, one could say that problems of mobilizing resources to the
center could not be overcome. Yet, during this period the Khojas
played a centripetal, even a centralizing role to counterbalance the
centrifugal tendencies of the local begs who were descendants of
the sedentarized steppe aristocracy. To this end they employed the
assistance of the Dzungar Qalmaqs even before they came directly
to power in 1679. Within the confines of a sedentarizing society,
which was increasingly associating itself with Islam, the rule of
the Khojas provided a common identity and later a common historical past for the heterogeneous populations of the oasis. It was
these centripetal tendencies of the Khojas that paved the way for
Ya'qūb Beg's rule of the northern area of this region from a southern vantage point, reversing the earlier trend of domination from
the north. All of these developments, which led to centralization
under a common identity, later contributed to an awareness of a
common historical past. As a result, the period of the Khojas
emerged in historical memory as a landmark in the heritage of
eastern Turkistan.

When this area came under Chinese suzerainty in 1759, it was
Islam and not töre or törü that provided the fuel for political dissent and rebellion.[9] In fact, there was a continuous chain of Khojas
who were sought after for leadership. This enthusiasm for the
Khoja line faded with the rule of Ya'qūb Beg (1867–1877), when
important members of the Khojas were killed or expelled. In the
words of Kim Ho-dong, who conducted a fascinating study of this
period, "the Sufis with saintly genealogies ceased to be a predom-
inant social group to be reckoned in the politics of eastern Turkistan, and their influence seriously diminished" (Kim, 1986).
Eastern Turkistan thus entered a new phase in its history, leaving
behind the old steppe principles of legitimacy and later moving
out of the silsila of the Khojas (Khwājagān).

The area under the rule of the Khojas is commonly described
as consisting of three distinct parts: (1) Kashgaria or Altishahr in
the west, (2) Mogholistan or Dzungaria in the north, (3) and Uighu-

ristan in the east. However, this commonly accepted geographical division was more a political than a geographical or ecological one. Moreover, such a division appears only after the Mongolian conquests. Before the thirteenth century, the area consisted of two general areas: the Muslim west and the "infidel" east. In yet earlier periods we can speak of city states in the south of the Tien Shan and parts of nomadic realms in the north extending into the south. Consequently, we can see that the area is characterized by a certain amount of flexibility in terms of its political center of gravity and even key economic areas.

During the time period under discussion, this region was divided between the nomadic north and the sedentary south. This was a process that started with the Mongolian conquests and was completed by Timur (Amir Temür) when the last strongholds in the north were destroyed, the area was depopulated, and the inhabitants of the northern region were settled elsewhere (Z. V. Togan, forthcoming: chap. 4). Thus the former integration of the north and south came to an end. Such a rigid division left the south at the mercy of any nomadic group in the north, as the south was not suitable for maintaining a military force. For two centuries, the khans of Mogholistan struggled to maintain a nomadic military force in the north while obtaining an economic surplus from the south in an attempt to find a balance between the two regions (I. Togan:1988). Maintaining a loyal military force consisting of nomadic groups required rulers who cherished the values of the steppe, and who would thus redistribute rather than accumulate resources, and arbitrate rather than dominate. Ruling from Altishahr and acting as a steppe ruler meant, in effect, distributing the riches of the sedentary population to the nomadic groups and leaving the administration of sedentary regions to nomads only. This was not a solution for the inhabitants of the oasis cities, nor was it sufficient for the nomadic groups who tried to exert their own dominance in political affairs by employing redistributive mechanisms such as booty raids. As a result, nomadic groups became dissatisfied with the rule of the khans of Mogholistan and in preference to the values of the steppe joined various other confederations, such as the Kazakh, Kirghiz, Oyirad, and later the Dzungars.

Changes in patterns of rule may be observed toward the middle of the sixteenth century. ʿAbd al-Rashīd Khān (1533–1559) eliminated the tribal power from government and killed the members of the leading Dughlat clan, who had virtually become rulers of eastern Turkistan since the days of Timur. Simultaneous with these developments, we see that the Sufi masters had gained considerable influence at the court of Sulṭān Saʿīd Khān, the father of ʿAbd al-Rashīd.[10] Among different groups, Sufis belonging to the *Silsila-i Khwājagān* (synonymous with the Naqshbandiya) seem to have been more influential than others (Kim, 1986:57). Our sources frequently mention missionary activities being carried out among the residents of Kashgar, Yarkand, Aqsu, and Khotan at the turn of the seventeenth century (Hartman, 1905:203, 209). It should be noted that Sufi influence, particularly Naqshbandi, occurred during a time in which members of the earlier tribal leadership as well as rulers showed a tendency toward sedentarization.[11] The tribal leadership dominant from the fourteenth century on (I. Togan, 1988) had earlier shown considerable resistance to sedentarization. By the late fourteenth and early fifteenth century, however, the same leadership showed tendencies of sedentarization in their rapprochement policies to the oasis settlers. By assuming a role that would satisfy the nomadic and the sedentary populations of the region, the tribal leadership began to assert itself as the new aristocracy. However, such aristocratic trends did not find continuous support in the region; while further sedentarization weakened the mediatory role of the tribal leadership, these trends vested opposition in a society in which social mobility had been a driving force. It was at this juncture that Sufi influence emerged as a counterbalancing force. In his *Tārikhi Rashīdī*, Mīrzā Ḥaydar Dūghlāt provides us with a sense of the struggles from the viewpoint of an aristocracy losing ground to Sufi masters.

Sufi influence was neither restricted to the court nor limited to the sedentary areas. While nomadic tribal leaders ceased to be the backbone of political rule, the nomadic population itself came increasingly under the influence of Sufi masters, shaykhs, and khojas (Hartmann, 1905:201–2). From the end of the sixteenth century on, the khojas were not only acting as religious and cultural leaders but were also active in the political and economic spheres. In the overall macrostructure of the state they had come to replace the former tribal leaders who had been the masters of politics in the days of Timur and after. Parallel with this change, the traditional role of the tribal leader as the organizer and manager of diplomatic and economic activities gradually was reduced to diplomatic activities alone. The tribal leader in his former role had been instrumental in providing tribesmen with an outlet to markets in war or peacetime. In the sixteenth and seventeenth centuries, markets reached nomadic communities when small merchant caravans accompanied the khojas on their visits to these communities. The *Anīs al-Ṭālibīn*, the spiritual work of Shāh Maḥmūd ibn Mīrzā Fāżil Choras, refers to such visits into the communities of the Kirghiz and Kazakhs. Staple products such as tea seem to have found their way to the nomads through these channels. By the end of the sixteenth century, khojas as well as Muslim traders were also active among Mongolian-speaking communities. In fact, later in the seventeenth century, Dzungar trading caravans to China were manned by Muslim traders. Many of these traders carried the epithet "khoja." This fact was explained to the Chinese court as the natural outcome of affairs with the following words: "The missions of the *taiji*'s have always consisted of Muslims."[12]

The missionary activities of the khojas, coupled with mercantile activities extending themselves into the nomadic population, satisfied the nomads' need for exchange, which in this case was within their homeland. These activities had, on the one hand, the effect of creating an economic dependency, and on the other hand, that of keeping the nomadic populations outside of the agricultural regions and trade routes, and thus led to an even flow of surplus to the center. As mentioned above, the employment of Muslim traders within nomadic societies such as the Dzungars had the same objective.

In conclusion, the khojas, by establishing themselves within both nomadic and sedentary communities, acquired a mediatory role. In addition, by becoming first the trusted advisors of the rulers and later the rulers themselves, they played an active political role and in fact became part of the political center. On the other hand, in their close connections with the trade guilds and merchants they were instrumental in channeling the commercial surplus to the centers in which they were active. In other words, their policy was not one of redistribution in the style of decentralized steppe culture, but of accumulation in the manner of a sedentary centralized rule which has its foundation in an agricultural surplus. Such accumulation, however small, may be seen in the increased *waqf* properties of the saintly families.[13]

Centralizing trends may be seen in the elimination of a variety of decentralizing elements. The leading tribal force, the Dughlat clan, was the first to be eliminated. Later, the number of leading Sufi masters was limited to the members of one family. Sixteenth-century Kashgaria and Turfan had both been frequented by various groups.[14] Already by the beginning of the seventeenth century, during Meḥemmed Khān's reign, the rivalry was reduced to the two branches of Makhdūm-i Aʿẓam's (1461–1515) family, known in this region as Makhdūmzāda. These branches later came to be referred to as Isḥaqiya and Afaqiya.[15] After the Afaqiya eliminated the Isḥaqiya through the help of the "infidel Dzungar Qalmaq" and tied themselves through marriage connections to the Chinggisid line, thus producing offspring who could claim sayyid ancestry on the father's side and Chinggisid ancestry on the mother's side, the legitimate line of rule or rebellion was limited to the descendants of Khoja Āfāq. It should be noted that eventually the line was not continued by descendants of the Chinggisid princess, the Khānim Pādshāh, daughter of ʿAbd al-Rashīd Khān. It was the descendants born from the Dughlat noble women who were destined to be the leaders. However, this was not important. Once Khoja Āfāq married into the Chinggisid line he was seen as having acquired legitimacy of rule and his descendants carried the title of *pādshāh*, khan, and töre regardless of whether their mothers were Chinggisid or not.

Khoja Āfāq's acquisition of legitimacy through marriage into the Chinggisid family might appear to be straightforward political maneuvering. However, it appears that this action also had a cultural value with which we might not be familiar. There are indications in our sources that seventeenth-century eastern Turkistani society did not follow patrilineal values alone. Matrilineal connections played an important role in genealogies. Key figures in the genealogies are shown with matrilineal connections.[16] Native accounts that provide the genealogies of these two Makhdūmzāda families do not only emphasize matrilineal connections; they also display a concentration of historically prominent lines. The Makhdūmzāda families are not only of sayyid ancestry going back to Fatima, the daughter of Muhammad, but they are also related to the much respected Qarakhanid saint and ruler Sulṭān Ilig

Māżī.[17] One of the sayyids who happened to visit Central Asia received the daughter of the Qarakhanid ruler as wife. However, in these accounts Sultān Ilig Māżī is seen as a descendant of Abū Bakr, thus connecting him with the Naqshbandi *silsila*. Qïlïch Burhān al-Dīn, the son of the sayyid, became both a ruler and a dervish, thus retaining claims for both spiritual and temporal rule. In spite of the differences between the Isḥaqiya and the Afaqiya, in their *silsila nāma* both make this claim of legitimacy to temporal rule through the much respected Qarakhanid ruler. Furthermore, in both accounts the maternal connections are emphasized. In this connection, the Isḥaqiya account makes claims on the Qarakhanid ruler Satuq Bughrā Khān, as the ancestor of the mother of Isḥāq Valī. The Afaqiya account, on the other hand, emphasizes that the mother in this line was a member of another sayyid family.[18] In other words, the Isḥaqiya who did not marry into the Chinggisid family derived their temporal legitimacy through their two connections to the Qarakhanid ruling family. The Afaqiya, however, had stronger spiritual connections but they also had the legitimate connection to temporal rule. In fact, Khoja Āfāq (r. 1679–1694), after whom the Afaqiya have been named, had married both a noble woman from the famous Dughlat family and a Chinggisid princess. Later the descendants of Khoja Āfāq become symbolically associated with eastern Turkistani independence and resistance and rebellion to Chinese rule. Members of this line were able to lead the populace for approximately two hundred years (1679–1867), until Ya'qūb Beg declared himself ruler in 1869 and exiled Buzurg Khān, the last of the Afaqi khojas to rule in eastern Turkistan. They were able to lead in this manner because the former centralization of rule had virtually rendered them legitimate on all fronts.

The genealogies themselves may be seen as a product and an example of such a centralizing effort, reflecting a variety of accumulated traditions. But they differ from the other Naqshbandi silsila, as we can see in the *Majmū'at al-Muḥaqqiqīn*, in going back to Fatima-i Zahrā, the daughter of the Prophet. The interpolation of Abū Bakr and the Qarakhanid rulers into the silsila is reminiscent of other historical works in which the ancestors of the Khojas have been inserted.[19] Such centralization, however, did not produce a centralized state, but rather operated more on the ideological level. In practice, the state did not possess the means to enforce a completely centralized bureaucracy, nor to produce a centralized military force for defense or offense. This lack of military power put the Islamic state at the mercy of those who had power, variously the Kirghiz or the Dzungar. In fact, it was this collaboration with Dzungar rule which further undermined the "Islamic state." The use of the term *Islamic state* is intentional, since it is a term frequently utilized. For instance, it is used at the beginning of the eighteenth century when the Dzungars had again invaded this region, and the properties of the collaborators were confiscated in the name of the "Islamic state."[20]

Despite the efforts to create a centralized treasury, it is doubtful whether it would have materialized without Dzungar occupation. Although Meḥemmed Amīn Bughrā, in his *Sharqī Türkistan Tārīkhi* (1946:336), speaks of two highly centralized state structures (one in Yarkand and the other in Turfan), he seems to refer to idealized circumstances rather than the reality. The available evidence on the bureaucratic network shows that there is a greater preponderance of local government than organs of central government, indicating a greater variety of local appropriation of surplus than a central one. Even in the nineteenth century there was centralized political power but hardly anything that we could call a "central government" (Kim, 1986:175). In spite of the lack of an efficient central control at the beginning of the eighteenth century, the situation was not hopeless, as there were no delays in collecting the annual tribute amounting to 100,000 *tenge*. The delivery of the tribute, on the other hand, presented another setback for the development of an efficient center.

The inability of the central rulership to maintain its own military power also prevented it from assigning a subordinate place to nomadic groups. Other centralizing powers in Asia were doing just that and keeping the nomadic tribal groups at bay. The inability of the Khoja rule to do this put them at the mercy of various nomadic groups. Eventually, they came under Chinese suzerainty in relation to their Dzungar connections that had developed out of this inability to produce a dependable military force either for offense or defense.

Seventeenth- and eighteenth-century Khoja rule, in general, showed tendencies of centralization without developing into a centralized government. It seems this was inevitable since the Khojas played only a centripetal role to counterbalance the centrifugal tendencies of the local begs at this juncture in time. During this time matrilineal connections strengthened the inclusive nature of the society. The exclusiveness of the Khoja line, as descendants of Makhdūm-i Aʿẓam, was counterbalanced by the incorporation of local groups into the silsila through matrilineal connections. It was through their role of preserving and furthering the values of the local populations that the Khojas acquired their long-lasting influence in the region. Their role as liberators of aristocratic elements gave the later Khoja descendants in the nineteenth century a legitimate source of political power to be used against their oppressors. However, their role and functions changed when the circumstances changed. Local begs, who were descendants of the sedentarized steppe aristocracy, were eliminated during the Muslim rebellions of 1864. Following these incidents we witness a disenchantment of the population with the line of the Khojas. As a result, during the second half of the nineteenth century the Khojas as well as the local begs disappeared completely from the administrative apparatus and channels of power. Thus ended also the legitimacy of rule in the line of Khojas.

Notes

1. Names and terms have been transcribed according to the system developed by János Eckmann in his *Chagatay Manual*, with the following changes: c is j, č is ch, ḡ is gh, ḥ is kh, and š is sh. For the Chinese names and terms the Wade-Giles system of romanization has been used. For names and terms that have been accepted into English either in dictionaries or on maps, the usual idiosyncratic style has been retained.

2. This case is illustrated in a nineteenth-century incident, when a Kirghiz leader named Ṣiddiq besieged Kashgar. "The begs inside sent him a 'letter of chastisement' (*siyāsat nāma*) in which they made it clear that they could not accept him as a ruler because he was neither a *sayyid* (descendant of Muhammad) nor a *pādishāhzāda* (king)." Kim Ho-dong (1986:63,95, n. 67), from an unpublished ms. on Yaʿqūb Beg.

3. The actual rule of the Khojas starts in 1679 with Khoja Afaq and ends in 1759 with the defeat of the two Afaqi brothers, Khoja-i Jihān and Burhān al-Dīn and their eventual death in Badakhshan. However, direct influence of the Sufis had started during Meḥemmed Khān's reign at the beginning of the seventeenth century.

4. This was not subordination, but assignment of a role of clientship to priesthood and religion. For a theoretical approach to this issue see Geertz (1980:36). The case of the early Mongols and their religious poli-

cies has been variously discussed in sources as well as in special studies (Ratchnevsky, 1954).

In the post-Mongolian era, *töre* or *törü* denoted a secular political rule according to established customs that were based predominantly on steppe values; later it also came to be used for political leaders (p. 135 of this chapter; Doerfer, vol. 1, #134).

5. The role of the ulama in central Islamic lands where transcendence of God is emphasized, and the role of the Sufi on the frontiers of Islam where the immanence of God is a more widespread notion, are discussed by John Voll (1979).

6. *Yasak/jasagh* denoted an army order or societal order according to steppe values. Later the same term was used for law reflecting these values (Haenisch, 1962:86; Doerfer, vol. 4, #1789).

7. For example, the characterization of a particular group of Muslims as infidels and the legitimacy of holy war carried out against them, a state of affairs reflected in the factional struggles in the eighteenth century (I. Togan, 1989).

8. In 1759 the last two Chinggisids, Manṣūr and Qāsim, were taken to Peking and were given the title of the *taiji* of the first degree (I. Togan, 1991).

9. In the case of the split of the Kazakhs from the Uzbeks, values of the steppe (töre or törü) had played the major role.

10. The author of the Tārīkh-i Rashīdī, Ḥaydar Mīrzā Dughlāt, was among the members who found refuge in India. His work tells us about these influences (Ross, 1972).

11. Those who did not cherish either sedentary life or Islam retained steppe values. According to one interpretation of the word, Mongolian-speaking groups among these were referred to as "Qalmuq or Qalmaq," i.e., the "remaining," from the Turkic *qal-* "to remain."

12. Ch'in-cheng p'ing-ting shuo-mo fang-lueh, p. 196, 1.34v.

13. According to reports from the beginning of this century, only one such *waqf* property near Kashgar amounted to more than 100,000 acres (43,470 hectares), including eighteen pairs of millstones, fifteen large farms, and a high school (Raquette, 1930:4, n. 1.). Many others had been turned into military colonies by the Chinese after the rebellions (Kim, 1986:24).

14. Ho-dong Kim ascribes a great influence to the Uvaysi Sufis living in Kucha (1986:56–60 and 1989). They were descendants of Arshad al-Dīn and his son Jalālal-Dīn, who were instrumental in the conversion of Tughluq Temür (r. 1347–61) to Islam. Because of that, they occupied a special place among eastern Turkistan saints. Apparently not all of their descendants were Uvaysi. Some were Naqshbandi. The importance ascribed to the Uvaysi takes on further meaning in terms of the immanence of God vis-à-vis the transcendence of God. A Sufi who was called Uvaysi was "the mystic who has attained illumination outside the regular mystical path and without the mediation and guidance of a living sheikh" (Schimmel, 1975:28–29, and Kim, 1986:58). Kim Ho-dong further clarifies this issue by using contemporary source materials such as *Tazkira-i*

Bughrā Khān by Khoja Meḥemmed Sharīf (d. 1565) and supplies us with an indigenous explanation by stating that the above author "defines an Uvaysi Sufi as the one who was taught by pure spirits of saints (*awliyalar*) and prophets (*payghambarlar*)" (Kim, 1986:58, and 1989). This postulation is very important for present purposes, as it shows a shift of emphasis in the immanence-transcendence of God. The early Sufis, who were more like the Uvaysi, were later replaced by the Nasqhbandis, in whose silsila the khojas played an intermediary role. Thus we can see that the Khojas' role recognized a hierarchy in relations between human communities as well as in relations with God.

15. Makhdūm-i Aʿẓam probably never visited eastern Turkistan. However, it was his second son, Isḥāq Valī (d. 1579), who first came to this region and stayed for a long time. He arrived during the reign of ʿAbd al-Karīm Khān (r. 1559–1590), but it was Meḥemmed Khān (1590–1609) who bestowed favors upon him, including land grants in Kashgar, Yarkand, and other cities. His descendants were known variously as Isḥaqiya or as Qarataghliq.

The other branch of the Makhdūmzādas were descendants of Meḥemmed Emīn (d. 1597), the eldest son of Makhdūm-i Aʿẓam. It was Meḥemmed Emīn's son, Khoja Yūsuf (d. 1652), who came to the area during the reign of ʿAbdullāh Khān (1636–1668). He and his son Khoja Hidāyatullāh (1693) established themselves in Kashgar. Khoja Hidāyatullāh was known as Khoja Āfāq/Apaq after he assumed the rule in 1697. This branch of the Makhdūmzāda was known as Afaqiya or Aqtaghliq. Sometimes they were also referred to as "Aqkhanlar" (I. Togan: 1991).

These two Makhdūmzāda families were at continuous war with each other from their bases in Kashgar and Yarkand respectively. However, for the purposes of this study these internal conflicts will not be touched upon (I. Togan:1989).

16. The importance of marriage, the adoption of the charisma of noble families through marriage, and the transmitting of that charisma to later generations had been advised by Khoja Āfāq himself. According to a source quoted by Joseph Fletcher, "he said, 'marry, like me, from the great and noble persons of this country,' advice which the companions obeyed"(Fletcher, "MS").

The whole question of matrilineal issues needs further examination. It is not common, either among the Naqshbandiya or within Islam in general, although on the frontiers of Islam, such as in Morocco with the Sharifi genealogies, parallel situations seem to exist. In the eastern Turkistan case, the situation seems to be related to Mongolian notions of origin and the role of the mother as the originator: Alan Ghoʾa, Monolun, Höleʾün, Börte. However, it seems the power of the woman was not only transmitted to her offspring, but also to her mates. The frequent marriages of noble women to associates of rulers could have its raison d'être here. In any case, we have an example of this notion in the case of Chinggis Khan. Chinggis had partaken in the charisma of Ong Khan by consummating the marriage with his granddaughter, Ibaqa Begi. When marriage seemed to have served its purpose, Chinggis bestowed her upon his most trusted, respected, and cherished ally. It should be noted that Jürchedei was not a subordinate, but an ally. He was the leader of the Uru'ud, one of the few tribes that had not been broken up (Cleaves, 1982: #208).

The genealogical work mentioned is from 1774. Thus we can see that former notions of matrilineal connections had found their way into the silsila.

17. This connection appears in the Ishaqi account of Muḥammad Ṣa-dīq Kāshgarī, the *Tazkira-i ʿAzīzān*, published in Hartmann in abbreviated translation (1905:196). In a note Hartmann expresses his doubts about the personality of Ilig Māzī. He is of the opinion that any identification of this ruler with the early Qarakhanids poses problems of anachronism, as the supposed husband, Sayyid Kamāl al-Dīn, could only be from around the fourteenth century (1905:196, n. 2). This anachronism is not of primary importance when we consider the genealogy from the perspective of pillars of legitimacy. The same information is repeated in the unpublished Afaqi account of Meḥemmed Ṣadīq Yārkandī, the *Majmūʿat al-Muḥaqqiqīn* (25, lines 9–10).

18. Meḥemmed Ṣadīq Yārkandī, *Majmūʿat al-Muḥaqqiqīn*, 32.

19. One of the most widely read and widely circulated (in different ms. versions) was the *Tazkira-i Bughrā Khān*. Apparently, ms. copies coming from this area show differences from those found in Transoxiana and the Golden Horde region (Z. V. Togan, 1962:25).

20. Joseph F. Fletcher, "MS."

References

[Bughra] Emīn, Meḥemmed (1359–1366 A.H./1940–46), *Sharqī Turkistān Tārikhī*. Kashmir.

Cleaves, Francis Woodman (1982), *The Secret History of the Mongols*. Cambridge, Mass.: Harvard University Press.

Doerfer, Gerhard (1963–75), *Turkische und Mongolische Elemente im Neupersischen*. 4 vols. Weisbaden.

Fletcher, Joseph (1985), "Integrative History: Parallels and Interconnections in the Early Modern Period, 1500–1800," *Niguca Bicig: An Anniversary Volume in Honor of Francis Woodman Cleaves. Journal of Turkish Studies* 9:37–57.

———— ("MS"), *Altishahr under the Khwajas. A Manuscript in Four Chapters. Chap. 1, "The Naqshbandi Tariqa or 'Path'"; Chap. 2, "The Khojas of Eastern Turkestan"; Chap. 3, "The Coming of Infidels"; and Chap. 4, "The Triumph of the Oasis Nobility." Harvard University Archives, HUG (B) F520.30 (box #2).

Geertz, Clifford (1980), *Negara: The Theatre State in Nineteenth Century Bali*. Princeton: Princeton University Press.

Haenisch, Erich (1962), *Worterbuch zu Manghol un Niuca Tobca'an*. Wiesbaden.

Hartmann, M. (1905), "Ein Heiligenstaat im Islam: Das Ende der Caghataiden und die Herrschaft der Chogas in Kasgarien," in *Der islamische Orient: Berichte und Forschungen.* Berlin, pts. 6–10, 193–374.

Kāshghārī, Meḥemmed Ṣadīq, *Tazkira-i 'Azīzān* (or, *Tazkira-i Khwājagān*). Written ca. 1768. For available copies, see H. F. Hofman, Turkish Literature (Utrecht, 1969), sec. 3, pt. 1, vol. 4, pp. 25–30. The copy in the Bodleian Library, Oxford (Ind. Inst. Pers. d. 20) is available in microfilm in the J. F. Fletcher Collection, the Middle East Section, Harvard College Libraries.

Kim, Ho-dong (1986), "The Muslim Rebellion and the Kashghar Emirate in Chinese Central Asia, 1864–1877." Ph.D. diss., Harvard University.

———— (1989), "Nomads and Saints in the 14th to 16th Centuries of Chinese Turkestan." A paper presented at the International Symposium in Memory of Joseph F. Fletcher, entitled "The Legacy of Islam in China," Harvard University, 14–16 April , 673–732.

Raquette, G. (1930), "Eine Kashgarische Wakf-Urkunde aus der Khodscha-Zeit Ost-Turkestans," *Lunds Universitaets Arsskrift* 26:1–24.

Ratchnevsky, Paul (1954), "Die Mongolischen Grosskane und die buddhistische Kirche," in *Asiatica: Festschrift fur Friedrich Weller zum 65. Geburtstag.* Leipzig, 489–504.

Ross, E. D. (1972), *A History of the Moghuls of Central Asia. Being the Tarikh-i Rashidi of Mirza Muhammad Haidar, Dughlat.* Ed. with commentary, notes, and map by N. Elias. New impression of the original, 1895. London.

Schimmel, Annemarie (1975), *Mystical Dimensions of Islam.* Chapel Hill: University of North Carolina Press.

SMFL: *Ch'in-cheng p'ing-ting shuo-mo fang-lueh.* Photographic print from the original of 1708. *Chung-kuo fang lueh tsung-shu.* Vol. 1, Series no. 2. Taipei: Ch'eng-wen ch'u pan shih, 1970.

Shaw, S. (1897), *The History of the Khojas of Eastern-Turkestan. Journal of the Asiatic Society of Bengal* 46: part 1. Extra number vi + 67 pp.

Togan, Isenbike (1988), "Moğollar ve Timurlular Devrinde Dogu Turkistan" ["Eastern Turkestan in the 13th–15th Centuries, under the Mongolian and Timurid Rulers"]. Presented to the "First Seminar on Turkestan Culture," Istanbul, 11–13 April.

———— (1989), "Differences in Ideology and Practice: The Case of the Black and White Mountain Factions." A paper presented to "The Legacy of Islam in China," an International Symposium in Memory of Joseph F. Fletcher, Harvard University, 14–16 April, 642–73.

———— (1991), "Chinese Turkestan under the Khojas (1678–1759)," in *Encyclopaedia Iranica*, vol. 5.

———— (forthcoming), Turfan-Çin Münasebetleri ve XVII. Yüzyilda Doğu Türkistan [Eastern Turkestan in the Seventeenth Century with an Emphasis on the Turfan Chapter of *Ch'in-ting wai-fan meng-ku hui-pu wang-kung piao chuan*]. Sources of Oriental Languages and Literatures Series.

Togan, Zeki Velidi (1962), *Karahanlilar. Ders Notlari.* Lectures Presented on the Qarakhanids Delivered at Istanbul University, 1961–62. Mimeo.

Voll, John (1979), "The Sudanese Mahdi: Frontier Fundamentalist," *International Journal of Middle East Studies* 10:145–66.

Yarkandī, Muḥammad Ṣadīq, *Majmūʿat al-Muḥaqqiqīn*. Staatsbibliothek, Marburg MS Orient. October, 1680. Available in microfilm in the J. F. Fletcher Collection, the Middle East Section, Harvard College Libraries.

III

Discourse as a

Cultural Expression

of Identity

7

Beyond Renewal

The Jadīd Response to Pressure for

Change in the Modern Age

Edward J. Lazzerini

During the nineteenth century, most visibly in its second half, certain of the Islamic communities of the Russian empire began to follow a path decidedly different from any they had embarked upon before. The initial inspiration for this "decision" came from a tiny but expanding segment of the population, primarily intellectuals, who dwelled in European Russia's Islamic territories (Crimea, Azerbaijan, and the Volga region). In time others within the empire's "oriental" holdings in Turkistan and Central Asia would join them. Most were educated men (and a few women), often trained in Russian and European institutions as well as Islamic ones, and frequently well traveled both inside Russia and abroad. Some were members of Islam's traditional learned class (*ʿulamā*; sing., *ʿālim*); some represented that characteristically modern type, the secular intellectual. Still others were businessmen engaged in various forms of commerce or industry, with their own reasons for underwriting the charting and construction of a new path. To a person they agreed that the cultural community with which they identified most, the Islamic, was faced with economic, social, intellectual, and political challenges necessitating urgent response that included a willingness to accept the need for an all-embracing reform effort.

Not surprisingly, the array of those challenges, as well as differing perceptions of their nature and acuteness, evoked considerable disagreement among attentive Muslims, rendering consensus increasingly problematic with the passage of time. Still, by the last decades of imperial Russian history, the phenomenon which might be broadly termed "Islamic reform" was pronounced and momentous for the thirteen million Muslims under tsarist rule. Moreover, it touched Islamic communities elsewhere, as, for that matter, reform touched non-Islamic peoples around the world under similar conditions and at roughly the same time. The universality of the experience, as much as its pivotal role among Russian Muslims, justifies its examination. That the phenomenon has reemerged in full force recently to affect global developments merely adds the weight of current relevance.

What follows is an attempt to identify in its formative stage some characteristics of the Russian variant of Islamic civilization's "modern" struggle, to offer an interpretation of the purposes and goals of reform its early advocates set, and to propose a critique of the "project"—captured by the term *jadīd*-ism (modernism)—that reform ultimately entailed.[1] Engagement of these themes, however, seems best preceded by attention to certain historical, philosophical, and theoretical considerations that will set a useful context.

For approximately a millennium following its establishment by the Prophet Muhammad, Islam dominated the heartland of the Near East and made considerable inroads into other, mostly bordering, territories. As early as the eighth century, Muslim political and cultural influence had already begun to penetrate those lands north of Iran and Afghanistan. Between the sixteenth and nineteenth centuries, those regions—Caucasia, the upper reaches of the Volga River, and Central Asia—would fall piecemeal before Russian advance. Islam's impact on the local, predominantly Turkic peoples inhabiting these regions naturally varied. Yet out of the religion's original successes emerged more than a few societies that attained sophisticated political and cultural levels and, as peripheral areas of large civilized networks are wont to do, contributed significantly to the storehouse of Islamic cultural achievement. This was especially true of the Central Asian milieu (in its broadest sense) that spawned some of Islam's most inspiring interpreters (e.g., Ibn Sīnā [Avicenna], al-Taftāzānī, and al-Bukhārī), as well as influential Sufi orders (above all, the Naqshbandiya).

Despite sporadic episodes of severe internal religious and political strife at the imperial center (as between Abbasid and Umayyad factions in the eighth century), and the calamitous military setbacks in the late fourteenth century at the hands of Timur's Turkic horde, Islamic vitality remained a major, shaping force in world history at least into the seventeenth century. And the argument can be made cogently, with Marshall Hodgson and others, that prior to the eighteenth century Islamic civilization possessed a unity anchored in the presence of (not unaltered) formative ideals that inspired and provoked at least some in every generation from the "Nile to the Oxus," and beyond (Hodgson, 1974). Significantly, the continuous dialogue with the original Qurʾanic message that resulted, notwithstanding variant forms that it took, was conducted by the "idealists" of each age not in geographic isolation, but in contact fostered to a remarkable degree by an international network of education, common literary languages that constructed and sustained a shared discourse, a habit of extensive traveling, as well as the prominence of mercantile interests that both reflected and exploited the geo-social character of the Irano-Turko-Semitic milieu.

The combination of civilizational unity and continuous dialogue with the original Qurʾanic message stimulated and legitimized a particular notion of reform for succeeding generations of Muslims that continues to find resonance today, despite the gradual weakening of Islamic cohesion in recent centuries. From the eighteenth century onward, however, this characteristic reformist "tradition" was slowly joined by another rooted in an unrelated perspective and reflective of a different, more recent, discourse. In subsequent pages the shape that "other" modality of reform took specifically in the Russian Islamic context will be examined; but its significance can be appreciated more by first decoding the approach organically linked to the Islamic experience. This is not to argue for an unambiguous connection between pre-modern and modern reformism—the easily apparent chronological link disguises a more significant caesura between them—but to emphasize that Islam has had a long experience with reformism and that tradition can be, in Marilyn Robinson Waldman's phrase, "a modality of change" (Waldman, 1986).

To begin with, it is useful to remember that throughout history complaints about "the times" are surely among the most commonly uttered sentiments. Even during periods of minimal social change within the experience of a single generation, some people have always found reason to grumble about or, worse, indict the current scene, let alone complain simply about day-to-day distress. From culture to culture, of course, and from period to period, the volume of complaint as well as its appropriateness (function) within the dominant discourse has varied, thereby illustrating again the marvelous diversity of human response to life. Franz Rosenthal, drawing from the rich treasury of Islamic sources, has analyzed the role of complaint within that civilization as one of the "poles of man's approach to life," balanced by the pole of hope, and concludes that: "Islam officially acknowledged the presumed fact of constant deterioration and decline from a glorious high point in its earliest history. . . . Subjectively, man was seen as possessing a natural predisposition toward dissatisfaction with his status. . . . Objectively, the times were seen as always bad enough to give rise to justified complaint" (Rosenthal, 1983:58). For the minority in each generation, then, who took upon themselves the task of conversing with the formative ideals of their civilization, sensitivity to the "more somber sides of human life" and the urge to complain seem characteristically Islamic (Rosenthal, 1983:58).

Complaint can, of course, take many forms, depending upon circumstance and personality. Its most common expression has been ordinary grumbling, likely a universal accompaniment to the human experience at least since the dawn of civilization. Yet, if Rosenthal is correct, religious attitudes within Dār al-Islām further conditioned especially the "piety-minded" (as Marshall Hodgson termed them) to be disposed toward pessimism and to participate in a "long and hallowed tradition" of complaining (Rosenthal, 1983:51).

Beyond such routine protest Islamic history has witnessed complaint that episodically reached such a degree of emotional and/or intellectual intensity, as well as popular support, as to engender actions resulting, on occasion, in dramatic and enormously consequential change. Sectarian controversy, emerging very early in the development of Islam and thriving to this day, is an obvious example. Initially the result of a two-and-a-half-century struggle to define orthodoxy and the myriad conflicts it entailed seemed to settle enough of the social, political, and moral issues that troubled the early generations of Muslims to permit, for most believers, establishment of a consensus based not only on the Qur'an and its interpretation but also on the sayings or actions (*sunna*) attributed to Muhammad and embodied in hadith reports.

Two other manifestations of complaint, however, deserve our special attention because they underscore the vitality of Islamic civilization through the centuries and represent modes of change predating "modern" notions of reform. The first has been Sufism, initially individual and ascetic, but increasingly an overtly anti-nomian mass movement organized in brotherhoods (*turuq*; sing., *tarīqa*), with its stress on the inner awakening and moral reformation of the individual. Along with emphasis on ecstatic communion with God and the legitimacy of esoteric knowledge, such appeals ensured Sufism's attraction not only to the uneducated but also, at least in its more moderate expressions, to many representatives of the ulama.

The second has been the often right-wing orthodox call for communal revitalization, epitomized intellectually, perhaps, in the writings of Ibn Taymiya (the thirteenth- to fourteenth-century Hanbali ʿālim) and realized in the numerous eighteenth- and nine-teenth-century reform movements ranging from the Wahhabi (Arabia) to the Idrisiya (North Africa) and the Faraizi (eastern Bengal).[2] The relationship between Sufism and orthodox reformism does not succumb easily to generalization. Typically, a basic tension (even explicit hostility) exists despite efforts from time to time to synthesize the former's methodology with the latter's doctrine, as al-Ghazālī attempted philosophically in the eleventh century. By the eighteenth century, however, evidence suggests that an integration of the two on a practical level was enjoying significant headway as Sufism absorbed the orthodox emphasis on the Qurʾan, hadith reports, and the person of the Prophet while reducing somewhat its own ecstatic practices and metaphysical tendencies. However that may be, and much more research needs to be focused on this question, Muslims have long accepted the legitimacy of periodic "renewal" (*tajdīd*) of the community (*umma*). But what did "renewal" mean in terms of the common discourse of Islamic civilization? One hadith offered its fundamental justification by declaring: "God will send to his umma at the head of each century those who will renew its faith for it." Human weakness thus recognized, the word of God promised hope through the actions of the renewer (*mujaddid*), who, by fixing on Islam's seventh-century "Golden Era" when Muhammad lived to guide the faithful, would labor to authenticate and implement the fundamental tradition then established. John O. Voll characterizes the mujaddid's function as being shaped by three doctrines: (1) faithfulness to God's revelation that insists upon an uncompromisingly literal reading of the Qur'an and the Prophet's life and words; (2) assertion of the right to independent analysis (*ijtihād*) of the guiding sources of Islamic teaching; and (3) affirmation of the Qur'anic experience as authentic and unique (Voll, 1983). Time after time these three doctrines served to limit the sources of truth to a fixed and narrow temporal setting so as to purge current Islamic experience of practices, rules, ideas, and opinions accumulated over the centuries from other sources, whether Islamic or non-Islamic. While it seems to suggest an openness to change for the sake of a different future, ijtihād in fact has been the prime instrument for eliminating inadmissible accretions, undermining the authority (*taqlīd*) of generations of ulama, and restoring what once was and should be again. Change yes, but with an unequivocal orientation to the past that is deliberately, if very selectively, preservationist.

As a modality of change, tajdīd had long served Islam's interests unchallenged, its power and legitimacy drawn from the larger discourse of which it was an expression. When much of the Islamic world since the eighteenth century, for reasons that still arouse intense debate, appeared to many to be in decline and (coincidentally?) showed itself less and less capable of successfully handling the political, economic, and ultimately cultural challenge from Western civilization, a typical response, intellectual and popular, was a call for renewal. Gradually, as failures mounted, efforts at tajdīd seemed only to confirm the anachronistic image of Islamic civilization under modern conditions, save to the most piety-minded, or conversely, the least thoughtful. The West's challenge "proved" to be overwhelming, thereby forcing (assisting?) a revolutionary transformation in the minds of more and more Muslims, leading them to accept not only non-Islamic (Western) representations of the past and present, but also, and more importantly, an alien, nontraditional modality of change. It is this—jadīdism—that will be addressed now using the Russian Islamic context. Within that context, two persons will be examined whose perspectives reflect the fundamental distinctions between classical Islamic and modernist approaches to reform: Abū Nāṣr Qursavī and Ismail Bey Gasprinskii. The purpose here is not to conflate wholesale the range of responses by Russian Muslims to the modern dilemma, but rather to address what appear to be the distinctions between dominant discourses, one longstanding, one new, rooted in fundamentally different epistemologies and social experiences.

A native of Kazan province, Qursavī was born in 1783, the same year that witnessed the absorption of another important Muslim region, Crimea, into the Russian empire. Educated in the usual manner, he passed through local schools before journeying to Bukhara (like generations of promising Tatar youths) for the advanced study that would open the ranks of the ulama to him. While we are able to reconstruct little more than the contours of his biography, the available sources invariably tell us that he found himself frequently at serious, sometimes dangerous, odds with established religious and political authority over his teachings. The charge of "apostate" (zandīq), in fact, hounded him both in Bukhara and, later, in his home town.[3] Most Western and Soviet commentators have sought to link him with that galaxy of reformers who in subsequent decades would be identified with the jadīd phenomenon. They have done so by stressing his analysis of Islamic fundamentals, pointing out his criticism of current practice and belief, and interpreting his perspective as something "modern," or at least different.

But was it? A divergent reading of the evidence suggests not. To be sure, his dissent from contemporary Islamic attitudes and practice placed him on the margin of acceptable discourse, but for all of his criticism he remained within its bounds (the charge of being an apostate notwithstanding). His insistence on change arose from the same assumptions (if not conditions) that had moved advocates in earlier centuries: the best of times was during the age of the Prophet and his Companions; the current times were bad; the jurists of the past have not rendered judgments applicable to all ages; the jurists of the present must exercise the right of independent analysis to deal effectively with current issues; and so forth. Moreover, he argued, the ulama obsession with disputation and logic (kalām) served mostly to distract the faithful from God's word and, in the process, to undermine belief in the validity of hadith reports compiled by such reliable scholars as al-Bukhārī and al-Muslim. Only a return to the roots of Islam in the Qur'an and sunna could renew the spirit of the true faith.

A more appropriate context, then, within which to read Qursavī is one wedded to the past, staking its legitimacy on revelation and the Prophet's traditions while dispensing with whatever stands between the believer and those inspirational sources. Proper education and study are crucial, and, like many before him, Qursavī makes much of philosophy and science as independent of theology and deserving of considerable attention. But he makes this only (mainly?) to strengthen the hold of a specific past on the present and to minimize superstition, false belief, and other departures from God's eternal truths (metaphysical and natural). Sunni Muslims, Kursavī wrote in the only work of his to survive, are those "who always and everywhere follow sunna. If anybody says he is Sunni but is not guided by sunna and does not follow in the footsteps of the Prophet's Companions, he is the most mistaken and foolish of men" (Abdullah, 1985:12). The call to be rightly guided, to restore the relationship between man and God and to place it again at the center of man's existence, and to renew the umma make of Qursavī a mujaddid. He is described as such by a leading figure among Soviet Muslims today, as he had been by two of the most prominent "Russian" ulama of the nineteenth century, Şihabbeddin Mercanī and Rizaeddin Fahreddin, who compared him favorably with the fourteenth-century reformer al-Taftāzānī (Abdullah, 1985:11).

A renewer, not an innovator; an implementer, not a challenger; a holder of the center, not its displacer. Qursavī deliberately upset many of his contemporaries by questioning their perception and practice of Islam, but his criticisms never bore revolutionary implications. He represented a legitimate, if usually understated and minimally popular, opinion within the discourse of Islam at a time, however, when critical voices began to multiply and attract mass support in those territories already or soon-to-be absorbed into the European portion of the Russian empire. Among the Volga and Crimean Tatars, as well as Azerbaijanis and other Caucasian Muslims, the late eighteenth to middle nineteenth century produced numerous ulama and Sufi adepts who echoed the complaints of Qursavī. In the absence of any detailed study of the subject, a situation that repeats itself at every turn for Russian Islam, it can only be suggested that a list of such men would likely include Abdürrahim Utïz-Imenī (1754–1836), Abdülmanïh Kargalī (1782–1826), Ibatulla Salih (1794–1867), and Abdülcebbar Kandalī (1797–1860) from the Volga region, as well as Mulla Panaha Vagïf

(1717–1797), Mulla Veli Vidalī (1709–1809), and Zeynülabeddin Şirvanī (fl. eighteenth century) from Azerbaijan, and the Crimean Tatar Eşmirza (1803–1883). In addition, through the mid-third of the eighteenth century along the Volga, and later in Caucasia, the tajdīd modality of change found expression in mass movements frequently inspired by Sufi ṭuruq and directed largely against Russian colonialism. The calls for jihad (holy war) by Imam Manṣūr (1785–1791), Shaykh Muhammad of Yaraglar (1825), and Imam Şamil (1834–1859) are but three examples.

Even as organic communal experiences and the shifting requirements of colonial relations between Russia and her Muslim subjects combined (with regional variations) to encourage a reformist spirit in the time-honored mode, increasingly some of the same factors fortuitously engendered native responses of a qualitatively different kind. Though not an exhaustive catalog, the following provide some sense of this momentous development's complex genealogy: (1) the policy of "enlightened imperialism" pursued during the "long" era of Catherine II, running from the 1760s to the 1830s, and entailing a proclamation of religious toleration, implementation of positive inducements to assimilation of minorities (including Muslims), the institutionalization and bureaucratization of Russian Islam by the creation of two Muslim assemblies (1788–89 and 1794) along with administrative apparatuses, the laying of a foundation for a printing revolution among Russian Muslims with the establishment of an "Asiatic" press in St. Petersburg in 1802, and the birth of Russian "oriental" studies at the universities of St. Petersburg and then Kazan; (2) the stimulation of socioeconomic change among the Volga Tatars (in the context of their communal diaspora and extensive commercial mobilization), among the Crimean Tatars (in the context of their catastrophic demographic decline along with the immigration of foreign colonists and entrepreneurs after 1783), and among the Azerbaijanis (in the context of their growing involvement in emerging venture capitalism associated largely with the exploitation of oil reserves in the Caspian Sea); and (3) the psychological challenge of the seemingly inexorable advance and power of Russia.

Taken together, these and other less obvious considerations fostered the emergence of a cadre of Russianized Muslims whose *Weltanschauung* reflected the effects of increasing contact with

Russian (Western) culture and various amounts of the "modern-ism" in which the greater Western complex was caught up. Some of these "new" Muslims, like Abbas Kuli Aga Bakihanov (1794–1848), Mirza Fetalī Ahundov (1812–1878), Çokan Valihanov (1835–1865), and Mirza Kazem-Bek (1802–1870), participated actively and fully in the Russian side of imperial life. They held various positions in military, governmental, or academic circles and en-gaged the modernist spirit to an exceptional degree (although in some cases, quite clearly, not without reservations). Of them, some ceased to be religious or even converted to Christianity, as did Kazem-Bek. Beyond these, however, others like Şihabeddin Mercanī (1818–1889), Abdülkayyum Nasirī (1825–1902), and Hasan Bey Zerdabī (1837–1907), adapted aspects of modern cul-ture without sacrificing as much of their Islamic identity in the process. Much more study needs to be undertaken to appreciate better the diversity within even these "groups," but through their collective activities and writings all contributed some measure to the emergence of the modernist discourse in their native cultural milieux.

That discourse, popularly known as jadīd-ism, had its most ar-ticulate and influential advocate in a Crimean Tatar, Ismail Bey Gasprinskii (1851–1914), who devoted his entire adult life to the goal of rendering the "new method" (uṣūl al-jadīd) acceptable to his co-religionists.[4] Distressed by the failure of Islamic (and other "Asiatic") societies to defend their political and economic inter-ests against Western competition, and determined to uncover the causes of Islam's contemporary limitations, he was led to con-clude that only by subjecting the traditional discourse to critical analysis and challenging its proponents' complacency, by making that discourse fully responsive to external influences and stretch-ing its self-definition, by reorienting and redefining it so as to bring it into conjunction with a "modern" alternative—only by these steps could Islamic peoples expect a brighter, more hopeful and productive future, one in which they could participate with full energy and creativity. In his struggle to understand the plight of Islamic societies, Gasprinskii believed something that Qursavī could not: that the times were not merely "bad," but were differ-ent from all others fundamentally, and that addressing the differ-ence required more than renewal.

Not that all the wisdom and experience of the Islamic past had been rendered irrelevant, but the painful consequences of not sharing in the West's engagement with technicalism and its many attributes and advantages revealed to Gasprinskii that more was needed than could be found already in any single culture. If the long-term goal of re-acquiring wealth, power, and dignity were to be attainable, the immediate agenda had to focus on developing instruments for appropriate change and more effective mobilization of material and human resources to supply what Islamic society lacked, which for Ismail Bey, was "alas, a great deal." Coordinated efforts had to be launched to generate public discussion of the structures of social life and their relationship to the Islamic discourse and to expand and reform education so as to create an awakened and critical spirit in people with which to forge a new society free from otherworldly concerns save in matters of personal ethics. "Rational" explanations of social behavior would lay the foundation for a calculable future undreamed of by former generations, but imaginable to the current one as soon as the past ceased to be approached as the unchallengeable tailor of posterity, and authority was fragmented and placed within the hands of the individual.

So that the technicalistic achievements of Western civilization would not remain the patrimony of Westerners alone, Gasprinskii struggled to use the modern medium of the periodical press to propagandize jadīd-ism. For him—to borrow and modify the cliché that Marshall McLuhan launched some years ago—the medium was part of the message. But only part. The message itself possessed numerous aspects; all ranged, however, around the central task of producing a new society, a new civilization. As formulated by Gasprinskii, the jadīd-ist message entailed the following key points:

1. Redefining and reading new lessons from history as well as adopting the analytical methodology (including critical use of sources) that had been evolving in Western historiography. The purposes were multiple: to dispel the notion of a model of perfection in some lost Golden Age (although lesser models might be employed for their inspirational value); to sanction change in keeping with an idea of progress; to justify an appeal for cultural borrowing from non-Islamic civilizations—and reliance on Russia—with the aim of achieving cultural synthesis; to strengthen the sense of community among Muslims (in an age of seeming

degeneration), stressing not only religious but also linguistic and ethnic ties, and to increase social consciousness through cooperative efforts; and finally, to generate optimism about the future by pointing with pride to appropriate past and current achievements.

2. Refocusing Islam as a cultural force, but also decentering it so as to place man in a logical as much as in a divine scheme. Religion may be regulative of human behavior; thus Gasprinskii emphasized Islam's ethics and commitment to social justice. But it is not the exclusive object of experience, from which men must also learn. Furthermore, contrary to common opinion among both Muslims and non-Muslims, Islam was served by, not opposed to reason. Thus, Ismail Bey declared the autonomy of philosophy and science from the Sharī'a and insisted upon free will along with the kind of toleration that ijtihad implies (though serving to open paths to the future, rather than to the past). Not surprisingly, Gasprinskii frequently appealed to Islam's wealth of unorthodox commentators and free-thinkers, such as Ibn Sīnā, al-Fārābī, and Ibn-Rushd, while turning as well to such Western exemplars as Voltaire and other philosophes. Lastly, jadīd-ism called for reform (tanẓīmāt) aimed at increasing the autonomy of Islam's religious leadership as institutionalized in the Russian empire, improving and extending the training of mullas, and rededicating pious endowments (awqāf; sing., waqf) to social purposes, particularly in support of education.

3. Redefining education and restructuring both its curricula and physical arrangements. Above all, education should serve to provide practical as well as theoretical training in the sciences, mathematics, and languages, while continuing to support the moral upbringing of children. Success in these efforts depended upon redesigning the school and the school day, compiling new instructional materials, employing "modern" pedagogical methods, and improving the training of instructors. Greater public (and private) support for education (of girls, as well as of boys) was a prerequisite for expanding the number and types of schools. And, in keeping with the openness of the new Muslim mentality, parents should be willing to send their children to non-Islamic institutions after a basic maktab experience.

4. Empowering women and moving them from marginal to more central status in society. On the one hand, in civil matters,

this meant enforcing a "fairness doctrine" rooted in the regulative spirit of the Qur'an and the lessons of experience. Many traditional restrictions placed on women, such as veiling and inequitable practices associated with polygamy and divorce, would be cleared away as a result. On the other hand, empowering women entailed allowing them expanded public roles—hence the importance of access to education—as much for social utility as respect for individual rights.

5. Strengthening material productivity so as to reverse economic stagnation and the consequent inability to compete with the technically more advanced and aggressive powers of the Christian West and the "pagan" East. Unless Muslims relished a future "as servants to the developed peoples, delectable morsels for them [to feast upon]," a vastly modified economic structure, based upon sophisticated technology and industrial mechanization, would have to be developed (Gasprinskii, 1975:40). Hence the pressing need for practical (vocational) education and mobilization of all community resources, including women.

Jadīd-ism was more than these few pages have outlined, more for some, perhaps less for others. Within the Russian sphere alone, the complexities and variations of practiced Islam, the differing experiences (historical and contemporary) of Muslims dwelling in Kazan as opposed to Bakhchisarai, Baku, Orenburg, Gök Tepe, Bukhara, or Khiva, and the timing of the phenomenon's awakening in different regions mean that it would not be the same for all who identified with the civilization of Islam. Change would come everywhere, but its advocates' priorities would be fixed more by local conditions than by any precise blueprint. Moreover, Gasprinskii's voice was only one of many contributing to this emerging discourse; when sufficiently analyzed, other voices will surely force modifications of and emendations to the larger interpretation of jadīd-ism offered here.

If anything, however, jadīd-ism represented a way of organizing thinking that differed fundamentally from, and thereby challenged implicitly, the prevailing dominant discourse that was Islam for many centuries, a discourse epitomized, perhaps, by a line attributed to Abū Ḥamīd al-Ghazālī: "There is not in possibility anything more wonderful than what is." The epistemological break with this traditional discourse and its attendant modality of change (tajdīd) that jadīd-ism denoted is captured in Gasprinskii's comment that "everything in life develops and improves from year to year; nothing remains the same." The future, therefore, is calculable, and man need not "expect only that which fate would provide" (Gasprinskii, 1891:15).

At the same time, jadīd-ism embodied pursuit of the technicalization that the West had institutionalized in working out its own transmutation, privileging efficiency, precision, "and a certain kind of person, the autonomous individual of humane and cooperative spirit" (Burke, 1979:252).

Finally, jadīd-ism was syncretic in its refusal to abandon Islam as a regulative authority even while adopting the technicalistic achievements of the West. There was in the phenomenon an abiding concern for the dehumanizing consequences of technicalism, consequences that must be controlled for the overall good of mankind. As a discourse, jadīd-ism spoke to a future that would be not only different but better; that is, better than the Islamic past, but also better than the future offered by a materially successful but spiritually deficient West. Thus, Gasprinskii asked: "Has there been no happiness or prosperity for the sons of Man outside of the European and Christian context? More simply stated: Is European civilization a necessity for prosperity? . . . Is it not necessary to look for a special path of progress for the Islamic world?" (Gasprinskii, 1885:5). And, an Azerbaijan contemporary, Ahmed Bey Agaoglu, charged: "Simply to transplant Western civilization to the Orient will only result in doubling the misery of the Oriental. One becomes neither Eastern nor Western, but something in-between, with all the weaknesses of the one without the qualities of the other. The Westernized Oriental is Western only on the surface; below the veneer is a degenerate Oriental soul almost intact" (Agaoglu, 1893:525–26).

Staying in touch with history, but leaving it behind; remembering and respecting the past, but refusing to be bound by it; breaking boundaries while proclaiming their preservation, jadīd-ism bore, januslike, the faces of orthodoxy and heterodoxy, authority and subversion. It was, to repeat, one of those rare epistemological shifts that could not fail to have a transforming effect upon all aspects of human experience, and with cultural variation it would recur over and again around the globe during the last century and a half.

Notes

1. I view "modernism" as a discourse reflecting innumerable material and technical changes in the character of Western civilization at least since the sixteenth century but entailing, most critically, an epistemological break with the past. Among the features of this discourse that distinguish it from those that represented and shaped all "pre-modern" societies is the belief that the future is not predictable, especially in some teleological sense, but is rendered calculable through the application of human reason. The future, thus, will not only be novel but will be better than the past, and mankind will continuously transcend its always (and merely) "current" limitations by treating knowledge not as a fixed commodity that mainly reflects reality, but as an instrument to push it into different directions.

The technicalism and economic advance that have accompanied the emergence of the modern discourse, however, should not suggest the equation of "modernism" with "modernization," a term justly criticized for its implicit determinism. Nor should one presume an identity between "modernism" and "Westernization" because Western civilization chanced upon the path leading to the "modern" first, and then exploited its advantages globally over the last one hundred and fifty years.

2. More than any of the other schools of jurisprudence recognized as legitimate by Sunnis, the Hanbali produced leaders less willing to respect taqlīd (the decisions of earlier authorities) and more likely to engage in ijtihād (individual inquiry to establish the ruling of the Sharī'a, or guide for Islamic life), and encourage puritanical reform.

3. On Qursavī see: Rizaeddin ibn Fahreddin, *Asar* (Kazan-Orenburg, 1900–1908), 95–130; Dzh. Validov, *Ocherk istorii obrazovannosti i literatury tatar* (Moscow: Gosudarstvennoe izd., 1923), 56–57; A. N. Khairullin, "Mesto G. Kursavi v istorii obshchestvennoi mysli," *Iz istorii tatarskoi obshchestvennoi mysli* (Kazan, 1979), 72–73; Abdulgani Abdullah, "The Reformist Activity of al-Kursawi," *Muslims of the Soviet East* 4 (1985):11–12; and A. Temir, "Abunnasir Kursavi," *Kazan*, 1, no. 4 (1971):44–45.

4. On Gasprinskii see my "Ismail Bey Gasprinskii and Muslim Modernism in Russia, 1878–1914," Ph.D. diss., University of Washington, 1973; "Ismail Bey Gasprinskii, the Discourse of Modernism, and the Russians," in *Tatars of the Crimea: Their Struggle for Survival*, ed. Edward Allworth (Durham: Duke University Press, 1988): 149–69; and "Ismail Bey Gasprinskii's *Perevodchik/Tercüman* : A Clarion of Modernism," *Central Asian Monuments*, ed. H. B. Paksoy (forthcoming).

References

Abdullah, Abdulgani (1985), "The Reformist Activity of al-Kursawi," *Muslims of the Soviet East* 4:11–12.

Agaoglu, Ahmed Bey (1893), "La Société persane," *La Nouvelle revue* 84, no. 3 (October 1, 1893):509–27.

Burke, Edmund (1979), "Islamic History as World History: Marshall Hodgson, 'The Venture of Islam,'" *International Journal of Middle East Studies* 10:241–64.

Gasprinskii, Ismail Bey (1885), *Avrupa Medeniyetine bir Nazar Muvazene*. Istanbul.

——— (1891), Untitled article, *Perevodchik/Tercuman*, no. 8 (March 8, 1891):15.

——— (1975), "Al-ʿālim al-Islāmī wa muhājimāt al-ajānib," quoted in T. Kuttner, "Russian *Jadidism* and the Islamic World: Ismail Bey Gasprinskii in Cairo, 1908." *Cahiers du monde russe et soviétique* 16 (3–4):383–424.

Hodgson, Marshall (1974), *The Venture of Islam: Conscience and History in a World Civilization.* 3 vols. Chicago: University of Chicago Press.

Rosenthal, Franz (1983), *"Sweeter Than Hope": Complaint and Hope in Medieval Islam.* Leiden: E. J. Brill.

Voll, John O. (1983), "Renewal and Reform in Islamic History: *Tajdid* and *Islah*," in John L. Esposito (ed.), *Voices of Resurgent Islam.* New York: Oxford University Press, 35–43.

Waldman, Marilyn Robinson (1986), "Tradition as a Modality of Change: Islamic Examples," *History of Religions* 25(3):318–40.

8

Interpreting the Poetry of Mäkhtumquli

Walter Feldman

The wholehearted acceptance within Soviet Turkmenia of Mäkhtumquli (Turkm. Maghtïmgulï; 1732?–1790?) as the greatest representative of Turkmenian literature is certainly a measure of the continuity between pre-Soviet and Soviet Turkmenian culture.[1] Mäkhtumquli is the most significant figure in the creation of Turkmenian written literature, a process which took place in the first half of the eighteenth century. This brief chapter will attempt to demonstrate how the aesthetic choices made by Mäkhtumquli made literary form into a strong symbol of the historical and the incipient national consciousness of the Turkmen people.

The preeminence of Mäkhtumquli in the Soviet period may be seen first of all in the fact that the Institute of Literature of the Turkmen Academy of Sciences is named "Maghtïmgulï." Research on the poet commenced early in this century and has been more or less continuous. During the 1930s, 40s, and 50s interviews were conducted among elderly Turkmen tribesmen who had preserved oral accounts of details of Mäkhtumquli's life (Baimyradov, 1983). In 1957 an edition of his poetry ("Selected Works") was published, and in 1958 it was translated into Uzbek and Russian (Makhtumquli/Shäripov). In 1960 the supposed 225th anniversary of the birth of the poet was commemorated in Ashkhabad with a large scholarly symposium, with the Turkish poet Nazim Hikmet among those attending (Batyrov, 1961). The 1970s and 1980s have seen more numerous and more scientific publications, almost all of them in the Turkmen language. A descriptive catalog of manuscripts containing works of Mäkhtumquli has recently been published in Ashkhabad (Ashyrov, 1984). More recent editions of Mäkhtumquli's poetry (M. 1977, 1983) take into account variants occurring in the manuscripts. While more scientific editions of the works of Mäkhtumquli are essential for serious critical work, significant characteristics of his output can be described even on the basis of the existing publications.

Mäkhtumquli has long been a figure of tremendous importance, not only in Turkmenia but among Turkmens in Afghanistan and Iran, Turks and Kurds in Iranian Khurasan, and among the Karakalpaks, Uzbeks, and Tajiks of Central Asia. Sung versions of his poetry have been collected as far afield as the North Caucasus and the Volga region. His verses are sung not only in Turkmen but also in Karakalpak and Uzbek translations (Garryev, 1961:277–86). Although he was a literate poet, an important medium for the diffusion of his verses has been oral transmission, a medium which has transcended both ethnic and rural/urban barriers. For these reasons alone his position not only within Turkmenian literature but throughout southern Central Asia is unique. The meager facts known about the life of the poet do little to convey either the great influence of Mäkhtumquli's poetry or the almost legendary status he holds in Central Asian folklore. He was widely known among the Uzbeks and Karakalpaks through oral translations of his poems sung by the *bäkhshis*, the oral bards of the three nationalities. An Uzbek bard from distant Nurata (N.W. of Samarkand), Ergäsh Jumanbulbuloghli (1868–1937), had composed a *dastan* (oral epic) relating his life story (Mirzaev, 1973:244). During the 1960s Western ethnomusicologists found his poetry well-established in the repertoires of the Turkmen and other bakhshīs of Afghanistan and Iran. Some interviews conducted by the American researcher Steven Blum in the area of Bujnurd, Iran, revealed significant attitudes toward Mäkhtumquli:

Several informants described him as "one who spoke many good *pandiyat*"—a genre of verse embodying ethical precepts. . . . "It was like this, like Makhdum Qoli—in those days, like the time when they were coming from that region to this region, looking over its good and bad aspects, and then returning—When they arrived in Khurasan, at that time Imam Reza had not yet been martyred, he was still living." (Blum, 1972:41)

Other remarks by Blum's Khurasani informants indicate that Turkmen was considered the "ancient language of the Turks" and that the Turkmen poets represent an ancient and prestigious culture to the local Khurasanian Turks and Kurds. Mäkhtumquli himself has become a figure of myth combining great antiquity with moral rectitude. The tomb of Mäkhtumquli, today on the Iranian side of the border at Aq Tuqay, thirteen kilometers from Gorgan, is still the site of pilgrimages at which offerings, prayers, and Sufi *dhikrs* are presented by members of several ethnic groups of the region.

The Turkmen language was not employed for courtly literature until the beginning of the eighteenth century, at which time written literature appears to emerge quite suddenly among the Turkmens. Turkmen poetry of the eighteenth century shows a remarkable freedom in the adoption of literary influences, in which each poet represents a different synthesis of the available material comprising (1) Turkmen folksong, (2) Turkmen oral epic, (3) courtly Chaghatay poetry, (4) Sufistic Chaghatay poetry, (5) religious-didactic Chaghatay poetry, (6) other sources, such as historical legends, etc. At one end of the spectrum were poets like Shabende, whose compositions are almost indistinguishable from folklore, and at the other Andalib (and to a lesser degree Azadi), whose work is partially within the mainstream of classical Central Asian literature. To gain an appreciation of Mäkhtumquli it is necessary to view him in this context of formal and thematic eclecticism and amalgamation.

The religious influence in Turkmenian poetry reflected both orthodox Islam and various strains of Sufism. Several of the writers voice strong social concern and even protest (especially Mäkhtumquli and Kemine). Folklore is consciously taken up by literate writers (Andalib, Maghrupi, etc.). Most writers exhibit a strong ethnic self-consciousness and political activism. While most Turkmen writers recall some elements from earlier Central Asian classical, religious, or folk literature, there does not appear to be any real precedent for such a tendency, certainly not in earlier Turkic-language writing. It proved to be Mäkhtumquli's synthesis of these elements which set the dominant tone for Turkmen literature throughout the later eighteenth, and all of the nineteenth century.

The Göklang poet Azadi and his son Mäkhtumquli probably

represent the first generations of madrasa-educated Turkmens. They adopted a largely didactic role toward their countrymen, who, while partly sedentary, retained a strong tribal identity and a strong desire for political independence. This desire was given some opportunity for expression in the mid-eighteenth century due to the chaotic situation in Iran and Transoxiana, following the end of the Safavid State and the debacle of Nādir Shāh (d. 1747). Nādir Shāh's incursion into Khiva and Bukhara had the result of creating turmoil in the Transoxiana region, where no strong ruler emerged until the last third of the eighteenth century in Khiva or the early nineteenth century in Bukhara. In addition, the rise of Aḥmad Shāh Durrānī, the Afghan who was approaching the southern border of the Bukharan emirate, was taken by some Turkmen groups as a signal to throw off their allegiance to Bukhara. Thus Mākhtumquli lived in a generation during which the states in which (or near which) the Turkmens lived (Khiva, Bukhara, Iran) were relatively weak. Mākhtumquli himself seems to have participated in warfare with the Persians, and his poetry was in part a vehicle for the assertion of Turkmen political aspirations. The strong "nationalistic" strain in Mākhtumquli's poetry must be understood as part of the same movement among the Turkmens as a whole. Mākhtumquli's poems employ the word *Turkmen* and specifically call for the union of the major tribes. Although in the early eighteenth century the Turkmens did not constitute a nation in the modern sense, it is clear that several factors gave the Turkmens as early as the seventeenth century a strong ethnic identity which could certainly have developed into true nationalism under different historical circumstances. These factors include (1) the combination of strong linguistic distinctiveness (especially in the non-Oghuzic linguistic environment of Turkic Central Asia); (2) preservation of Oghuzic tribal traditions, including a distant memory of royal charisma (the latter canceling out the acceptance of the Chinggisid charisma which dominated Central Asia as a whole); plus (3) the religious cohesion provided by popular Sufism centered on tomb sites and sacred lineages, rather than the larger *ṭarīqats* (Sufi brotherhoods) of Central Asia (Basilov, 1984). Had the Turkmen tribes achieved the political success of the contemporaneous Afghans they might have reached a degree of national consciousness at least as strong as the latter.

Any reading of the Turkmenian poetry of the eighteenth century must include this proto-nationalistic element. Most of the poets writing in Turkmen during the eighteenth century envisaged a role for literature in the reshaping of the Turkmenian tribal/ ethnic consciousness into something more like a nation. This proto-nationalistic concern is evident both in the form and the themes of the Turkmen literature of the entire period, and cannot be explained as a backward projection of the Soviet period. In this connection both the themes and the form of the literature are critical because the distance from or closeness to existing Islamic literatures of the region would have the effect of placing the Turkmens in a particular historical context.

The Uzbeks of the sixteenth century furnish an example of a contrasting cultural strategy. The Uzbeks took over the rule of Transoxiana not as a nation but as a dynasty in nominal control of a tribal confederation. Their relationship to the existing literary tradition was one of assimilation; their greatest desire appears to have been not to stand out as cultural and political parvenues (Subtelny, 1983). Despite the literary activity of Shaybani Khan himself, the imposition of Uzbek rule was neither preceded nor succeeded by distinctive literary activity which had as one of its aims the definition of the Uzbeks as a cultural entity. On the contrary, the appearance of the Uzbeks in Transoxiana led to a decline in the use of Turkic as a literary medium for original literature, that is to say a reverse in the cultural trend which had been encouraged by the Timurids during the previous century. It is impossible to predict how a Turkmen dynasty with strong links to the Turkmen tribes would have behaved on the throne of Khiva, but the literary activity of the Turkmens of the eighteenth century in the absence of centralized political patronage is certainly without precedent in the recent history of Central Asia. The distinctiveness of the Turkmen literary strategy can be seen in the literary works of the major Turkmen poets of the eighteenth century.

The earliest figure who appears in any published survey of Turkmen literature is Dövletmemmet Azadi (b. 1700), the father of Mäkhtumquli. A slightly younger contemporary of Azadi was the poet Andalib (b. 1712). While Azadi and Mäkhtumquli lived in the extreme southwest of Turkmenia, along the Atrak River, Andalib was from Urgench near Khiva (Garryev et al., 1975:83–100). These three major figures of the first half of the eighteenth century represent rather different tendencies. In his choice of gen-res and style, Andalib was perhaps as original as Mäkhtumquli, but his emphasis was rather different. Andalib cultivated the classical genres, *ghazal, ruba'ī,* and *mukhammas,* using the quantitative 'arūz meters, but in the Turkmen language. He wrote many "imitations" of or "responses" *(takhmis)* to classical Chaghatay verse, principally the ghazals of 'Alī Shīr Navā'ī (Andalib, 1975:67–102). Andalib also wrote several *mathnavis,* the most famous of which is about the life of the fourteenth-century Iraqi Turkmen mystic Nesimi (Andalib, 1978). Unlike Azadi, Andalib's religious position was heterodox Sufi. The appearance of Nesimi raises the question of non-Chaghatay Turkic literary sources for the poetry of Andalib, and for other eighteenth-century Turkmenian poets. It is not clear whether Nesimi's work was better known in Khiva than elsewhere in Central Asia, or whether Andalib as a Turkmen-speaker wished to establish a conscious link with the earlier literature written in the related old Azerbaijani language, with the heterodox elements in this literature, or with the general historical consciousness of the earlier Oghuzic Turkmen dynasties of the Middle East. Andalib furnished further evidence of a self-conscious nationalism by composing a narrative poem called "Oghuzname" in which he relates the legendary history of the Turkmens based largely on the "Shejere-yi Tarakima" by Abu'l-Ghāzi Khan. In the past, the composition of legendary histories and genealogies of the Oghuz Turks had been associated with post-Mongol Turkic dynasties such as the Aqquyunlu and the Ottomans striving to establish their legitimacy against the Chinggisid charisma (Woods, 1976:5, 7, 67, 187–96). In this exceptional instance a much later Turkmen poet was attempting to accomplish a similar task without any dynastic support.

It was Andalib who initiated the trend of literate poets writing texts for the originally oral epics of the Turkmen *bäkhshis.* He cultivated the Turkmen *dessan (= dastan)* form as a vehicle for originally classical tales, such as "Leili va Mazhnūn," "Yusup ve Zuleykha," and the semi-folk "Tahir ve Zuhra." The choice of a folkloristic oral form for the creation of literary works by a mad-rasa-educated urban poet was a significant departure from the literary precedents of Central Asia, where from the fourteenth century the only literary models had been Persian and Chaghatay poetry and prose. This experiment of Andalib's was continued and developed in the second half of the eighteenth century by the poet Maghrupi, who composed several dessans of purely Turkmen rather than classical provenance (i.e., "Yusup ve Ahmad" and "Ali Bek bilän Boli Bek") and the semihistorical "Dövletler," treating an uprising against the Khivan Khan in 1770 (Kor-oghly, 1972: 152–53). By the mid-nineteenth century these written dessans were coming to replace the oral epical performances of the Turkmen bäkhshis. The manuscript collected by Hermann Vambery in Khiva of "Yusuf bilän Ahmad" appears to be very close stylistically to the Uzbek oral dastan, so it can be assumed that by the early nineteenth century "Yusuf bilän Ahmad" had become an Uzbek oral dastan. Later in the century "Ali Bek bilän Boli Bek" had become an Uzbek dastan as well, appearing in the repertoire of the Uzbek bard Ergäsh Zhumänbulbuloghli (Mirzaev, 1973: 243). Thus the creation of the Turkmen literary dastan had a large impact on the direction of both Turkmen and Uzbek folk literature. Although it is of great interest to observe this development during the nineteenth century, this should not obscure the rather different situation of Andalib, who initiated this movement in the eighteenth century as part of a larger cultural agenda which included the modeling of the young Turkmen literary language along the lines of Chaghatay, the inclusion of Sufistic literature in older Western Turkic (the language of the medieval Turkmens), the creation of a national chronicle-epic (Oghuzname), and the elevation of the oral epical form dessan to literary status.

The Biography of Mäkhtumquli

Mäkhtumquli's grandfather was a weaver who immigrated into the area. His name was also Mäkhtumquli, indicating a religious attachment to one of the sacred Makhtum (maghtïm) lineages. The senior Mäkhtumquli composed folksongs (goshghï). His son, Dövletmemmet, born around 1700, studied in the Khivan madrasa Shirghazi. He was therefore a mulla and returned home to teach at the maktab level, there being no local madrasa. As a poet he took the makhlas "Azadi." Dövletmemmet is in fact the first poet to write in the Turkmen language of whom any record survives (Garryev, 1975:37–73). His major work is preserved, a didactic mathnavi of over 2,300 couplets named "Vaghz-i Azad" (roughly,

"The Sermon of the Free" playing on his makhlas Azadi = Persian "freedom"). He also wrote a shorter mathnavi (400 couplets). A few quatrains also survive (Azadi, 1982). "Vaghz-i Azad" is a thoroughly orthodox didactic mathnavi. Aside from the language, which is Turkmen, there is nothing to suggest a Turkmen origin for the work, which is not even touched by mainstream, orthodox Sufism, let alone the heterodox type favored by the Turkmens. Although Soviet scholars sometimes depict Azadi as a potential revolutionary, his calls for justice are no stronger than was conventional in the Mirror for Princes literature. By comparing the output of Mäkhtumquli with that of his father the thoroughness of the literary break between them may be seen.

Despite the widespread recognition of his importance as a poet, very little information, none of it documented, has been preserved about the life of Mäkhtumquli. He was born around 1730 (possibly in 1732) in what is today the extreme southwest of Turkmenia, near the Atrak River, north of the Iranian city of Gorgan. He belonged to the Gökleng tribe. This area was beyond the territory of the Khivan khanate, and was at times claimed or held by the Iranian shahs. In one of his poems ("Gökleng") he urges his fellow tribesmen to attack Gorgan: "Pïragi dïyr, goshun tartïp / Barar sen Gurgene, Gökleng!" (Mäkhtumquli, 1977:202; "Firagi says, you shall muster an army and go as far as Gorgan, Göklengs!"). Another variant urges them on to Tehran (Mäkhtumquli, 1983:120). The enemy is always the Persians, not the Khivans. Mäkhtumquli is said to have studied, like his father, in the Khivan madrasa Shirghazi—the Khivans today point out the cell in which he is supposed to have lived. He also learned the goldsmith's trade and is reputed to have earned his living from this trade, rather than from teaching. He is said to have traveled widely in Central Asia and Iran. He wrote many of his poems to his beloved, named Mengli. His inability to obtain her hand in marriage was the greatest tragedy of his life. He eventually married another woman, and had two children by her, both of whom died young. Turkmen raids against the Iranians and Iranian raids into the Turkmen region both figure in his poems. In one of them he laments the loss of his manuscripts, which had been tossed into the Atrak River by the Persians. Legends about his life relate that he was taken prisoner and escaped several times. The above constitute more or less the extant facts about his life, although certain references in his poems have been used to flesh out a number of other events. The poet used two distinct noms de plume (makhlas), Mäkhtumquli and Firagi (Pïragi). Mäkhtumquli = "slave of the *makhtum*," the latter being one of the sacred lineages among the Turkmens. Firagi is derived from Ar. *firāq* = "separation," hence "the one separated from," "deprived from" happiness, or union with his beloved.

Poetry of Mäkhtumquli

Mäkhtumquli's extant poetic output is reported to consist of approximately eight hundred poems, many of which may be apocryphal, however. Soviet editions regularly print about four hundred poems (generally the same ones). No autograph of the poet exists. The vast majority of the numerous manuscripts of his works, housed in Ashkhabad, Tashkent, and Leningrad, date from the second half of the nineteenth or the first quarter of the twentieth century. Early manuscripts total less than half a dozen (Ashyrov, 1984:17–19). Unlike his father Azadi, or his contemporary Andalib, Mäkhtumquli left no long poems, whether classical mathnavis or folklike dastan. The majority of his poems are in the forms of Turkmen folk songs, goshghï, including a number of the musical contest, *aydïs*. These poems are syllabic, employing strophic form, usually quatrains.

Approximately one-fifth of the published poems are in the form of classical ghazal, utilizing the simpler meters, such as *ramal* or *hazaj*. However, these poems are quite distant in their use of language and theme from the true classical ghazal, whether in Chaghatay or Persian. They do not resemble Andalib's Turkmen-language ghazals, for these are either direct imitations (takhmis) of classical works, or else show a more direct influence of the classical models. Mäkhtumquli avoids the altered syntax so typical of the Chaghatay ghazal, and in particular the Persian syntactic constructions. The relation of his language to classical Azerbaijani has been noted (Benzing, 1964:39), and this is probably a result of the influence of poetic models in that language, seen also in the work of Andalib. Mäkhtumquli's ghazals display a blend of classical imagery and Sufistic philosophical attitudes with highly personal emotion and idiosyncratic imagery. The fact that the poet wrote both goshghïs and ghazals to his own beloved, Mengli, mentioning her by name, is highly unusual for the classical ghazal, although not unknown in the *āshiq* tradition in Ottoman and Azerbaijani. The abrupt transitions from personal to more conventional expression in these ghazals render accurate interpretation most hazardous. The following brief analysis of a single ghazal can suggest the issues involved in their interpretation.

1. Köyse ömrüm zhebr ïshqïna ïzïnda Mezhnunï bardïr
    Yüzleri khandan eylese cheshmide khunï bardïr

    Should my life be destroyed in a torturing love, it follows in the steps of Majnūn,
    Though his face is smiling, his eye is filled with blood

2. Peshe birlen pilni tutup gör bu pelek oyun qïlar
    Peshe diyip aghïrtmagïl zhesedide zhanï bardïr

    Setting the gnat against the elephant, see the game played by
        the spheres!
    Though but a gnat, please hurt it not, in its form there lives a soul.

3. Gözel ilden gider dövlet merdi namarda döner
    Namarda til merde gülki bir bigadïr khanï bardïr

    Fortune passes from the beautiful land; its heroes become cowards
    Speech to the coward is a joke to the hero;
        Its khan is without power.

4. Kher gözelde bir ayïp bar on iki sïna ornuda
    Suyde singe nazar salsang ichresinde ganï bardïr

    In every beauty there's no perfection, there's a fault;
    If you but glance within her breast, the place within is
    filled with blood.

5. Leb üstüne leb goyup sen zerreche tagham bilmeding
    Emmä ki yarïng lebinde ïshqïng zhavudanï bardïr

    Placing lip upon the lip, a drop of pleasure you haven't known;
    It's only in your true love's lip that love eternal can be found.

6. Azashïban dang säharda vasïl olsang ki bir gapa
    Bagh ichinde shecher atlïgh ki bir arghuvanï bardïr

Lost at dawn, if you search for a word with her,
you'll find within the garden a Judas-tree, whose leaves are red
with the blood of the tears you shed for her!

7. Mezhnun kibi ïshqa köyseng adam oghlï unutmaghïl
   Dovzahnïng odundan beter atash-ï suzanï bardïr

   If, like Majnūn, you burn with love, oh man do not forget
   that worse than Hellfire is the flame of love.

8. Pelek salsa kher bir yola yöregil sen gayïtmaghïl
   Chünki pelekning goluda bir ulugh permanï bardïr

   On whatever road you're put by Fate, go on and turn not back,
   For in his hand there's a decree put there by Almighty God.

9. Maghtïmgulï bu vatanï sen terk qïlïban yörmegil
   Khüyr u peri ghulman besher ancha ki zhananï bardïr

   Mäkhtumquli you must this homeland not forsake,
   For in it are beloved ones as many as the celestial maids.

                                             (Mäkhtumquli, 1983:72).

This is a ghazal ending with the *radīf* (monorhyme) *bardïr* (long
rhyme: *-any bardïr*), which can be translated as "there is," "it has"
or in several other ways depending on its context. Some of the
characteristics of this poem are evident even in translation, while
others depend on the original language. Apart from the language
of the poem, which is based on the West Turkic literary language
plus modern Turkmen elements, the reader of the original text
will sense a distance from the Chaghatay literary norm in the extreme regularity of the syntax, which very rarely departs from the
Turkic word order. This tendency is probably increased by the use
of the radīf *bardïr*, which necessitates a certain amount of Turkic
word order to be intelligible. The vocabulary is middle-range classical. It includes many standard words of the poetic vocabulary,
but without the recondite vocabulary of both Persian and Chaghatay origin which abound in the poetry of Mīr ʿAlī Shīr Navāʾī. The
major structural technique of the poet is to create a contrast between the first and second *miṣraʿ* (stich) of each *bayt* (couplet).
This contrast may be a simple development, as in bayts 1, 4, 8, or
a surprising new aspect of the original statement, as in bayts 2, 5,

7, or 9. This in itself is standard technique of the ghazal tradition in several languages. However, by the eighteenth century it was not the normal strategy of a classical ghazal to rely on this so exlusively without other rhetorical or syntactic techniques. Thus the syntactic and rhetorical structures of this poem are simpler than the classical norm (whether in Chaghatay, Persian, Azerbaijani, etc.). However, it would be a mistake to regard this as a simple poem, akin to the many didactic or popular Sufi poems produced for liturgical or other purposes in Persian or Turkic, which also employ a simplified classical vocabulary and syntax. There is a complexity here despite the surface simplicity of the work.

In the opening bayt *(matla')* the most emphasized words are found immediately preceding the radīf. This is a function of Turkic word order, and in the translation they appear last: *Majnūn* and *blood*. It is these two words which set the tone for entire ghazal, and it is therefore not accidental that it is only these two out of the vocabulary of the matla' (not counting the omnipresent *ïshq*, "love") which are repeated later in the poem. *Blood* appears in its Turkmen form *gan* in the second misra' of bayt no. 4, while *Majnūn* appears in the first misra' of bayt no. 7. Note that *Majnūn* appears in the first misra' of both bayt 1 and bayt 7 and "blood" *(khūn* or *gan)* in the second misra' of bayts 1 and 4. The use of *Majnūn* in the first and particularly in the seventh bayt where the literal meaning of the second misra' is: "there is a burning flame which is worse than Hellfire," both suggest an association of *Majnūn* with this-worldly love. Although *Majnūn* has been used to symbolize an essentially Sufi mystical lover, at least for a part of the story (in its various versions), he is still to be viewed as a lover in this world, not as the archetypical 'ashiq of the eternal divine Beloved. In any case the poet here seems to be using Majnūn's name to evoke a worldly love. This impression is strengthened by the word *blood,* in both bayts.

The second major theme of the poem is the tyrannical dominion of Fate, the revolving sphere *(pelek* = Persian *falak)*. In bayt no. 2 the poet introduces the image of the elephant and the fly, which seems to have originated in Sufi parable. The addition of the verb *oyun qïlmaq* (to play) gives a very informal tone to this misra', quite different from the first bayt. The second misra' refers to the poetic matrix (Rifaterre, 1978:19–22), otherwise topos, which could be paraphrased "the great or truly significant may be concealed within the apparently small and insignificant." This matrix is a cliché of Sufi-influenced poetry which usually prefers to compare the ant (*mûr, naml*) to Soliman (Süleyman). The rather activistic, or at least not totally fatalistic conclusion of bayt no. 8 is a feature of Mäkhtumquli's poetry wherein the tyranny of Fate is paradoxically viewed as a necessary condition for the exercise of man's will. A surprise awaits the reader in the final bayt where the celestial maidens (in the original, youths as well) are brought down to this world, in particular to the homeland of the Turkmens. This introduction of an overtly nationalist theme is found in many of Mäkhtumquli's poems. Due to the rather loose thematic coherence of most ghazals, it would be unnecessary (or wrong) to read back the national reference to the earlier bayts, thereby creating a nationalist allegory, in which the homeland becomes the real beloved, whose love is eternal (bayt no. 5). There is the suggestion that some of the bayts may have more to do with the Turkmen national struggle than was first apparent. In particular bayt no. 8 may in fact urge the Turkmen people to pursue their destiny.

Ghazal writers have tended to introduce several themes into a single ghazal, so that a single image can be interpreted as relating to one or another theme. Apart from the better-known ambiguities of wine and divine intoxication and their entire semantic fields, in one ghazal tradition—the Ottoman—an ambiguity is created involving the beloved and the worldly sovereign (Andrews, 1985:89–108). Mäkhtumquli here is consciously creating another type of ambiguity involving the beloved, paradise, and the national homeland, and fitting it into the framework of the ghazal.

Soviet criticism tends to emphasize the undoubtedly sincere social protest found in many of Mäkhtumquli's poems, as well as the personal lyrics. The ghazals also provide statements that, taken out of context, sound particularly antinomian or revolutionary: for example, "Dini hödür eyleyir sen, azhap Kur'an gerekmes" ("You yourself reveal the faith, the wonderous Qur'an is not needed") or "Her kes özige soltandïr, khan-u soltan gerekmes" ("Everyone is his own sultan; khan and sultan are not needed"). In cases like these Mäkhtumquli should not be confused with the Uzbek poet Mashrab, who was hanged in 1712, and was primarily an antinomian heterodox Sufi, and is therefore described today as an "isyankar shair" ("revolutionary poet"). Antinomian heterodoxy does not seem to be the major trend in Mäkhtumquli's thought, and he certainly does not adopt the "Ana'l-Haqq" (self-deification) stance of a Nesimi. In fact his usual stance is the Sufi station of khajrät ("bewilderment"). These poems are a charming blend of conventional expression and individual emotion, and even snatches of autobiography. The poet does voice strong social protest, but at the same time his political thought seems to have been primarily directed toward the unification of the Turkmen tribes and the establishment of some sort of independent political entity. In modern Turkmenia these "nationalist" poems are of course much beloved. Such poems as "Türkmening" or "Türkmen binasï" are very impressive works, which draw on many sources including the oral folk-epic, particularly the heroic das-tans of "Göroghli." The poet cites Göroghli in several places, thus showing his familiarity with these epics, which undoubtedly ex-isted in his time. Mäkhtumquli also wrote a number of poems on purely personal subjects, such as the death of his father and the absence of his elder brother Abdullah. He is also well known for his vision in which 'Alī, Muḥammad, and the three caliphs (as well as Selim Khoja and Baba Selman) initiate him into the poetic vocation.

The nationalist aspect of Mäkhtumquli's poetry is expressed clearly in a poem in which the long rhyme is -li Türkmening, and which appears in Soviet editions under the title "Türkmening" ("of the Turkmens"). The form of this poem is related to the folk-loristic goshghï form. Its structure is abab / aaab / cccb / dddb, etc.[2]

1. Zheykhun bile bakhr-ï Khazar arasï
   Chöl üstünden öser yeli Türkmening
   Gül-gunzhasï gara gözüm garasï
   Gara daghdan iner sili Türkmening

   Between the Jeyhun and the Khazar Sea
   Over the desert blows the breeze of the Turkmen
   Its rose-bud is the pupil of my black eye;
   From the black mountain descends the river of the Turkmen

2. Khak sïlamïsh bardïr onung sayasï
   Chïrpïnshar chölünde peri mayasï
   Reng be reng gül achar yashïl yaylasï
   Ghark bolmush reykhana chöli Türkmening

The Lord has exalted him and placed him under His protection
His camels, his flocks range over the desert
Flowers of many hues open on his green summer pastures
Drenched in the scent of basil is the desert of the Turkmen

3. Al yashïl bürenip chïkar perisi
    Kükeyip bark urar anbarïng ïsï
    Beg töre aqsaqal yurdung eyesï
    Küren tutar gözel ili Türkmening

    His fairy-maids go forth clad in red and green
    From them wafts the scent of ambergris
    Bek, prince, and elder are the lords of the country
    Together they uphold the beautiful land of the Turkmen

4. Ol merding oghludïr mertdir pederi
    Göroghlï gardashï serkhoshdïr seri
    Daghda düzde kovsa sayatlar diri
    Ala bilmez yolbars oghlï Türkmening

    He is the son of a hero—a hero his father
    Göroghli his brother, drunken his head;
    Should they pursue him on mountain or plain,
    The hunters cannot take him alive,
            this panther's son of the Turkmen!

5. Köngüller yürekler bir bolup bashlar
    Tartsa yïghïn erer topraqlar dashlar
    Bir suprada tayar kïlïnsa ashlar
    Göteriler ol ïqbalï Türkmening

    Hearts, breasts, and heads are at one
    When he holds a gathering earth and mountains crumble,
    When food is prepared at one table
    Exalted is the destiny of the Turkmen!

6. Köngül khovalanar ata chïqanda
    Daghlar laghla döner gïya baqanda
    Bal getirer zhoshup derya aqanda
    Bent tutdurmas gelse sili Türkmening

    His heart rejoices as he mounts his horse
    At his glance the mountains turn to rubies
    The sea overflows, bringing him honey
    It will not be contained when it comes,
            the river of the Turkmen!

7. Ghapïl galmaz dövüsh güni khar olmaz
   Garghïsha nazara giriftar olmaz
   Bilbilden ayrïlïp solup saralmaz
   Dayïm anbar sachar güli Türkmening

   On the day of battle he is not caught unaware
   He is captured neither by curse nor evil eye
   It is not deprived of its nightingale, does not wilt or wither,
   Always smelling of musk is the rose of the Turkmen

8. Tireler gardashdïr urugh yarïdïr
   Iqballar ters gelmez khakïng nurudïr
   Mertler ata chïqsa sövesh sarïdïr
   Yav üstüne yörär yolï Türkmening

   The tribes are brothers, clans are good friends,
   Fate does not oppose him, he is God's light,
   When heroes mount their horses, facing the battle,
   Toward the foe goes the road of the Turkmen!

9. Serkhosh bolup chïqar zhiger daghlanmaz
   Dashlarï sïndïrar yolï baghlanmaz
   Gözüm ghayra düshmez köngül eglenmez
   Maghtïmgulï sözler tili Türkmening

   He sets out in high spirits, sorrow feels not,
   He smashes through rocks, his way is not blocked,
   My eye alights on none else, nor will my heart rejoice elsewhere,
   Mäkhtumquli speaks in the tongue of the Turkmen!

   (Mäkhtumquli, 1983:11)

   In contrast to the preceding poem, a ghazal, whose couplets are on the whole thematically distinct, this poem is tightly unified. Although it has the form of a folkloristic goshghï, this level of thematic unity is not characteristic of this genre either, but must be regarded as a conscious innovation of the poet. This formal innovation constitutes as much of a statement as the substantive elements in the poem itself, and is another expression of the rationalism which characterizes Mäkhtumquli's work.

   The long rhyme, in which the major element (virtually a monorhyme) is the ethnonym Turkmen with the genitive suffix, is both the formal and substantive focus of the entire poem. This contrasts sharply with the ghazal tradition in which the mono-rhyme (radīf) may or may not bear a significant substantive meaning. In a sense the essence of the poem is encapsulated in the final phrase of each quatrain: the river, the desert, the land, the son, the destiny, the river, the rose, the road, the tongue of the Turkmen (sili, chöli, ili, oghlï, ïqbalï, sili, güli, yolï, tili Türkmening).

In most of the quatrains the four stichs constitute a single semantic unit, except for no. 3, whose couplets are connected only by rhyme. It is noteworthy that unlike the rubāʿi and the Turkic tuyugh, the Turkmen goshghï is arranged aaab, so that the fourth and not the third line is the "turning point" of the quatrain. In Mäkhtumquli's opus (and unlike Turkmenian folklore) the goshghï generally contains nine quatrains, the last of which bears the takhalluṣ of the poet. It is clear that the first quatrain should have been the opening quatrain, as it geographically locates the Turkmenian land. Other than these there seems no fixed order in the quatrains, except that the first three speak of the land and its inhabitants, while the last six quatrains celebrate the heroism of the Turkmenian warriors. In the last couplet Mäkhtumquli very significantly closes his praise of the warrior with praise of his language: "Mäkhtumquli speaks in the tongue of the Turkmen."

This remarkable poem contains virtually a national program for the Turkmens. It opens with a clear location in space of the Turkmen national territory, coupled with an idealized description of their environment. This poetic idealization, both deft and hyperbolic, continues for the following two quatrains. The second couplet of quatrain 3, however, departs from the natural environment to the social structure, in which the poet takes an affirmative (and nonrevolutionary) view of the latter. With the fourth couplet the poet assumes a bardic tone as he begins his praise of the Turkmen warrior with his heroic lineage, in which the epical hero Göroghli is not omitted. This fourth quatrain contains an enjambment between the third and fourth lines (highly unusual both in the folk and in the classical traditions); the phrase "say-atlar diri / ala bilmez" is divided between these two lines. Quatrain 7 very effectively introduces the symbols of the ghazal— nightingale, rose, and musk, completely out of their natural semantic context. Quatrain 8 brings up the issue of segmented social structure, and summarily solves this barrier to Turkmenian political unity.

The poem with the monorhyme "yar senden" ("oh beloved, from you") appears to be one of Mäkhtumquli's simplest pieces. It uses syllabic meter and uninvolved syntax. In addition to being printed in all Soviet editions, it was also recorded during the 1960s in the sung repertoire of a Turkmen bäkhshi of Gorgan, probably an indication of its nearness to folk taste.

1. Bilbilleri esir eden gül-i khandan
    Ya Reb khabar bilerinmi yar senden
    Yedi ïqlïm manga görünür zïndan
    Ya Reb khabar bilerinmi yar senden

    The smiling rose has captured the nightingale
    Oh Lord, let me have news of You, my beloved!
    The seven climes for me have become a dungeon
    Oh Lord, let me have news of You, my beloved!

2. Ispendiyar Ruinten, Rüstem Zalğnda
    Sham, Nezhefde, Mekke, Dïmshïq ilinde
    Arz-i Karsda, Kerebelanïng chölünde
    ya Reb khabar bilerinmi yar senden

    From Isfandiar, Rustam, and Zal,
    In Syria, Najaf, Mecca, and Damascus
    In Erzerum, Kars, in the desert of Kerbela
    Oh Lord, let me have news of You, my beloved!

3. Sherap ichip serkhosh bolup seresem
    Ganïm zhanïm gïyïm-gïyïm doghrasam
    Göroghly dek daghdan dagha ughrasam
    Ya Reb khabar bilerinmi yar senden!

    Let me drink wine, besotted leap and spring;
    If I shred to pieces my blood and my soul,
    If I dash from mountain to mountain like Goroghli—
    Oh Lord, will I hear from You, my beloved?

4. Bir gül qoqar gözel yarïng baghïnda
    Bilbil khüzhüm eyler sol-u saghïnda
    Beytullanïng Safa, Mina daghïnda
    ya Reb khabar bilerinmi yar senden

    A rose exudes perfume in the garden of your beloved
    Nightingales throng around it right and left,

In the House of Allah, in the mountain of Mina
Oh Lord, will I hear from You, my beloved?

5. Shïkh Senghan dey uzïn gaygha ulansam
   Shibli kimin toz-topragha bulansam
   Käbä barïp yedi keret dolansam
   Ya Reb khabar bilerinmi yar senden

   If I get caught in the whirlwind like Shaykh Sanʿān,
   If I cover myself in the dust and dirt like Shiblī,
   If I go to the Kaaba and seven times circle it,
   Oh Lord, will I hear from You, my beloved?

6. Yusup kibi zïndan ichre aghlasam
   Zhirzhis kibi zhan yolunda chaghlasam
   Yunus kibi khaka qulluq baghlasam
   Ya Reb khabar bilerinmi yar senden

   If I weep in the dungeon like Joseph,
   If I fight the soul's battle like St. George,
   If I serve the True One like Jonah,
   Oh Lord, will I hear from You, my beloved?

7. Dogha qïlïp elim göge galdïrsam
   Gül Ferkhad dek gïzïl mengzim soldursam
   Gopuz alïp beyik naghra chaldïrsam
   Ya Reb khabar bilerinmi yar senden

   If I pray, hands raised toward Heaven,
   If I make my red cheeks to wither like Gül and Farhar,
   If I take the *kopuz* and make a great jangling
   Oh Lord, will I hear from You, my beloved?

8. Isa kibi khïlvat tutsam semada
   Idris kibi qulluq etsem ziyada
   Khïzyr Ilyas kibi girsem zulmada
   Ya Reb khabar bilerinmi yar senden

   If I retreat in the Heavens like Jesus,
   If I serve You perfectly like Idris,
   If I enter the darkness like Khidhr-Ilyās
   Oh Lord, will I hear from You, my beloved?

9. Maghtïmgulï ashïqlarïng mestinde
   Khïra gözi khayran olar dostunda

Yedi yerde doquz pelek üstünde
Ya Reb khabar bilerinmi yar senden

Mäkhtumquli is drunk with love of You
His dazzled eye stares in amazement at his Friend
In the nine spheres above the seven earths,
Oh Lord, will I hear from You, my beloved?

(Mäkhtumquli, 1983:38)

Although there does not appear to be much evidence of what Turkmen Sufi devotional poetry was like in the eighteenth century, on the surface it would appear that this poem cannot be very distant from a model within such a tradition. The first stanza with its twice-repeated erotic/devotional refrain, its nightingale-capturing rose and seven climes suggests innumerable poems in several popular Sufi traditions. The rest of the poem presents a list of places and personages seemingly like other Sufi litanies. But a closer look at this cast belies such an identification. Isfandiar, Rustam, and Zal are linked with Najaf, Mecca, and Damascus, Erzerum and Kars with Kerbela. In the next stanza Mäkhtumquli is drinking wine, then mortifying his flesh and then identifying with the hero Göroghli. Then the Kaaba is mentioned several times, then two Sufi saints, and then two stanzas each mentioning three figures from biblical and esoteric lore. Characteristic for the author is the "amazement" or "bewilderment" (khayrät, khayran) with which he stares at his Beloved. While many of the figures in the poem are familiar from other Sufi poems and hymns, the juxtaposition of sacred and profane figures and places is not expected. The poet is begging for "news," "communication" (khabar) from his Beloved, but also seeking guidance on the best manner to obtain this communication. In doing so he presents a catalog of the various religious, esoteric, and secular figures, or perhaps the cultural options available to the poet, and hence to his people. Orthodox figures are apparently absent, although the Kaaba is mentioned, along with Najaf and Kerbela, two major Shi'ite centers of pilgrimage. The secular heroes include both the native Göroghli and representatives of the classical Iranian tradition. Thus the poet is casting his glance widely across the entire field of his cultural vision and perhaps beckoning his countrymen to do the same, although he confesses to a bewilderment which prevents him from knowing with certainty the correct path.

Khalyk Kor-oghly has remarked that, although Mäkhtumquli was a Sufi poet, were he exclusively a mystic he would not be of great interest to a Soviet reader (Kor-oghly, 1972:127). Mäkhtumquli has been read as a mystic, as a nationalist-warrior, as a protorevolutionary, and as a lyricist. What is most striking about this poet is his complexity and the frankness with which he borrows from several genres and poetic traditions. In all this he was also part of a unique period in the cultural history of Central Asia, but his own extraordinary talent projected his personal poetic synthesis onto the next generation of writers, and beyond them to the majority of Turkmen poets even into the Soviet era. Despite the differences among them, the Turkmenian poets of the eighteenth century share an attitude which can be described as rationalist, especially in the sense in which that term has been used in discussions of Islam in the early modern period (seventeenth through nineteenth centuries). That is, both the religious and social structures were held to be inadequate in terms of the contemporaneous historical conditions. In religious terms this referred to the tribal quasi-Sufism and cult of saints which has been described in recent Soviet ethnographic literature, and in social terms it referred to the fragmented and politically ineffective tribal society. What is most striking in Andalib, Maghrupi, and above all in Mäkhtumquli is the attempt to refashion and reinterpret what was significant in the Turkmenian national and literary tradition. Even Azadi, who at first glance appears so unoriginal, must be viewed in his historical circumstance as a neo-orthodox reformer, attempting to bring Turkmenian Islam into conformity with Central Asian Sunni standards. Azadi's brand of rationalism was more akin to the type which would become influential elsewhere in the Muslim world in this period and afterward. His son's rationalism, like that of most other major Turkmenian literary figures in the eighteenth century, contained a strong secular element, and a more mystical and even personalized view of religion. What makes for the uniqueness of Turkmenian poetry in the eighteenth and nineteenth centuries is the fact that it was this latter type of rationalism, and not the religious orthodoxy of Azadi, which set the tone for literary creation.

Notes

1. The name of the poet in modern Turkmen pronunciation is Magh-tïmgulï. The Russian form is Makhtumkuli, apparently based on the Uz-bek form Mäkhtumquli, which is widely used in Central Asia. I am employing the Uzbek form to which I have become accustomed. Modern literary Turkmen (unlike modern literary Uzbek), has vowel harmony based on the eight-vowel system of Common Turkic. Like many Turkic languages, the front form of *a* has two variants—*ä* and *e*. Persian words which are well known in English-language criticism of Persian literature (e.g., *ghazal, radif*) have been written as they usually appear in English.

2. The provenance of the formal structure of the Turkmen stanza is not entirely clear. Although there is some resemblance to the *tarjiʿ-band* of classical Persian poetry, the Turkmen form is much closer to the Turkic verses found in the *Divān Lughāt al-Turk* of Maḥmūd al-Kāsh-gharī (c. 1075).

The only difference between the Turkmen stanzas and those of al-Kāshgharī is that in the latter the opening stanza is arranged *aaab*, rather than *abab*. The Turkmen stanza form is used by eighteenth-century poets such as Mäkhtumquli and Andalib (and their successors), as well as the *bäkhshis* who created the epics of Gör-oghlï. See, for example, *Gör-oghlï: Türkmen gahramanlïk eposï*, Moscow, 1983; Nurmukhämmet Andalyp, *Yusup-Zuleykha*, Ashkhabad, 1987. The early appearance of this stanza form in al-Kāshgharī, in heroic genres which have no relation to the *tarjiʿ-band*, would seem to rule out simple borrowing from the Persian form. A similar problem exists in connection with the relation of the Turkic *tuyugh*, the Uzbek *dastan* stanza, and the Persian *rubāʿī*. It is possible that a now lost Soghdian stanzaic form underlies all of these Persian and Turkic stanzas, or perhaps all of these Persian and Turkic forms evolved in mutual contact. In any case the Turkmen form was widely accepted in both written and oral genres during the eighteenth century.

References

Andalib (1976), *Lirika*. Ashkhabad: "Ilym."

——— (1978), *Nesimi* (Tankydy Tekst). Ashkhabad: "Ilym."

Andrews, Walter (1985), *Poetry's Voice, Society's Song: Ottoman Lyric Poetry*. Seattle: University of Washington Press.

Ashyrov, A. (1984), *Maghtïmgulïnïng Golyazmalarïnïng Tesviri*. Ash-khabad: "Ilym."

Azadi, Dövletmämmet (1982), *Saylanan Eserler* (Tanqydy Tekst). Ash-khabad: "Ilym."

Baimyradov, Amanmyrat (1983), *Maghtïmgulï Khakïnda Rovayatlar ve Legendalar*. Ashkhabad: "Ilym."

Basilov, V. N. (1984), "Honour Groups in Traditional Turkmenian Societies from the Atlas to the Indus." London: Routledge.

Batyrov, Sh. B. (1961), *Maghtïmgulï: Beyik Türkmen Shakhïrï Maghtïmgulïnïng Dolghan Günününg 225 Yillïgïhnda Baghïshlanan Yubiley Yïgïndïsï.* Ashkhabad: "Ilym."

Benzing, J. (1964), "Die türkmenische Literatur," *Philologica Turcicae Fundamenta*, vol. 2. Wiesbaden: Franz Steiner.

Blum, Steven (1972), "The Concept of 'Asheq in Northern Khorasan," *Asian Music* 4:1.

Garryev, Sejit (1961), "Maghtymguly Ozbek ve Garagalpak Khalklarïnïng khem Söygüli Shakhïrdïr," in Ashyrov, 1984.

———— (1975), *Türkmen Edebiyatïnïng Tarïkhï,* vol. 2. Ashkhabad: "Ilym."

Hodgson, Marshall (1974), *The Venture of Islam,* vol. 2, Chicago: University of Chicago Press.

Kor-oghly, Khalyk (1972), *Tiurkmenskaia Literatura.* Moscow: "Vysshaia Shkola."

Maghtïmgulï (1957), *Saylanan Eserler.* Ashkhabad: "Ilym."

———— (Makhtumquli) (1958), *Izbrannye Proizvedenia* (trans. Zhumäniyaz Shäripov). Tashkent: "Fän."

———— (1977), *Saylanan Goshghïlar.* Ashkhabad: "Türkmenistan."

———— (1983), *Saylanan Eserler* (2 vols). Ashkhabad: "Türkmenistan."

Mäkhtumquli Fragi (1965), *Mäkhtumquli Fragining Eseri.* Gonbad-e Qabus: Qabus Nashriyatï.

Mirzaev, Torä (1973), "Ulkän Khälq Shairi," in Ergäsh Zhumänbulbuloghli, *Bulbul Täranäläri*, vol. 5. Tashkent: "Fän."

Rifaterre, Michael (1978), *Semiotics of Poetry.* Bloomington: University of Indiana Press.

Subtelny, Maria Eva (1983), "Art and Politics in Early Sixteenth Century Central Asia," *Central Asiatic Journal* 27, no. 1–2:121–48.

Woods, John (1976), *The Aqquyunlu: Clan, Confederation, Empire.* Minneapolis: Bibliotheca Islamica.

9

Abdullah Qadiriy and the Bolsheviks

From Reform to Revolution

Christopher Murphy

Abdullah Qadiriy was one of those Uzbek men of letters who began writing in the years just prior to the Russian revolution and whose work continued after the events of 1917.[1] Considered to have played the major role in establishing the genre of the novel in modern Uzbek literature, Qadiriy is particularly singled out for his powerful prose style and his mastery of the complex thematic, symbolic, and narrative structures which must be integrated in order to create a successful novel.

Qadiriy came of age during a period when Uzbek intellectuals were forced to come to grips with the powerful traditions of Central Asian folk literature and classical Chaghatay and Persian Islamic literature, as well as modern (nineteenth- and twentieth-century) Russian literature. The sorting out and reintegration of these diverse venues of literary discourse into a new literary tradition progressed parallel to the social and economic realignments that occurred in Uzbekistan during the late tsarist and early Soviet periods. The literary work created by Adbullah Qadiriy clearly reflects the social and political context in which he worked. The writer's progress from a reformist orientation (which held that the proper education of individuals would bring about the changes in behavior necessary to reinvigorate Uzbek society) to a revolutionary orientation (which held that the solution to the problems of Uzbek society was a general overturn and reorganization of that society) is clearly displayed in the works he published between 1913 and 1923. This evolution of outlook on the author's part reflects his changing understanding of the circumstances of Uzbek life under the late tsarist and early Soviet regimes.

As numerous scholars and observers have noted, the tsarist conquest of Uzbekistan had far-reaching results, producing economic changes and their sociocultural consequences. The economic developments can be described as a general displacement of certain local products by manufactured goods from Russia, which resulted in business failures and significant changes in the goods and services provided by Central Asian merchants. Also, cotton, which had been a crop raised for local consumption, became under the Russian administration a major cash crop around which grew an active entrepreneurial class of Central Asians (Bacon, 1966:105–15).

While economic change progressed in Central Asia there was a concurrent cultural development. This stemmed partially from economically induced social change as a growing merchant class with ties to the tsarist colonial system redefined its Muslim Central Asian identity. The process of redefinition also had pre-conquest roots in a literary and intellectual revival along traditional lines, such as that which occurred in the khanate of Kokand during the 1820s and 1830s (Hayit, 1975:129–32).

Russian contact greatly influenced the *Jadidchilar*, one of the two contending schools of thought that took on clear form during the final years of tsarist colonial rule. The Jadidchilar, or reformers, sought to redefine a Central Asian Muslim identity combining a European social organization with a Muslim religious and cultural base. Their opposition, the *Qadimchilar*, or traditionalists, wished to retain an identity based on a traditional Islamic social and cultural base. The basic tenet and belief of the Jadidchilar was that Central Asia fell under the control of the Russians because traditional Central Asian society had stagnated and allowed its masses to sink into a morass of ignorance in every field of thought and endeavor. In order to awaken and enlighten the people the Jadidchilar worked to establish modern schools and they experimented with such media as newspapers and theater.

Abdullah Qadiriy was born into this atmosphere of identity redefinition, social change, and economic development in Tashkent on April 10, 1894. His family has been described as *orta dekkanlik*, middle class farmers ("Abdulla Qadiriy," p. 19). In many ways Qadiriy's family history is a textbook example of the effects of the social, economic, and cultural changes that took place among the Uzbeks during tsarist colonial rule. Qadiriy's father's career shows clearly the forces at work after the Russian conquest. By all accounts Qādir Bābā led an adventuresome life. As a young man he served as a soldier in the army of the Khan of Kokand before finally settling in Tashkent a few years before the city was taken by the Russians. There he opened a shop where he sold housewares and textile goods. With the coming of the Russians and the introduction of Russian manufactured goods Qādir Bābā went out of business. He then, with the help of his family, began to grow vegetables on some land he had previously purchased (H. Qadiriy, 1973:73–74).

Qadiriy's maternal grandfather, ʿAzīz Ṣūfī, was a *muazzin* in a local mosque. The famous Uzbek/Chaghatay poet Shair Miskin (1880–1937), like Abdullah Qadiriy, was also one of ʿAzīz Ṣūfī's grandsons. After receiving a traditional education in a madrasa Shair Miskin went on to write both traditional lyric poetry and to experiment with new poetic forms. That two of ʿAzīz's grandsons were important literary figures in Uzbekistan during the first third of this century is indicative of the level of cultural awareness and activity in Abdullah Qadiriy's family. Coming as they did from the religious tradition of their grandfather, these writers are also clear examples of the intellectual renewal taking place not only among the new Russian-connected, European-oriented middle class but also among traditional intellectual groups (H. Qadiriy, 73–74).

After attending a *maktab*, a traditional primary school, Qadiriy began to act as a servant for a merchant in the neighborhood. This neighbor, with the concurrence of Qadiriy's parents, sent him to the Russo-native school number seven in Tashkent (H. Qadiriy, 1973:18–19). Upon the completion of this education, his family found him a position as the private secretary to a merchant who imported Russian manufactured goods. At this point, through his family, education, and employment, Abdullah Qadiriy became fully immersed in the social milieu that was creating the reformist movement of the Jadidchilar. At the merchant's shop he began to become acquainted with the writings and persons of the reform movement. This cultured and educated young man began to try his hand at writing, and this writing was clearly *Jadidchi* in inspiration.

Qadiriy's son reports that Qadiriy acted as a correspondent for the following Jadidchi newspapers: *Sada-yi Turkistan, Samarkand,* and *Ayna.* These papers were, from 1913 until 1917, the flagships of Jadidchi expression in Uzbekistan. *Ayna* and *Samarkand* were founded by Mahmudkhoja Behbudi, a leading Central Asian reformer who in 1902 founded in Samarkand the second "new method" school in Central Asia. Behbudi was continuously involved in publishing and literary activities during the first two decades of the twentieth century. *Sada-yi Turkistan* was established by Munavvar Qari of Tashkent, who was perhaps the leading reformer among the Uzbeks. Qari had created the first "new method school" in Central Asia in 1901 in Tashkent. He also published one of the first Uzbek newspapers, *Khurshid,* in 1906. The famous literary scholar, playwright, and producer Abdullah Avlaniy was a major participant in *Sada-yi Turkistan.* Abdullah Qadiriy's association with these papers and the circle of writers and reporters involved with them, especially *Sada-yi Turkistan,* placed Qadiriy in the center of the Jadidchi movement. During these years and later, Qadiriy was also closely associated with the famous Uzbek poet Kamiy, who formed part of the circle of reformer poets who preceded the Jadidchilar. Kamiy was very close to Zavqiy, Muqimy, and Furqat, all of whom were outstanding poet reformers during the latter half of the nineteenth century (H. Qadiriy, 1973:74).

The following lines of a poem published in 1913 (Aybek, 1979:114) illustrate this young writer's concerns.

> Kor bizning ahvalimiz ghaflatda qanday yatamiz
> Oqhlimizqa na adab, na fan, na yakhshi soylamaq
> Na khudani buyruqhi bolgan ulum orgatamiz

> Look how we lie heedless of our condition
> We are teaching our youth neither God's commandments
> Nor manners, nor science, nor proper speech

Here portrayed in simple and direct language are the major themes of the reformers. The people have become paralyzed in stagnated social conditions and as a result they have neglected to educate their youth even in the basics of religion. During this period Qadiriy wrote a short story and a play, both of which decried the uneducated, heedless actions of young men and their disastrous consequences. In the play *Bakhtsiz Kuyev,* "The Unlucky Bridegroom," a young man borrows money to pay for a wedding and through his inability to repay the loan destroys himself and his wife. In the short story *Juvanbaz*, "The Pederast," a young man gives himself over to a life of dissolute pleasure and destroys his family's fortune and himself (Sultanov, 1956:vii).

These writings, which take Qadiriy up to the year 1915, are definitely in the mainstream of Jadidchi reformist thought. They decry the lack of education and base selfishness which the author sees as causes of the social problems besetting his people. As has been pointed out by the Uzbek scholar Hamil Yaqubov, Abdullah Qadiriy did not have any political program in these writings; rather he was concerned with personal behavior (Yaqubov, 1973: 388). This attitude may stem from the influence of his mother's family and its religious outlook, which was focused on the personal actions of individuals. This interest in the individual may also indicate that at this time Qadiriy conceived of personal actions as affecting society rather than as results of social conditions. Whatever the source, his lack of political orientation is significant because it gave Qadiriy the freedom to explore literature unfettered by the considerations of any party line.

The literary results of this freedom can be seen in his short story *Ulaqda*, "At the Goat Game." Here the author sets aside the didactic style of his previous work and presents a humorous and lively vignette of Uzbek life. Another example of this new direction in Qadiriy's writing is *Jinlar Bazm*, "The Jinns' Party," where the writer experiments with onomatopoeia and presents a very lively and funny tale. During these same years, 1916–17, Qadiriy's companions report that he had almost totally immersed himself in the study of literature and in his writing (H. Qadiriy, 1973:28).

At this point, the reformist writer, who was becoming simply a writer, was confronted with revolution. With the February and October revolutions Qadiriy's literary endeavors were influenced by the politics of reform and revolution far more than in the prerevolutionary period. As he himself states, before this time he was uninformed as to the programs of any of the various political parties or groupings. He was initially attracted to the *Turan* society, which was interested in creating a Central Asian Muslim self-identity through education and consciousness-raising activities such as theatrical performances (Allworth, 1964:32; H. Qadiriy, 1973:32). Qadiriy's attraction to the organization was probably twofold. First, from his earliest literary attempts he had been con-

cerned with the need to educate people; secondly, Abdullah Avlaniy, a famous author and folkorist, was a major figure in the
organization (Allworth, 1964:109). It should also be noted that, as
mentioned above, Avlaniy was an important figure in the group
that published *Sada-yi Turkistan*, and in 1915 he produced Qadiriy's play, *Bakhtsiz Kuyev* (H. Qadiriy, 1973:25). Thus Abdullah
Qadiriy was already well acquainted with this important Jadidchi
when he became involved with the Turan Society.

In early 1918 when Qadiriy became secretary to the Tatar socialist revolutionist Ismail Abidov, he moved away from this Central Asian political program and became involved in promoting
the cause of the Bolsheviks. Ismail Abidov, despite his being a socialist revolutionary, had very close connections with the Jadidchilar. In 1906 he founded *Taraqqi*, one of the first reformist
newspapers in Tashkent (Devlet, 1985:145, 220). Qadiriy used his
now proven literary talent to criticize the ulama and the wealthy.
An early example of this is the story *Tinch Ish*, "Easy Work," in
which Qadiriy criticizes a stereotypical mulla. For instance, he
writes that after spending twenty-five to thirty years studying in
a madrasa the mulla knows all about geography. America, in the
mulla's view, is a tribe of the Franks who work with lacquered
leather (i.e., *amirkan teri*), and the English are called rulers of the
sea because they build their cities on the ocean. In another place
the mulla is seen to be puzzled by the word *ḥurriyat*, "liberty," so
he consults a dictionary, after which he has a slight understanding
of the word. In the end it is related that the mulla has found a
permanent place as an imam, a prayer leader, a rather humble position for one so well educated. Qadiriy says, "Truly Akhund
Damla had a job for which he was well suited" (A. Qadiriy,
1969:16–21). The bare bones of the story present an attack on religious professionals. Interestingly, the fault that Qadiriy finds in
this stereotypical character is the fault of ignorance, the same
fault he decried in his earliest poems. Ignorance as a root cause of
opposition to the Bolsheviks is often a theme in Qadiriy's polemical works.

If the story were only a bald polemic against the religious
professionals it would not have been as effective as it probably
was. The story gains greater effect because Qadiriy has become a
powerful stylist. In the work he incorporates a biting sarcasm and
an almost slapstick stereotypical characterization. He uses a num-

ber of quotations from the mulla, displaying the proper dialect, which adds a greater dimension of pleasure for the audience. This is particularly significant when one remembers that much of this material was read aloud to gatherings of illiterate people. Qadiriy even employs rather simple ironic symbolism in the case of the mulla's name, Damla Sharif Akhund, which literally means "well-educated honored teacher."

It is important to realize that Qadiriy is attacking a certain kind of Muslim, not Islam itself. Qadiriy is consistent in this approach throughout his writings. It is difficult to ascertain whether Abdullah Qadiriy was a practicing Muslim, or at what level he may have practiced Islam. However, there is at least some circumstantial evidence that the author never gave up Islam as part of his personal identity as an Uzbek, even a revolutionary Uzbek. An example of this is the report by his son (H. Qadiriy, 1973:53) that Abdullah Qadiriy participated with the local imam in the funeral rites and prayers for Qadiriy's mother. Another inference as to the author's adherence to Islam is the fact that during the winter of 1916–17 he attended a madrasa in Tashkent (H. Qadiriy, 1973:29). Habibullah Qadiriy also indicates that one of his father's closest friends was Rasulmuhammad Damla, who had been a qadi (religious judge) and a mufti (Muslim legal consultant) during tsarist times (p. 106). Another of his friends was Allahqul, a *kalandar* (dervish) and a well-known reciter of old-style poetry (p. 113).

Another piece that displays Qadiriy's literary ability as well as his strong pro-Bolshevik sentiments is the story *Atam va Bolshevik*, "My Father and the Bolshevik," published in 1922 in the journal *Inqilab*, "Revolution" (Sultanov, 1956:ix). This story, which is presented as a son's report about a conversation with his father, is based on Qadiriy's familiar theme of the necessity of having correct information in order to act properly. The conversation revolves around two points: (1) who the Bolsheviks are, that is, whom they represent, and (2) the contention that the Bolsheviks are not anti-Muslim. The father's first impression is that the Bolsheviks are in fact a single person who has overthrown the tsar and the provisional government and taken their places. The son assures the old man that the Bolsheviks are in fact the leaders of the masses, particularly the poor. He states that since the old man has always been poor he should be especially supportive of the Bolsheviks. When the father then voices the opinion that the Bolsheviks are *kāfir*, non-Muslim, again he is corrected by the son who tells him that many Muslims are working with the Bolsheviks, including some in leadership positions. As a result of his corrected understanding of the Bolsheviks the old man is reported by the son to have blackened his hair and joined the Bolsheviks as a "loyal soldier" (Qadiriy, 1969:27–29).

Qadiriy strengthens the effect of this conversation by prefacing its description with a brief account of the old man's life. He is said to have grown up during the last years of independence for Turkistan and to have been a soldier in the forces that defended Tashkent against the Russians (p. 27). The symbolic message of this defense against the tsarist Russians and aid to the Bolshevik Russians by the same good Muslim man is inescapable. The father is also said to be initially no friend of the new workers' government because of his experience under tsarist rule (p. 27). The conversational part of the story demonstrates that this attitude is a mistake and the old man changes when given the proper information. It should be noted that this story would lend itself very well to oral presentation since three-fourths of it is written in the colloquial oral style of a conversation.

The issue of the Bolsheviks being anti-Muslim was extremely important, as there was strong feeling against Russians in general because they were non-Muslims. Qadiriy personally experienced this anti-Russian anger in 1918. He and two friends were on their way to a polling place when they were approached by a Russian and an Armenian who gave them some Bolshevik election leaflets. Upon their entering the polling place someone noticed the leaflets and raised an outcry against the three young men who had kāfir materials in their hands. Consequently the three were struck with canes and driven from the polling place (H. Qadiriy, 1973:32–34). This incident demonstrates well the intense feeling which any party having a Russian leadership had to overcome in Central Asia.

In many of the writings of Qadiriy discussed thus far there is a clear theme of the necessity of education, or at least a true understanding of the situation. This theme also exists in *Atam va Bolshevik*, but a closer look at the piece suggests a more powerful, indeed a revolutionary, reading of the story. Izzat Sultanov, the editor of a volume of short works by Qadiriy, presents *Atam va Bolshevik* as a humorous work (Sultanov, 1956:ix). The story is funny but in a very special way. The son, in relating the conversation, holds the old man up to a kind of ridicule, gentle though it is. In a society and culture that venerates age, this is a blow struck against traditionally constituted authority. This overturn of tradition is further reinforced by the fact that it is the son who, in essence, sends the father to war rather than the usual circumstance of the father sending the son. This story can be read as a call to mature, vigorous sons to set aside the stifling hand of the past represented by the confused and irrelevant father.

Had Qadiriy, at this point in his career, passed from the reformist orientation of his earlier work to a revolutionary orientation? The resolution of this question becomes particularly interesting when it is remembered that in the next year, 1923, Qadiriy began to publish serially his historical novel *Otgan Kunlar*, "Past Days," in the journal *Inqilab* (H. Qadiriy, 1973:74–75). This subtle and complex work, which is still considered to be among the first rank of Uzbek novels, is open to various and even contradictory readings and interpretations.[2] The novel's clear connections with traditional Uzbek narrative, and the book's depiction of life during the last period of independence in Uzbekistan, lend strong support to arguments that this is a nationalist work. In fact, the portrayal of nineteenth-century attitudes toward Russians was deemed to be so inflammatory that when *Otgan Kunlar* was republished in 1956 a number of offensive passages were edited out (S. Qadiriy, 1990:12–13). Beyond this surface reading of the text there are some jarring departures from traditional Uzbek narrative practice. A particularly salient example is the title, *Otgan Kunlar*. It was a common practice among the Uzbek singers of oral narratives to compose late in life an autobiographical song usually entitled *Otgan Kunlarim*, "My Past Days" (Cirtautas, 1981). Qadiriy's use of a title echoing this type of composition is an action designed to raise questions in the minds of his audience. It is obvious that the novel is neither an oral work nor written by an author late in life. A title such as this one, which has meaning in the traditional literary discourse of the Uzbeks, alerts the audience at the book's very outset that the work is a departure from the usual Uzbek narrative literature. The audience, having had these questions raised, must resolve them in some meaningful way. One resolution is to see Qadiriy's choice of title as a statement that the role of the traditional literary artist has been replaced by a new type of literary figure both younger and using a different genre. Thus the young nontraditional artist is essentially the same type of person as the son who gently corrects and leads his father. The old man has experienced a great deal of life but his experience does not allow him to lead in such new conditions.

Qadiriy's use of the theme of the tragic lovers in *Otgan Kunlar*, a traditional theme from classical Chaghatay and Persian literature, also demonstrates the author's adoption of a revolutionary orientation. In the classical tradition the conflict among the lovers and their parents is seen to symbolize both the mystic and God on the part of the lovers and the world and its temptations and demands on the part of the parents. The reader cannot resolve the conflict among the characters in Qadiriy's novel in the traditional manner, because the novel is explicitly presented as a realistic work and therefore the destruction of the couple must be understood in worldly terms. This very negative presentation of parental demands, an important symbol of traditional authority, is a symbolic call for a reorganization of society. An opposite reading of the novel, that traditional authority is being upheld by the example of the destruction of disobedient children, is not possible. The tragic couple are the hero and heroine and therefore the sympathy of the audience must lie with them and their activities must be viewed positively.

The theme of the necessary overturning of traditional authority is constantly presented in the novel. For example, when Atabek falls in love with Kumush he is incapable of acting. However, his slave, Hasanali, takes it upon himself to engage a friend of Atabek's to approach Kumush's father and arrange the marriage which brings the couple their brief period of bliss (*Otgan Kunlar*, pp. 42–49). Here the symbolism of a man's slave acting in the place of his master's older male relative is an unmistakable indication of the overturn of the normal traditional order of society and the happy results arising from the overturn.

When the blissful outcome of the slave's actions is contrasted with the disastrous results of Atabek's compliance with the demands of traditional authority, as represented by his acceptance of his mother's and Kumush's mother's demands (that Atabek allow Kumush to remain in Marghilan and that he marry Zaynab), the reader is again presented with a symbolic discourse on the necessity to confront and overcome traditional authority. This aspect of the novel is further reinforced in Atabek's attempt to abandon his family, including Zaynab, and remain in Marghilan. Kumush's father then confronts the young man, and Atabek succumbs to the older man's arguments and returns to Tashkent and the eventual disaster of Kumush being poisoned by Zaynab (*Otgan Kunlar*, pp. 146–58, 376–82). Atabek's final abandonment of his parents (*Otgan Kunlar*, pp. 382–83) and the girl's death also serve to develop the theme of the necessity for revolution. The parents as paragons of traditional authority lose their very future—their children—through their adherence to traditional social values.

Finally, the epilogue, which has the hero, Atabek, going off to fight the tsarist conquerors, should not be seen as a nationalist statement. Rather, it is the final tragic denouement of Atabek's failure to rebel. Early in the novel, when Atabek points out the superiority of the tsarist military-colonial forces to those of the Khanate of Kokand, he clearly understands the hopelessness of fighting the Russians. Thus his inability to assert himself against the traditional authority of his society leads him to an act he clearly understands as hopeless (*Otgan Kunlar*, pp. 16–18; 384–85). This is another powerful symbolic example for the audience to ponder. The importance of this epilogue as a guidepost for the readers should not be overlooked, as it is reminiscent of the type of explanatory epilogue used by classical Islamic writers such as ʿAlī Shīr Navāʾī, for example, in his *Layla va Majnun* (Levend, 1967: 285–88).

From the beginning of his literary career Abdullah Qadiriy was concerned with educating his fellow Uzbeks. By 1922, after ten years of literary effort and the experience of political and incipient social revolution, Qadiriy appears to have come to the conclusion that not only is education necessary but the educated should not wait for the rising tide of education among the people to reform Uzbek society. Rather, the educated should actively put themselves forward to replace the old leadership, as the son replaces the father in the role of advisor and corrector in *Atam va Bolshevik*. In fact Qadiriy's use of literary devices reminiscent of traditional Uzbek themes and symbols in ways that produce revolutionary interpretations indicates that by 1923 the author had taken up a clearly revolutionary orientation.

Notes

1. The transliteration system used in this paper is that found in Edward Allworth's *Uzbek Literary Politics* (The Hague, 1964).

2. Gaining an accurate understanding of the Uzbek evaluation of Abdullah Qadiriy is made difficult by the political nature of literary criticism that has existed in Uzbekistan during the Soviet period. Two works that concern themselves with literary matters and political-literary affairs, rather than simply the latter, are Aybek's 1936 work "Abdulla Qadiriy Ijadi Yolda" and Ibrahim Mirzayev's *Abdulla Qadiriyning Ijadiy Evolyutsiyadi* (Tashkent, 1969). It is interesting that recently Matyaqub Qushjanov published an article entitled *"Otgan Kunlar* Tanqid Kozgusida" (*Otgan Kunlar* in the Mirror of Criticism) in *Uzbek Tili va Adabiyati* 6 (1989):7–13. Qushjanov reviews the critical controversy that preceded the publishing of Aybek's article in 1936. First he looks at M. I. Sheverdin and Satti Husayn's criticism of the novel as being insufficiently proletarian in nature, particularly the fact that the life of a merchant, not a peasant, is portrayed. Qushjanov then discusses and supports Aybek's analysis of the novel. That is, the work's importance does not stem from its portrayal of merchants or peasants, but rather from its functioning as a literary work. This is perhaps the beginning of an Uzbek effort to analyze Qadiriy's work from a purely literary point of view.

Another indication of the Uzbeks' coming to grips with not only Qadiriy's literature but the system that destroyed him are the articles that appeared in *Sharq Yulduzi* 9 (1989):171–88. The first article by Aziz Abdurazzaq, entitled "Otgan Kunlarimiz Qursin" (May Our Past Days Be Truly Understood) is an eyewitness account of the arrest of Abdullah Qadiriy and the subsequent silence which surrounded the subject. The second, by Enver Khurshut, entitled "Amir Umarkhanning Kanizi" (Amir Umarkhan's Slave) looks at the literary question of Qadiriy's use and portrayal of historical events in his second novel, *Mehradban Chayan* (The Scorpion from the Mehrab). Interestingly, these two articles are followed by the reprint of the 1974 article of Ergash Rustamov, entitled "Lenindan Ruh Alib Marksdan Ilhamlangan" (Taking Lenin's Spirit and the Being Inspired by Marx). This article basically repeats the justifications of Izzat Sultanov's 1956 article, which was published when Qadiriy was officially rehabilitated. It should be noted that Sherkan Qadiriy, in *Gulistan* 9 (1990):12–13, published documentation concerning the rehabilitation of Qadiriy and the republishing of his works.

References

"Abdullah Qadiriy" (1971), *Uzbek Sovet Entsiklopediyasi*, vol. 1. Tashkent.

Abdurazzaq, Aziz (1989), "Otgan Kunlarimiz Qursin," *Sharq Yulduzi*, no. 9.

Allworth, Edward (1964), *Uzbek Literary Politics*. The Hague.

Aybek (1979), "Abdulla Qadiriy Ijadi Yolda," *Mukammal Asarlar Toplami*, vol. 14. Tashkent.

Bacon, Elizabeth E. (1966), *Central Asians under Russian Rule*. Ithaca, N.Y.

Cirtautas, Ilse (1981), "The Continuing Importance of Autobiographical Writings in Eastern Turkic Literature." A paper presented at the 1981 Middle East Studies Association Annual Meeting.

Devlet, Nadir (1985), *Rusya Turklerining Milli Mucadele Tarihi (1905–1917)*. Ankara.

Hayit, Baymirza (1975), *Turkistan Rusya ile Cin Arasinda*. Istanbul.

Khurshut, Enver (1989), "Amir Umarkhanning Kanizi," *Sharq Yulduzi*, no. 9.

Levend, Aga Sirri (1967), *Ali Sir Nevai*, vol. 3. Ankara.

Mirzayev, Ibrahim (1969), *Abdulla Qadiriyning Ijadiy Evolyutsiyadi*. Tashkent.

Qadiriy, Abdullah (1956), *Otgan Kunlar*. Tashkent.

Qadiriy, Abdullah (1969), in Izzat Sultanov (ed.), *Kichik Asarlar*. Tashkent.

Qadiriy, Habibullah (1973), *Atam Haqida*. Tashkent.

Qadiriy, Sherkan (1990), "Aqlav ve Tazyiq," *Gulistan*, no. 9.

Qushjanov, Enver (1989), "*Otgan Kunlar* Tanqid Kozgusida," *Uzbek Tili va Adabiyati*, no. 6.

Rustamov, Ergash (1989), "Lenindan Ruh Alib Marksdan Ilhamlangan," *Sharq Yulduzi*, no. 9.

Sultanov, Izzat (1956), "Abdulla Qadiriy Ijadi Haqida." *Otgan Kunlar*. Tashkent.

Yaqubov, Hamil (1973), "Yirik San'atkarning Tonghich Romani." *Otgan Kunlar*. Tashkent.

Postscript

Remarkable and dramatic events have occurred during the past weeks in the Soviet Union, and they continue to occur with astonishing speed. Following the attempted coup d'état that took place between 19–21 August and its defeat by democratic forces, a series of transformations have spelled the end of the Pax Sovietica. These transformations include the suspension of Communist Party activities on 30 August 1991, the dismantling and reorganization of the KGB, the Soviet and international recognition of Lithuania, Estonia, and Latvia as independent sovereign states, and a surge of secessionist and nationalist activity throughout the republics. The true ethnic, religious, and cultural pluralism of the former Soviet USSR is forcefully emerging. As for Soviet Central Asia, it should now be possible to more correctly conceive of this region within the wider historical and cultural map of the Eastern Islamic world of Iran, China, and Northern India.

A multitude of new possibilities face the peoples of Central Asia. If, for example, the Central Asian republics remain tied to a newly conceived center, and if Nursultan A. Nazarbayev, the increasingly powerful leader of Kazakhstan (the third largest republic), continues to exert considerable influence at the center, Muslim and Central Asian identities (Turk and Tajik) will likely take on a new meaning and exercise new political weight. However, it is a perilous time for all the peoples of the Soviet Union. As winter draws closer, the threat of inadequate food supplies increases. As the decentralization process continues, interethnic conflicts persist and intensify, and restive populations long hoping to regain lost territories, such as the Tatars, actively press for independence. Populations that spill across international borders—such as Tajiks and Uzbeks into Afghanistan, or Turkmen and Azeris into Iran—raise critical issues concerning identity and political loyalty on both sides of the frontiers.

The present situation and that of 1917 are very different with respect to the status of ethnic and national identity. This is made clear by the declaration of the Congress of People's Deputies on 5 September 1992: "The new union must be based on the principles of independence and territorial integrity of states, and observance of the rights of the nation and the individuals, and social justice and democracy" (*New York Times*, 6 Sept. 1991). Precisely what such a declaration will mean in practice for the large population of Muslims in Central Asia and what implications the ongoing events have for Muslims in other areas of Central Asia—particularly in northwest China, where rebellions have already been reported during the past year—remain to be seen. However, it is clear that, increasingly, nationalism and ethnic separatism are replacing the false vision of closed, homogeneous nation states.

Jo-Ann Gross
Pennington, N.J., *8 September 1991*

Glossary

Note that complete diacritical marks are given for all words in the glossary. In the text some of these words appear without diacritics, according to common English usage.

ʿālim, pl. *ʿulamā* (*ulama*)	religious scholar
ahong	imām (prayer leader or spiritual leader)
aṣlī	lit. original; term used to refer to Uzbeks who came to N. Afghanistan in the sixteenth century
bakhshī/bäkhshi (Turkm.)	oral bard (Uzbek); musician and singer of didactic religious texts (Turkmen); also used to refer to scribe
bayt	couplet
Dār al-Islām	Muslim territory
dastan/dessan	oral epic (Uzbek); long oral narrative (Turkmen)
dhikr	Sufi term for repetition of specific formulas in praise of God (v.); the ceremonial chanting praising God (n.)
fatwā	formal legal opinion, issued by a qualified jurist
ghazal	a kind of poem about love, the number of couplets is between 7 and 15

habitus	a term coined by Pierre Bourdieu to refer to a set of schemes resulting in habitual actions and representations
ḥadīth	reported words and deeds of the Prophet Muḥammad, handed down by a line of authorities
ḥajj	pilgrimage to Mecca
ijtihād	the use of individual reasoning
imām	prayer leader; spiritual leader
īshān	polite Persian form of saying "he"; honorific title often used for Central Asian Sufi shaykhs
jihād	holy war for the cause of Islam
kāfir	unbeliever in the Islamic revelation
kalām	speculative theology; philosophy applied to Revelation
khān	local leader or chief (Turkic term)
khad	Afghan secret police
khoja/khwāja	Sufi master, title of learned person
madrasa	school, often associated with a mosque
maktab	traditional primary school
manla	Hui term derived from mulla, meaning village preacher
mathnavī	long narrative poem
muhājir	term used to refer to Uzbeks who came to N. Afghanistan in the late 1920s
mudarris	teacher
mujaddid	renewer
Mujāhidīn	Muslim resistance fighter, Muslim freedom fighter
mukhammas	a five-line stanzaic form based on an original couplet
mullā	Muslim preacher
murīd	a Sufi term for student or disciple

qāḍī	religious judge
qawm	a segment of society bound by solidarity ties (family, clan, occupational group, village)
radīf	monorhyme; word repeated at the end of every couplet of a ghazal
Ramaḍān	lunar month of fasting
rubāʿī	a quatrain of a certain meter with a rhyme of *aa/ba*
sayyid	descendant of the Prophet
shahāda	declaration of faith
Sharīʿa	the revealed, or canonical, law of Islam
shaykh	tribal or religious leader
silsila	chain, patrilineal geneaology
sunna	the traditions of the Prophet Muhammad
tajdīd	renewal
taqlīd	imitation
ṭarīqa	Sufi brotherhood, the Sufi "path"
tekke	religious lodge
töre/törü	a secular political rule based on steppe values (post-Mongol era); later used for political leaders
ulūs	territories into which Chinggis Khan divided his steppe empire
umma	Islamic community
yāsā; yasaq/jasaq	Mongol customary law; also denoted an army order or societal order according to steppe values
waqf, pl. *awqāf*	pious endowment

General Bibliography

Abdullah, Abdulgani. "The Reformist Activity of al-Kursawi." *Muslims of the Soviet East* 4(1985):11–12.

Abramzon, Z. M. *Kirgizi i ikh etnogeneticheskie i istoriko-kulturnye.* Afghanistan Council, the Asia Society. New York: Occasional Papers.

Aini, K., and Y. S. Maltsev. "Oriental Studies in Tajikistan." *Iranian Studies* 21(1988):18–22.

Akiner, Shirin. *The Islamic Peoples of the Soviet Union.* London, 1984.

Algar, Hamid. "The Naqshbandi Order: A Preliminary Survey of its History and Significance."*Studia Islamica* 44(1976):123–52.

Allsen, Thomas T. "Changing Forms of Legitimation in Mongol Iran." In *Rulers from the Steppe: State Formation on the Eurasian Periphery,* ed. Gary Seaman. Los Angeles: Ethnographics Press, 1990, pp. 186–204.

———. *Mongol Imperialism: The Politics of the Grand Qan Möngke in China, Russia, and the Islamic Lands, 1251–1259.* Berkeley: University of California Press, 1987.

———. "Mongolian Rule in East Asia, 12th–14th Centuries: An Assessment of Recent Soviet Scholarship." *Mongolian Studies* 3(1976):5–27.

Allworth, Edward. *Uzbek Literary Politics.* The Hague, 1964.

——— (ed). *The Nationality Question in Soviet Central Asia.* New York: Praeger, 1973.

——— (ed.). *Central Asia: 120 Years of Russian Rule.* Durham: Duke University Press, 1989.

Alstadt-Mihradi, Ayşe. "The Azerbaijani Bourgeoisie and the Cultural-Enlightenment Movement in Baku: First Steppes toward Nationalism." In *Transcaucasia: Nationalism and Social Change,* ed. G. Suny. Ann Arbor: University of Michigan, pp. 197–208.

Arjomand, Said (ed.). *From Nationalism to Revolutionary Islam.* Albany: State University of New York Press, 1984.

Ashyrov, A. *Maghtïmgulïnïng Goyazmalarïnïng Tesviri.* Ashkhabad: Ilym, 1984.

Atkin, M. "Iranian Studies in the USSR." *Iranian Studies* 20(1987):223–51.

———. *The Subtlest Battle: Islam in Soviet Tajikistan.* Philadelphia: Foreign Policy Research Institute, 1989.

Aubin, Jean. "Le Khanat de Cagatai et le Khorasan (1334–1380)." *Turcica* 7, no. 2, 1976.

Aybek. "Abdulla Qadiriy Ijadi Yolda." *Mukammal Asarlar Toplami,* vol. 14. Tashkent, 1979.

Bacon, Elizabeth E. *Central Asia under Russian Rule.* Ithaca, N.Y.: Cornell University Press, 1966.

Baimyradov, Amanmyrat. *Maghtïmgulï Khakïnda Rovayatlar ve Legednalar.* Ashkhabad: Ilym, 1983.

Banuazizi, Ali, and Myron Weiner (eds.). *The State, Religion, and Ethnic Politics: Afghanistan, Iran, and Pakistan.* Syracuse University Press, 1986.

Barfield, Thomas T. *The Perilous Frontier: Nomadic Empires and China.* Cambridge: Basil Blackwell, 1989.

———. *The Central Asian Arabs of Afghanistan.* Austin: University of Texas Press, 1981.

Barth, Fredrik (ed.). *Ethnic Groups and Boundaries.* Boston: Little, Brown, 1969.

Barthold, V. N. *Four Studies on the History of Central Asia.* Vol. 3, *Mir 'Ali-Shir* [and] *A History of the Turkman People.* Trans. from the Russian by V. Minorsky and T. Minorsky. Leiden, 1962.

———. *Turkestan Down to the Mongol Invasion.* 3rd ed. Edited by C. E. Bosworth. E. J. W. Gibb Memorial Series, n.s., vol. 5. London, 1968.

Barthold [Bartol'd], V. V. "Sheikh Zaynullah Rasulev, 1833–1917." *Musul'manskii Mir* 1, no. 1. Petrograd, 1917.

Basilov, V. *Honour Groups in Traditional Turkmenian Societies from the Atlas to the Indus.* London: Routledge, 1984.

———. *Drevnie obriady verovanii a i kul'ty narodov Srednei Azii: istoriko-etnografischeskie ocherki.* Moscow: Nauka, 1986.

——— (ed.). *The Nomads of Eurasia* (trans. Mary Fleming Zirin). Seattle: National History Museum of Los Angeles County in Association with the University of Washington Press, 1989.

Battal-Taymas, Abdullah. *Kazan Türkleri.* Ankara, 1966.

Bawden, C. R. *The Modern History of Mongolia.* 2nd ed. London: Kegan Paul, 1989.

Bennigsen, A., and Ch. Lemercier-Quelquejay. *La presse et les mouvements nationaux chez les musulmans de Russie avant 1920.* Paris and the Hague: Mouton, 1964.

———. *Islam in the Soviet Union.* New York/London, 1967.

Bennigsen, A., and S. E. Wimbush. *Muslims of the Soviet Empire: A Guide.* London, 1985.

———. *Mystics and Commissars.* Berkeley: University of California Press, 1987.

Bentley, G. Carter. "Ethnicity and Practice." *Comparative Studies in Society and History* 29(1987):24–55.

Benzing, J. "Die türkmenische Literatur." *Philologica Turcicae Fundamenta* II. Wiesbaden: Franz Steiner, 1964.

Bourdieu, P. *Outline of a Theory of Practice* (trans. R. Nice). Cambridge/New York: Cambridge University Press, 1977.

Bregel, Iu. *Dokumenty Arkhiva Khivinskikh Khanov po istorii i etnografii Karakalpakov.* Moscow: Nauka, 1967.

———. "The Role of Central Asia in the History of the Muslim East." Afghanistan Council, the Asia Society of New York. Occasional Paper #20, 1980.

Bromley, Iu. "Ethnic Processes." In *Soviet Ethnographic Studies*, No. 3. Moscow, 1983.

———. *Theoretical Ethnography.* Moscow: Nauka, 1984. Brown, 1969.

Burke, Edmund III, and Ira M. Lapidus. *Islam, Politics, and Social Movements.* Berkeley: University of California Press, 1988.

Centlivres, Pierre. "Problèmes d'identité ethnique dans le Nord de d'Afghanistan." In *Actes du XVIème Congrès des Orientalistes, L'Iran Modern, L'Asiathèque.* Paris, 1976.

Charlseley, S. R. "The Formation of Ethnic Groups." In *Urban Ethnicity*, ed. Abner Cohen. London/New York: Tavistock, 1974.

Chu Wen-djang. "Ch'ing Policy towards the Muslims of the Northwest." Ph.D. diss., University of Washington, 1955.

Cleaves, Francis Woodman. *The Secret History of the Mongols.* Cambridge, London: Harvard University Press.

Cohen, Abner. "Introduction: The Lessons of Ethnicity." In *Urban Ethnicity*, ed. Abner Cohen. London: Tavistock, 1974.

Cohen, R. "Ethnicity: Problem and Focus in Anthropology." *Annual Review of Anthropology* 7(1978):379–403.

Comaroff, John. "Of Totemism and Ethnicity: Consciousness, Practice, and the Signs of Inequity." *Ethnos* 5(1987):301–23.

Connor, Walker. *The National Question in Marxist-Leninist Theory and Strategy.* Princeton: Princeton University Press, 1984.

Crossley, Pamela Kyle. "Thinking About Ethnicity in Early Modern China." *Late Imperial China* 11(1990):1–34.

Davidovitch, E. A. "Some Social and Economic Aspects of 16th Century Central Asia." *Central Asian Review* 112(1964):265–70.

Deweese, Devin A. "The Kashf al-huda' of Kamal ad-Din Husayn Khorezmi: A Fifteenth-Century Sufi Commentary on the 'Qasidat al-burda' in Khorezmian." Ph.D. diss., Indiana University, 1985.

D'Encausse, Hélène Carrère. *Islam and the Russian Empire: Reform and Revolution in Central Asia* (originally published in French, 1966; trans. Quintin Hoare). Berkeley: University of California Press, 1988.

de Planhol, Xavier. "Sur la Frontiere turkmene de l'Afghanistan." *Révue Géographique de l'Est* 13, no. 1–22:1–16.

de Rachewiltz, Igor. "Some Remarks on the Ideological Foundations of Chingis Khan's Empire." *Papers on Far Eastern History* 7(1973):21–36.

Dickson, Martin. "Uzbek Dynastic Theory in the Sixteenth Century." In *Trudy XXV-ogo Mezhdunarodnogo Kongressa Vostokovedov* 3(1960): 208–16.

Dreyer, June. *China's Forty Million: Minority Nationalities and National Integration in the People's Republic of China.* Cambridge: Harvard University Press, 1976.

Eckmann, János. "Die Tcshaghataische Literatur." *Philologiae Turcicae*, vol. 1. Wiesbaden: F. Stein, 139–60.

———. "Das Tschaghataische." *Philologiae Turcicae Fundamenta*, vol. 1. Wiesbaden: F. Steiner, 1959, pp. 139–402.

Eickelman, Dale. *The Middle East: An Anthropological Approach,* 2nd ed. New Jersey: Prentice-Hall, 1989.

———. "The Study of Islam in Local Contexts." In *Islam in Local Contexts,* ed. Richard Martin. Leiden: 1982, pp. 1–16.

Evans-Pritchard, E. E. *The Nuer.* Oxford: Clarendon, 1940.

Fletcher, Joseph. "The Mongols: Ecological and Social Perspectives." *Harvard Journal of Asiatic Studies* 6(1986):11–50.

———. "Altishahr under the Khwajas." A Manuscript in Four Chapters. Harvard University Archives, HUG(b) F520.30.

Garryev, Sejit. *Türkmen Edebiyatïnïng Tarïkhï,* vol. 2. Ashkhabad: 1975.

Gasprinskii, Ismail Bey. *Avrupa Medeniyetine bir Nazar Muvazene.* Istanbul, 1885.

Gellner, Ernest. *Soviet and Western Anthropology.* New York: Columbia University Press, 1980.

———. *Nations and Nationalism.* Ithaca: Cornell University Press, 1983.

Gladney, Dru C. "Muslim Tombs and Ethnic Folklore: Charters for Hui Identity." *Journal of Asian Studies* 46(1987):495–532.

———. "Qing Zhen: A Study of Ethnoreligious Identity among Hui Muslim Communities in China." Ph.D. diss., University of Washington, Seattle, 1987.

———. "The Ethnogenesis of the Uighur." *Central Asian Survey* 9(1990): 1–28.

Golden, Peter. "The Qipčaqs of Medieval Eurasia: An Example of Stateless Adaptation in the Steppes." In *Rulers from the Steppe: State Formation on the Eurasian Periphery,* ed. Gary Seaman. Los Angeles: Ethnographics Press, 1990.

Golombek, Lisa, and Donald Wilber. *The Timurid Architecture of Iran and Turan.* 2 vols. Princeton: Princeton University Press, 1988.

Gross, Jo-Ann. "The Economic Status of a Timurid Shaykh: A Matter of Conflict or Perception?" *Iranian Studies* 23(1988):84–104.

Hartmann, M. "Ein Heiligenstaat im Islam: Das Ende der Caghataiden und die Herrschaft der Chogas in Kasgarien." *Der islamische Orient: Berichte und Forschungen,* parts 6–10. Berlin, 1905, pp. 193–374.

Hicks, George L., and Philip Leis. *Ethnic Encounters: Identities and Contexts.* Belmont, Calif., 1977.

Hobsbawm, E. J. *Nations and Nationalism since 1780: Programme, Myth, Reality.* Cambridge: Cambridge University Press, 1990.

Imart, Guy. *The Limits of Inner Asia: Some Soul-Searching on New Borders for an Old Frontier-Land.* Papers on Inner Asia, no. 1. Bloomington: Indiana University Research Institute for Inner Asian Studies, 1987.

Israeli, Raphael. *Muslims in China.* London & Atlantic Highlands: Curzon & Humanities Press, 1978.

Jagchid, Sechin, and Van Jay Symonds. *Peace, War, and Trade along the Great Wall.* Bloomington: Indiana University Press, 1989.

Karmysheva, B. Kh. *Uzbek-i lokaitsy Iushnogo Tadzhikistana.* Stalinabad, TadzhSSR, 1954.

Kor-oghly, Khalyk. *Tiurkmenskaia Literatura.* Moscow: Vysshaia Schkola, 1972.

Keyes, Charles. "The Dialectic of Ethnic Change." In *Ethnic Change*, ed. C. Keyes. Seattle: University of Washington Press, 1981, pp. 3–30.

———. "Towards a New Formation of the Concept of Ethnic Group." *Ethnicity* 3(1976):202–13.

Khazanov, A. M. *Nomads and the Outside World*, trans. Julia Crookenden. Cambridge: Cambridge University Press, 1978.

Kim, Ho-dong. "The Muslim Rebellion and the Kashghar Emirate in Chinese Central Asia, 1864–1877." Ph.D. diss., Harvard University, 1986.

Kor-oghly, Khalyk. *Tiurkmenskaia Literatura.* Moscow: "Vysshaia."

Krader, Lawrence. *Peoples of Central Asia*, 3rd ed. Bloomington: Indiana University Press, 1971.

Lattimore, Owen. *Inner Asian Frontiers of China.* New York: American Geographical Society, 1951.

———. "The Geographical Factor in Mongol History." In *Studies in Frontier History: Collected Papers 1928–1958*, ed. Owen Lattimore. London: Oxford University Press, 1962.

Leach, Edmund. *Political Systems of Highland Burma.* Cambridge: Harvard University Press, 1954.

Leslie, Donald Daniel. *Islam in Traditional China: A Short History to 1800.* Canberra: CCAE, 1986.

Li, Charles, and Dru Gladney (eds.). *Minority Nationalities of China: Language and Culture.* Amsterdam: Mouton Press, forthcoming.

Lipman, Jonathan. "The Border World of Gansu, 1895–1935." Ph.D. diss., Stanford University, 1981.

———. "Patchwork Society, Network Society: A Study of Sino-Muslim Communities." In *Islam in Asia*, ed. Raphael Israeli and Anthony H. Johns, vol. 2. Boulder, Colo.: Westview Press, 1984.

Maghtïmguli. *Izbrannye proizbedenia* (trans. Zhumäniyaz Shäripov). Tashkent, 1958.

——. *Saylanan Eserler* (2 vols.). Ashkhabad: Türkmenistan, 1983.

——. *Saylanan Eserler*. Ashkhabad: Ilym, 1957.

Manz, Beatrice Forbes. "Central Asian Uprisings in the Nineteenth Century: Ferghana under the Russians." *Russian Review* 46(1987):267–81.

——. "Tamerlane and the Symbolism of Sovereignty." *Iranian Studies* 21(1988):104–22.

——. *The Rise and Rule of Tamerlane*. New York: Cambridge University Press, 1989.

McChesney, Robert. *Waqf in Central Asia: Four Hundred Years in the History of a Muslim Shrine*. Princeton: Princeton University Press, 1991.

Mirzayev, Ibrahim. *Abdulla Qadiriyning Ijadiy Evolyutsiyadi*. Tashkent, 1969.

Morgan, D. O. "The Great Yāsā of Chingiz Khān and Mongol Law in the Īlkhānate." *Bulletin of the School of Oriental and African Studies* 49(1986):163–76.

——. *The Mongols*. New York/Oxford: Basil Blackwell, 1986.

Naby, Eden. "The Ethnic Factor in Soviet-Afghan Relations." *Asian Survey* 20(1980):237–56.

Pillsbury, Barbara L. K. "Cohesion and Cleavage in a Chinese Muslim Minority." Ph.D. diss., Columbia University, 1973.

——. "Factionalism Observed: Behind the 'Face' of Harmony in a Chinese Community." *China Quarterly*, June 1978.

——. "Islam 'Even unto China.'" In *Change and the Muslim World*, ed. Philip H. Stoddard, David C. Cuthell, and Margaret W. Sullivan. New York: Syracuse University Press, 1981.

Piscatori, James P. *Islam in a World of Nation States*. Cambridge: Cambridge University Press, 1986.

Qadiriy, Habibullah. *Atam Haqida*. Tashkent, 1973.

Rakowska-Harmstone. *Russia and Nationalism in Central Asia: The Case of Tadzhikistan*. Baltimore: Johns Hopkins University Press, 1970.

Roff, William R. (ed.). *Islam and the Political Economy of Meaning: Comparative Studies of Muslim Discourse*. Berkeley: University of California Press, 1987.

Rorlich, Azade-Ayşe. "Islam under Communist Rule: Volga-Ural Muslims." *Central Asian Survey* 1(1982).

——. *The Volga Tatars: A Profile in National Resilience*. Stanford, Calif.: Hoover Institution Press, 1986.

Rossabi, Morris. *China and Inner Asia: From 1368 to the Present Day*. London: Thames and Hudson, 1975.

——. *Khubilai Khan: His Life and Times*. Berkeley: University of California Press, 1988.

Roy, Olivier. *Islam and Resistance in Afghanistan*. Cambridge: Cambridge University Press, 1986.

Royce, A. P. *Ethnic Identity*. Bloomington: Indiana University Press, 1982.

Saray, Mehmet. *The Turkmens in the Age of Imperialism: A Study of the Turkmen People and Their Incorporation into the Russian Empire*. Ankara: Turkish Historical Society Printing House, 1989.

Schimmel, Annemarie. *Mystical Dimensions of Islam*. Chapel Hill: University of North Carolina Press, 1975.

Schwartz, Henry G. *The Minorities of Northern China: A Survey*. Bellingham, Wash.: Western Washington University Press, 1984.

Seaman, Gary (ed.). *Ecology and Empire: Nomads in the Cultural Evolution of the Old World*. Los Angeles: Ethnographics Press, 1989.

———. *Rulers from the Steppe: State Formation on the Eurasian Periphery*. Los Angeles: Ethnographics Press, 1990.

Shahrani, M. Nazif. "Ethnic Relations under Closed Frontier Conditions: Northern Badakhshan." In *Soviet Asian Ethnic Frontiers*, ed. W. O. MacCagg, Jr., and B. D. Silver. New York: Pergamon Press, 1979.

———. *The Kirghiz and Wakhi of Afghanistan: Adaptation to Closed Frontiers*. Seattle: University of Washington Press, 1979.

Shalinsky, Audrey. "Islam and Ethnicity: The Northern Afghanistan Perspective." *Central Asian Survey* 1(1982):2–3.

Shaw, S. "The History of the Khojas of Eastern-Turkestan." *Journal of the Asiatic Society of Bengal* 46(1897), part 1.

Smith, Anthony D. *The Ethnic Origins of Nations*. London: Basil Blackwell, 1986.

Spuler, B. "Central Asia: The Last Centuries of Independence." In *The Muslim World*, pt. 3, ed. F. R. C. Bagley. Leiden, 1965, pp. 219–59.

Subtelny, Maria Eva. "Art and Politics in Early Sixteenth Century Central Asia." *Central Asiatic Journal* 27(1983):121–48.

———. "Centralizing Reform and Its Opponents in the Late Timurid Period." *Iranian Studies* 21(1988):123–51.

———. "Socioeconomic Bases of Cultural Patronage under the Later Timurids." *International Journal of Middle East Studies* 20(1988):479–505.

Sultanov, Izzat. "Abdulla Qadiriy Ijadi Haqida." *Otgan Kunlar*. Tashkent, 1956.

Ṭāhir, Maḥmūd. "Rizaeddin Fahreddin." *Central Asian Survey* 8(1989): 111–15.

Tambiah, Stanley J. "Ethnic Conflict in the World Today." *American Ethnologist* 16(1989):1–13.

Tapper, Richard. "Ethnicity and Class: Dimensions of Conflict." In *Revolutions and Rebellions in Afghanistan*, ed. M. Nazif Shahrani and Robert Canfield. Berkeley: Institute of International Studies, 1979, pp. 230–46.

Togan, Isenbike. "Chinese Turkestan under the Khojas (1678–1759)." *Encyclopaedia Iranica* (1991).

Voll, John. *Islam: Continuity and Change in the Modern World*. Boulder, Colo.: Westview Press, 1982.

———. "Muslim Minority Alternatives: Implications of Muslim Experiences in China and the Soviet Union." *Journal of the Institute of Muslim Minority Affairs* 6(1985):332–55.

――――. "Renewal and Reform in Islamic History: *Tajdid* and *Islah.*" In *Voices of Resurgent Islam,* ed. John L. Esposito. New York: Oxford University Press, pp. 35–43.

Waldman, Marilyn. "Primitive Mind / Modern Mind: New Approaches to an Old Problem Applied to Islam." In *Approaches to Islam in Religious Studies,* ed. Richard Martin. Tucson, Ariz.: University of Arizona Press, 1985, pp. 91–105.

Williams, Brackette F. "A Class Act: Anthropology and the Race to Nation across Ethnic Terrain." *Annual Review of Anthropology* 18(1989):401–44.

Woods, John. "The Rise of Timurid Historiography." *Journal of Near Eastern Studies* 46(1987):81–108.

――――. *The Timurid Dynasty.* Papers on Inner Asia, No. 14. Bloomington: Indiana University Research Institute for Inner Asian Studies, 1990.

――――. *The Aqquyunlu: Clan, Confederation, Empire.* Minneapolis: Bibliotheca Islamica, 1976.

Contributors

Hamid Algar is a professor of Near Eastern Studies at the University of California, Berkeley. He received a Ph.D. from Cambridge University, Institute of Oriental Studies in 1965. His research interests are Islam, Sufism, and the history of Iran. He has published numerous articles and books, including *Religion and State in Iran, 1785–1906: The Role of the Ulama in the Qajar Period* (University of California Press, 1969), and *Mirza Malkum Khan: A Study in the History of Iranian Modernism* (University of California Press, 1973).

Muriel Atkin is associate professor of history at George Washington University. She holds a doctorate from Yale University. Her research specialities are the Muslims of Russia's southern borderlands and Russo-Iranian relations. She is the author of numerous articles on these subjects and the monographs *Russia and Iran, 1780–1828* and *The Subtlest Battle: Islam in Soviet Tajikistan*.

Walter Feldman is a full-time lecturer at the University of Pennsylvania, Department of Oriental Studies. His Ph.D. dissertation from Columbia University, 1980, was "The Uzbek Oral Epic—Documentation of Late Nineteenth and Early Twentieth Century Bards." His research specialties are traditional Turkic literatures and the musicology of Turkic peoples. He has written several articles on Turkish music and is preparing two books for publication: one on the Uzbek oral epic and a second on early Ottoman court music.

Dru C. Gladney is assistant professor of anthropology at the University of Southern California, Los Angeles. After almost three years of fieldwork in China, he completed his Ph.D. in cultural anthropology at the University of Washington, Seattle. His book, *Muslim Chinese: Ethnic Nationalism in the People's Republic* (Harvard University Press, 1991) addresses the identity of Hui Muslims in divergent communities across China, including the northwest, Beijing city, and along the southeast coast.

Jo-Ann Gross is assistant professor of history at Trenton State College. She received her Ph.D. from New York University in 1982. She specializes in the social history of the late Timurid period and the role of Sufism in Islamic Central Asia. Her writings include "The Economic Status of a Timurid Sufi Shaykh: A Matter of Conflict or Perception?" *Iranian Studies* 21 (1980); and "Multiple Roles and Perceptions of a Sufi Shaikh: Symbolic Statements of Political and Religious Authority," in *Naqshbandis*, ed. M. Gaborieau, A. Popovic, and T. Zarcone (Istanbul: ISIS Press, 1990).

Edward J. Lazzerini is professor of Russian and Asian history at the University of New Orleans, having earned the Ph.D. from the University of Washington in 1973. His research specialty is the history of European Russia's major Turkic peoples (Volga Tatars, Crimean Tatars, and Azerbaijanis), particularly as regards their cultural and intellectual evolution since the eighteenth century and their problems of adaptation to Russian/Soviet dominance. He is presently completing a study of Ismail Bey Gasprinskii, the nineteenth-century Tatar reformer.

Beatrice Forbes Manz is assistant professor of history at Tufts University. She received her Ph.D. from Harvard University in Inner Asian and Altaic studies. She specializes in the Timurid period (1370–1507) and works particularly on questions of nomad-sedentary relations. Her scholarly works include a book, *The Rise and Rule of Tamerlane* (Cambridge University Press, 1989), and articles in numerous journals, notably *Central Asiatic Journal, Iranian Studies, Russian Review,* and *Harvard Ukrainian Studies.* She has contributed articles to the *Encyclopaedia Iranica* and the *Encyclopaedia of Islam.*

Christopher Murphy is the Turkish area specialist at the Library of Congress, Washington, D.C. He received his Ph.D. from the University of Washington, Seattle in 1980. His dissertation was "The Relationship of Abdullah Qadiriy's Historical Novels to the Earlier Uzbek Literary Traditions." His research interests are Turkish culture and literature, and nineteenth- and twentieth-century Uzbek literature.

Olivier Roy is a researcher at the French National Center for Scientific Research (CNRS). He made eight journeys with the Afghan resistance between 1980 and 1988 and has written several articles on politics, religion, and ethnicity in Afghanistan, Iran, and Central Asia. He is currently doing research on Uzbekistan and Tajikistan. He is the author of *Islam and Resistance in Afghanistan,* translated from the French (Cambridge University Press, 2nd ed., 1990).

Isenbike Togan received her Ph.D. in 1973 from Harvard University. She has taught in Turkey and the United States and is currently Visiting Associate Professor of Inner Asian History at Washington University in St. Louis. Her work focuses on the interaction of nomadic and sedentary peoples in Inner Asia and their encounter with Islam. Her writings include an article, "Chinese Turkestan under the Khojas (1678–1759)," in *Encyclopaedia Iranica,* 1991.

Index

Library of Congress Cataloging-in-Publication Data

Muslims in Central Asia : expressions of identity and change / edited
by Jo-Ann Gross.
    p. cm. — (Central Asia book series)
    Includes bibliographical references and index.
    ISBN 0-8223-1187-9. — ISBN 0-8223-1190-9 (pbk.)
    1. Muslims—Asia, Central. 2. Asia, Central—Ethnic relations.
I. Gross, Jo-Ann, 1949– II. Series.
DS328.4.M87M87 1992
958'.00882971—dc20   91-13772
                                    CIP